Also covers the new English GCSE

AQA GCSE

Series editor: Steve Davies

English

Language & Literature

HIGHER

Authors:
John Clare
Helen Clyde
Steve Davies
Mike Devitt
Shelly Etheridge
Sarah Forrest
Robert Francis
Joanna Haffenden
Chris Hawkes
Linda Hill
Sharon McCammon
Kathryn Simpson

DYNA LEARN

HODDER EDUCATION

The Publishers would like to thank the following for permission to reproduce copyright material:

Photo credits Unit 1 image: © Niels Poulsen DK / Alamy; **page 2:** © Imagestate Media Partners Limited - Impact Photos / Alamy; **page 4:** © Ingram Publishing Limited; **page 5 and APPLE image throughout:** © Ingram Publishing Limited; **Unit 2 image:** © David Hancock / Alamy; **page 8:** © Rex Features; **page 9:** © Design Pics Inc. / Alamy; **page 10 and 89 (top):** © Geoffrey Robinson / Rex Features; **page 11:** © Christopher Furlong/Getty Images; **page 12:** © Design Pics Inc./Alamy; **page 13:** © 1997 Doug Menuez / Photodisc / Getty Images; **page 14:** © Russell Illig / Photodisc / Getty Images; **page 15:** © Jane Jackson; **page 18:** © Peter M. Fisher/Corbis; **Unit 3 image:** © Bernhard Lang / Riser / Getty Images; **page 29:** © Steve Davies; **Unit 4 image:** © Larry Lilac / Alamy; **page 37:** © David Pearson / Rex Features; **page 38:** © Ingram Publishing Limited; **page 40:** © Keystone/Getty Images; **page 42:** © Carlos's Pemium Images / Alamy; **page 47:** © Royalty-Free/Corbis; **Unit 5 image:** © Steven Lam / Stone / Getty Images; **page 50:** © Ingram Publishing Limited; **page 55:** © Design Pics Inc. / Alamy; **page 56:** © Kevin Peterson / Photodisc / Getty Images; **page 57:** © OJO Images / Rex Features; **Unit 6 image:** © Daniel Kerek / Alamy; **page 65:** © The Granger Collection, NYC / TopFoto; **page 66:** Battle of Balaclava. Brilliant charge of the Scots Greys, 25th October 1854, engraved by Augustus Butler, published by Stannard and Dixon, London, 6 January 1855 (colour litho) by Butler, Augustus (fl.1854) © National Army Museum, London/ The Bridgeman Art Library; **page 69 (left):** © Ullstein Bild / TopFoto; **(right):** © Popperfoto/Getty Images; **page 71 (left):** © ERIK C PENDZICH / Rex Features; **(right):** © Neville Elder/Corbis; **(top):** © Jess Alford / Photodisc / Getty Images AP/Press Association Images; **page 73:** © Image Source / Alamy; **Unit 7 image:** © Mira / Alamy; **page 77:** © Jacob Wackerhausen/istockphoto.com; **page 78:** © Colin McPherson/Corbis; **page 81:** © OJO Images / Rex Features; **page 84:** © Design Pics Inc. / Alamy **Unit 8 image:** © CreativeAct - Emotions series / Alamy; **page 85 (top):** With kind permission by Facebook, Inc.; **(bottom):** © Fremantle Media; **page 86:** © Ingram Publishing Limited; **page 87:** © Purestock; **page 89 (bottom):** © Design Pics Inc / Rex Features; **page 91 (top):** © Blend Images / Alamy; **(middle):** © Image Source Pink / Alamy; **(bottom):** © Photofusion Picture Library / Alamy; **page 92:** © Kristy-Anne Glubish/Design Pics/Corbis; **Unit 9 image:** © Margarita Sarri / Flickr / Getty Images; **page 93:** © AA World Travel Library/TopFoto; **page 95 (left):** © Britain On View/VisitBritain; **(right):** © Bryan & Cherry Alexander Photography / Alamy; **page 99:** © John Springer Collection/Corbis; **page 100 and 122 (right):** © Peter Cade / Iconica / Getty Images; **page 102 (left):** © Olivia Edward/Photographer's Choice/Getty Images; **(middle):** © Tanya Constantine/Blend Images/Getty Images; **(right):** © Alex Segre / Rex Features; **Unit 10 image and page 106:** © The London Art Archive / Alamy; **page 105:** © akg-images / British Library; **page 108:** © Richard Caton Woodville/The Bridgeman Art Library/Getty Images; **page 109:** A Ward in the Hospital at Scutari, engraved by E. Walker, 1856 (colour litho) by Simpson, William 'Crimea' (1823-99) © Florence Nightingale Museum, London, UK/ The Bridgeman Art Library; **Unit 11 image:** © Will Stanton / Alamy; **page 113 and 114:** © Paramount / Everett / Rex Features; **page 117:** © Stephane Cardinale/People Avenue/Corbis; **Unit 12 image:** © Mohamed Sadath / Alamy; **page 119 (top):** © 1997 Steve Mason / PhotoDisc Inc./ Getty Images; **(bottom):** © Hulton Archive / Getty Images; **page 121:** © Ross Fraser / Alamy; **page 122 (left):** © Design Pics Inc. / Alamy; **page 124:** © Classic Image / Alamy; **page 125:** © Jules Frazier / Photodisc / Getty Images; **Unit 13 image:** © Harriet Cummings / Alamy; **page 127:** Burra, Edward: The Snack Bar ©Tate, London 2009 / © Estate of the Artist c/o Lefevre Fine Art Ltd, London; **page 129:** © Clive Barda/ArenaPAL/TopFoto; **page 131 (bottom):** © Donald Cooper / Rex Features; **(middle):** With kind permission by www.marlboroughplayers.co.uk; **Unit 14 image:** © BE&W agencja fotograficzna Sp. z o.o. / Alamy; **page 135:** © THE KOBAL COLLECTION / 20TH CENTURY FOX / MORTON, MERRICK; **page 139:** © Rex Features; **page 141:** © Geraint Lewis / Rex Features; **Unit 15 image:** © Peter Cavanagh / Alamy; **page 143 (top):** © Sipa Press / Rex Features; **(bottom):** © David Fisher / Rex Features; **page 144:** © 1997 Karl Weatherly / PhotoDisc Inc. / Getty Images; **page 145 (all):** © Kevin Peterson / Photodisc / Getty Images; **page 147:** © Jonathan Hordle / Rex Features; **page 148:** © Stephane Masson/Kipa/Corbis; **page 149:** © World Illustrated/Photoshot. All rights reserved; page 150: © Elle Holland / Alamy; **Unit 16 image and page 43:** © Corbis. All Rights Reserved; **page 151:** © Janine Wiedel Photolibrary / Alamy; **page 155:** © Design Pics Inc. / Alamy; **page 156:** © BBC; **Unit 17 image:** © Richard Newstead / Lifesize / Getty Images; **page 159:** © Design Pics Inc / Rex Features; **page 161 and 163:** © zak/istockphoto.com; **page 162:** © Larry Brownstein/Photodisc/Getty Images; **page 165:** © Comstock Images / Photolibrary Group Ltd; **page 166:** © Markku Ulander / Rex Features.

Acknowledgements Page 4 and Unit 13: extract from *Of Mice and Men* by John Steinbeck (Penguin 2000), copyright © John Steinbeck, 1937,1965, reproduced by permission of Penguin Books Ltd; **page 8:** 'History of Crufts', extract from www.crufts.org.uk/history-crufts (2009), copyright The Kennel Club, reproduced with their permission; **page 11:** 'You and Your Dog in the Countryside' from www.countrysideaccess.gov.uk/dog/ reproduced by permission of Natural England; **page 13:** dog food advert from www.uk.pedigree.com/our-product-promises.aspx, reproduced by permission of Mars Petcare UK; **page 14:** 'Part Friend, Part Family' article from www.improvementaudio.com/dogcareguide.htm; **page 19:** 'My Rottie, Henry' by Joy C. Rogers from www.petstation.com/henry.html; **page 20:** 'Why are dogs man's best friend?' by Sara Elliott from http://dogs.suite101.com/article.cfm/why_r_dogs_mans_best_friend (July 2008), reproduced by permission of the author; **pages 21–24:** Avon Fire & Rescue leaflets, www.avonfire.gov.uk/Avon/ (2009); **page 25:** 'Things to know about Sanday' from www.sandayorkney.co.uk/leaflet.php (2007), reproduced by permission of Sanday Tourism Association; **page 26:** Lewisham Council, 'Re-Cycling - Why Bother?' from *Lewisham Life* (June/July 2003); Viking worksheet from www.parents.dfes.uk/discover, reproduced by permission of Qualifications & Curriculum Development Agency; **page 28:** *Sprocket Man* from http://www.cpsc.gov/CPSCPUB/PUBS/341.pdf, reproduced by permission of U.S. Consumer Product Safety Commission; **page 30:** front cover of *Lewisham Life* magazine (April 2007 edition), reproduced by permission of Lewisham Council; 'Safe driving for life – it's all about attitude!' (2009), reproduced by permission of The Big Red L Company; **page 32:** Children's Workforce Development Council, 'Do you want someone to be there for you?' from http://www.newcastlechildrenservices.org.uk; **page 34:** 'Who Do You See?' (2009), reproduced by permission of Wyre Community Safety Partnership; **page 36:** Disneyland Resort Paris leaflet, reproduced by permission of Holiday Discount Centre; **page 38:** article on Nickelodeon by Arif Durrani from mediaweek.co.uk, 09/07/2007, reproduced by permission of the author; **page 44:** Change4Life leaflet (2008), reproduced by permission under Click-Use PSI Licence C2009002464; Tessa Jowell, letter to David Currie (2009), reproduced by permission under Click-Use PSI Licence C2009002464; **page 46:** Department of Health, smokefree leaflet (2009), reproduced by permission under Click-Use PSI Licence C2009002464; **page 51:** Drug Driving leaflet, reproduced by permission of Department for Transport; **page 53 and 101:** extracts from *A Kestrel for a Knave* by Barry Hines (Michael Joseph, 1968), copyright © Barry Hines, 1968, reproduced by permission of Penguin Books Ltd; **page 54:** road safety information, reproduced by permission of Brake; **page 59:** Kent County Council flooding leaflet, reproduced by permission of Environment Agency; **page 76:** 'It ain't what you do it's what it does to you' from *Selected Poems* by Simon Armitage (Faber & Faber, 2001); **page 80:** 'Medusa' from *The World's Wife* by Carol Ann Duffy (Picador, 2000); **page 81:** 'Belfast Confetti' from *Collected Poems* by Ciaran Carson (Gallery Press, 2008), reproduced by permission of the author and The Gallery Press, Loughcrew, Oldcastle, County Meath, Ireland; **page 84:** 'My Pen Has Ink Enough' from *Collected Poems 1950–1993* by Vernon Scannell (Robson Books, 1993), reproduced by permission of The Estate of Vernon Scannell; **page 87:** extract from *Boy: Tales of Childhood* by Roald Dahl (Jonathan Cape, 1994), reproduced by permission of David Higham Associates; **page 89 and 90:** extract from *Notes from a Small Island* by Bill Bryson (Doubleday, 1995), reproduced by permission of The Random House Group Ltd; **page 98:** extract from *New Moon* by Stephenie Meyer (Atom, 2007), copyright © 2006 Stephenie Meyer, reproduced by permission of Little, Brown & Company; extract from *Private Peaceful* by Michael Morpurgo (HarperCollins Children's Books, 2004), reproduced by permission of HarperCollins Publishers Ltd; **page 111:** review of *Public Enemies* by Simon Thompson from http://www.heartlondon.co.uk (2009), reproduced by permission of the author; **page 112:** review of *Up* by Jonathan Romney from http://www.uncut.co.uk (2009); **page 114:** review of *Transformers: Revenge of the Fallen* by Peter Bradshaw from *The Guardian* (19 June 2009), copyright Guardian News & Media Ltd 2009, reproduced by permission of the publisher; **page 117:** *Twilight* review from http://eshed.net (2009); **Unit 13:** extracts from *An Inspector Calls* by J. B. Priestley, (Heinemann, 1992), © J. B. Priestley, 1988, reproduced by permission of PFD (www.pfd.co.uk) on behalf of The Estate of J. B. Priestley; **page 148:** 'Unrelated Incidents – No. 3' by Tom Leonard, reproduced by permission of the author, © Tom Leonard from *outside the narrative: poems 1965–2009*, (Etruscan/WordPower 2009); **page 156 and 157:** extract from Waterloo Road reproduced by permission of and © Shed Productions (WR) Limited.

Every effort has been made to trace all copyright holders, but if any have been inadvertently overlooked the Publishers will be pleased to make the necessary arrangements at the first opportunity.

Although every effort has been made to ensure that website addresses are correct at time of going to press, Hodder Education cannot be held responsible for the content of any website mentioned in this book. It is sometimes possible to find a relocated web page by typing in the address of the home page for a website in the URL window of your browser.

Hachette UK's policy is to use papers that are natural, renewable and recyclable products and made from wood grown in sustainable forests. The logging and manufacturing processes are expected to conform to the environmental regulations of the country of origin.

Orders: please contact Bookpoint Ltd, 130 Milton Park, Abingdon, Oxon OX14 4SB. Telephone: (44) 01235 827720. Fax: (44) 01235 400454. Lines are open 9.00 – 5.00, Monday to Saturday, with a 24-hour message answering service. Visit our website at www.hoddereducation.co.uk

Clare, Clyde, Davies, Devitt, Etheridge, Forrest, Francis, Haffenden, Hawkes, Hill, McCammon, Simpson © 2010

First published in 2010 by
Hodder Education,
An Hachette UK Company
338 Euston Road
London NW1 3BH

Impression number 5 4 3 2 1
Year 2014 2013 2012 2011 2010

All rights reserved. Apart from any use permitted under UK copyright law, no part of this publication may be reproduced or transmitted in any form or by any means, electronic or mechanical, including photocopying and recording, or held within any information storage and retrieval system, without permission in writing from the publisher or under licence from the Copyright Licensing Agency Limited. Further details of such licences (for reprographic reproduction) may be obtained from the Copyright Licensing Agency Limited, Saffron House, 6–10 Kirby Street, London EC1N 8TS.

Cover photo from © Nation Wong / Corbis
Illustrations by Andrew Roberts and Julian Molesdale
Typeset in Garamond 10pt by 2idesign Ltd
Printed in Italy

A catalogue record for this title is available from the British Library

ISBN: 978 1444 108 699

Contents
Introduction to your book

Exam Units

5

Tell Me About It – Explaining, Advising and Informing

In this unit you will develop your skills in speaking and listening and writing to explain, advise and inform (including role-play and giving a presentation).

AQA spec link:
This unit will help you prepare for:
- GCSE English – Unit 1, Section B: Writing
- GCSE English – Unit 2, Speaking and Listening
- GCSE English Language – Unit 1, Section B: Writing
- GCSE English Language – Unit 2, Speaking and Listening

Approx teaching time: 8–10 hours

6

Poetry – Contemporary and Heritage

This unit will help you prepare for Section A of the Poetry Across Time exam paper in English Literature. You will develop your skills in comparing poems by concentrating on five poems from the Conflict cluster in the AQA Anthology.

AQA spec link:
This unit will help you prepare for:
- GCSE English Literature – Unit 2, Section A

Approx teaching time: 8–10 hours

7

Poetry – Unseen

This unit will help you prepare for Section B of the Poetry Across Time exam paper in English Literature. You will develop your confidence and knowledge of how to approach any poem.

AQA spec link:
This unit will help you prepare for:
- GCSE English Literature – Unit 2, Section B

Approx teaching time: 6–8 hours

Controlled Assessment Units

8 — Creating a Personal Voice

This unit will help you prepare for the Creative Writing Controlled Assessment Tasks. You will learn how to write in an interesting way about people, places and events from your life.

AQA spec link:
This unit will help you prepare for:
- GCSE English – Unit 3 Creative Writing: Prompts and Me. Myself. I.
- GCSE English Language – Unit 3 Creative Writing: Commissions

Approx teaching time: 4–6 hours

9 — Creating Characters, Mood and Atmosphere

This unit will help you prepare for the Creative Writing Controlled Assessment Tasks. You will learn how to create mood and atmosphere in your writing and create effective characters.

AQA spec link:
This unit will help you prepare for:
- GCSE English – Unit 3 Creative Writing: Moving Images and Prompts and Me. Myself. I.
- GCSE English Language – Unit 3 Creative Writing: Commissions and Re-Creations

Approx teaching time: 4–6 hours

10 — Re-creations

This unit will help you prepare for the Creative Writing Controlled Assessment Tasks. You will learn how to transform one text into another.

AQA spec link:
This unit will help you prepare for:
- GCSE English – Unit 3 Creative Writing: Prompts and Re-Creations
- GCSE English Language – Unit 3 Creative Writing: Re-Creations

Approx teaching time: 4–6 hours

11 — Linking Words and Images

This unit will help you prepare for the Creative Writing Controlled Assessment Tasks. You will learn about the typical features of a review, and the skills and understanding you need to write a good review.

AQA spec link:
This unit will help you prepare for:
- GCSE English Language – Unit 3 Creative Writing: Moving Images

Approx teaching time: 4–6 hours

12

Themes and Ideas – Family Relationships

This unit will help you prepare for the Reading and Literature Controlled Assessment Tasks. Using three William Wordsworth poems, you will learn about the key things you need to comment on when analysing themes in poetry.

AQA spec link:
This unit will help you prepare for:
• GCSE English and GCSE English Language – Unit 3 Understanding Written Texts: Themes and Ideas
• GCSE English Literature – Unit 3 The significance of Shakespeare and the English Literary Heritage: Themes and Ideas

Approx teaching time: 4–6 hours

13

Presenting People

This unit will help you prepare for the Reading and Literature Controlled Assessment Tasks. You will consider the techniques that writers use to create character and learn how to explain how a character is presented to a reader or audience.

AQA spec link:
This unit will help you prepare for:
• GCSE English and GCSE English Language – Unit 3 Understanding Written Texts: Characterisation and voice
• GCSE English Literature – Unit 3 The significance of Shakespeare and the English Literary Heritage: Characterisation and voice

Approx teaching time: 4–6 hours

14

Genres and Form – Openings

This unit will help you prepare for the Reading and Literature Controlled Assessment Tasks. Using the opening scenes from two Shakespeare plays, you will look at themes, ideas, characters and language used.

AQA spec link:
This unit will help you prepare for:
• GCSE English and GCSE English Language – Unit 3 Understanding Written Texts: Themes and Ideas
• GCSE English Literature – Unit 3 The significance of Shakespeare and the English Literary Heritage: Themes and Ideas

Approx teaching time: 4–6 hours

Introduction to your book

Welcome! It is with excitement that the writing team presents this book to you. We set ourselves two challenges when writing it ...

The first challenge was to write a book that prepared you for whichever of the AQA GCSE English courses you decide to follow – English, or English Language and/or English Literature. Over the next 17 units, we have provided material that will allow you to achieve the best results, whichever course you have chosen.

The units which help you with your exams

After **Unit 1** – which tunes you into reading and writing at GCSE level – the book moves on to **Units 2–5** which support you in getting ready for the English and English Language exams. **Units 6 and 7** will help you in the GCSE Literature exam – in particular the poetry sections. For further exam guidance, the section Doing Well in the English and English Language Exam (pages 167–72) gives you advice about how to boost your marks in the exam.

The units which help you with your Controlled Assessment Tasks

Units 8–17 support the Controlled Assessment Tasks that your teacher will choose for you. They cover the Creative Writing tasks for English and English Language; the Reading and Literature tasks for English, English Language and English Literature; and the Spoken Language Investigation tasks for English Language.

Features of the book

You will notice that we have explained important words in the **Concept Banks** at the side of the page (these are collected together at the end of the book in the Concept Bank for easy reference, pages 182–84). We have also included some Grammar Links throughout. These link to a section at the end of the book – Grammar (page 173–81) – which gives you help with grammar and punctuation.

The second challenge we set ourselves was as important – we wanted the activities and tasks to be demanding but always do-able; we wanted the tasks to involve all sorts of ways of learning, and we wanted the work you will be doing to be interesting and fun. You will find role-play, drama, discussion, image and media study, and writing and reading of all kinds of texts. We hope this variety keeps you interested, makes your learning fun and gives you the confidence, skills and understanding to go for those good grades in your exams and Controlled Assessment Tasks.

Enjoy the journey!

Steve Davies

Learning aim

In this unit you will revise some of the features of texts you already know. You will begin to build up a range of ways of looking at texts so that you understand how they are constructed to influence their audience and how you can create texts for your own purposes and audiences.

1.1 What do we mean by text?

ⓘ Concept bank

Lexical: refers to the words of language that help shape texts and construct meaning.

Text: How we define a text is changing. Once, the word 'text' meant simply longer writing such as novels, but now texts include images and film as well as written and spoken texts.

2

Text type	Text features

> By the end of this section, you will understand that there are many different types of text, each with particular **lexical** and textual features.

↻ For starters

Look at the materials below and decide which are **texts**. Give reasons for your choices, identifying the features that suggest a particular text type.

1 Riding a bike. First make sure that the saddle is at the right height. Check that your feet are flat on the floor. Now find a flat area without obstacles that you might ride into. Begin by pushing yourself along with your feet. Do not try using the pedals at this stage. Try out the brakes and test out your steering.

3 '… guaranteed to keep the reader flipping through the pages.' *The Guardian*

You will be analysing and writing many text types throughout your GCSE course.

↻ Task

Note down as many different text types as you can think of in two minutes and record them in the first column of a table like the one on the left.

↻ Taking it further

1 Compare your list with a partner, adding any text types you had forgotten about.
2 Think about each of the text types you have listed and note down in the second column any features you remember them having.
3 Compare your list of features with a partner.

1.2 Context and purpose

You will understand how context and purpose influence text types.

ⓘ Concept bank

Context: the situation in which a text is found. The language, structure and presentation of a text are influenced by context.

↺ For starters

Think about your journey to school. You will have passed several texts displayed as signs or symbols on your way. Some of these will have become so familiar to you that you will hardly have noticed them. Try to remember as many as you can and note their conventions. Think about:

- size, shape and colour
- position and **context**
- image and language
- audience and purpose
- effect and impact.

↑ *A starving child in Africa*

↺ Task

Look at the image above.

1 Write a short description of the image. Be as accurate as you can so that a reader could imagine the image in their mind's eye.
2 Now turn this description into a diary entry written in the first person by the child's parent.
3 How does this image affect you personally as a 'reader' of the text?
4 How might your reaction differ if you were the parent of the child?
5 What is your view of using these kinds of images in charity campaigns, for example? Explain your reasons.

↺ Taking it further

1 With a partner, prepare a short, spoken presentation to persuade an advertising company that using this type of image is inappropriate.
2 Present your speech to the class.

ᐤ Grammar link

The first person singular is 'I' and 'me'. Persuasive texts also use the second person: 'you' and 'your'.

1.3 Fiction texts – audience and reader

You will learn how writers of fiction try to keep their reader's interest.

⊃ For starters

Read this opening to a work of fiction:

> There are not many people – and as it is desirable that a story-teller and a story-reader should establish a mutual understanding as soon as possible, beg it to be noticed that I confine this observation neither to young people nor to little people, but extend it to all conditions of people: little and big, young and old: yet growing up, or already growing down again – there are not, I say, many people who would care to sleep in a church.

1 What kind of story do you think it is introducing?
2 How well does the text attract the reader's attention? Explain your answer.
3 When do you think this passage might have been written? What features of the text give you a clue that this was written in the past?
4 What difficulties does this text present to readers?

🔗 Grammar link

The first person singular uses 'I' and 'me'. You have already seen how non-fiction texts can use the first and second person. Although many novels are written in the third person ('he', 'she', 'it', 'they'), many are written in the first person.

⊃ Task

Now read the extract below from a modern children's novel:

> Some things start before other things.
>
> It was a summer shower but didn't appear to know it, and it was pouring rain as fast as a winter storm.
>
> Miss Perspicacia Tick sat in what little shelter a raggedy hedge could give her and explored the universe. She didn't notice the rain. Witches dried out quickly.
>
> From *The Wee Free Men* by Terry Pratchett (2003)

1 What kind of story do you think it is introducing?
2 How does the text try to attract the reader's attention? How successful is it at gaining your interest? Explain your answers.
3 Terry Pratchett uses some short, powerful sentences. Choose one short sentence and explain why it grabs the reader's attention.
4 How does this modern text differ from the older text above?

⊃ Taking it further

Write your own story-starter imitating Terry Pratchett's opening, including some short sentences, a description of the weather and a simile. Read it to a friend and see if it 'grabs their interest'.

The World of Texts

1.4 Fiction texts – form and genre

You will learn about genre and some forms of texts.

⊃ For starters

Look only at the **form** of the two texts on the right. What **genres** are they likely to be? Note down the aspects of form that gave you a clue.

⊃ Task

Analysing form and genre means you need to look at the shape of a text on the page, the types of sentences within it and the actual words used to create those sentences. To achieve the higher grades you need to use a technical vocabulary to write about texts. However, don't forget the 'So what?' aspect. It is not enough to spot the features. You need to say what their effect is.

Read this short extract from *Of Mice and Men*:

> Lennie dabbled his big paw in the water and wiggled his fingers so the water arose in little splashes; rings widened across the pool to the other side and came back again. Lennie watched them go. 'Look, George. Look what I done.'

What impression does the writer want to give you about Lennie? How does the writer do this? Write about the extract making sure you use appropriate technical terminology in your writing.

⊃ Taking it further

1 Imagine you are going to develop this extract into a science fiction text. Write the next two or three sentences that would signpost the science fiction genre to the reader.

2 Imagine you are going to develop this extract into a horror text. Write the next two or three sentences that would signpost the horror genre to the reader. (The weather often plays a role in **pathetic fallacy**, so you might like to concentrate on that to help build your text.)

3 Now write a brief commentary on your writing, explaining what features you have included that belong to the appropriate genre.

00 Xxxxx Street
Xxxx xxxx
London
XXX XXX

tel 0800 000 000
fax 0800 000 000

00 Xxxxx Street
Xxxx xxxx
London
XXX XXX

To whom it may concern

odcvdoividjvij nGaitMolor ing ero con henibh ea feugue molenim alisit vulla commy num veliquis eugait eu faccum dolutatem illutem dolobore min velendignis nulla feugait iusto diam

Yours faithfully

Mr X Xxxxxxx

odcvdoividjvij nGaitMolor ing ero con henibh ea feugue molenim alisit vulla commy num veliquis eugait eu faccum dolutatem illutem dolobore min velendignis nulla feugait iusto diam

odcvdoividjvij nGaitMolor ing ero con henibh ea feugue molenim alisit vulla commy num veliquis eugait eu faccum dolutatem illutem dolobore min velendignis nulla feugait iusto diam

odcvdoividjvij nGaitMolor ing ero con henibh ea feugue molenim alisit vulla commy num veliquis eugait eu faccum dolutatem illutem dolobore min velendignis nulla feugait iusto diam

odcvdoividjvij nGaitMolor ing ero con henibh ea feugue molenim alisit vulla commy num veliquis eugait eu faccum dolutatem illutem dolobore min velendignis nulla feugait iusto diam

ⓘ Concept bank

Form: the way in which subject matter is presented, or its conventions and rules. For example, a sonnet is a form of poem that has 14 lines.

Genre: comes from French and means style or type. There are genres of fiction and non-fiction.

Pathetic fallacy: where the weather or surrounding landscape reflects the mood of the scene. Clouds could be hanging threateningly in the sky, for example.

1.5 Non-fiction texts – purpose, audience and intention

You will learn a checklist of features to call upon when analysing and writing a variety of non-fiction texts.

⊃ For starters

One of the things you need to remember about non-fiction texts, even those with facts in them, is that they are not always true or reliable. You may have seen a TV advert that claims that 8 out of 10 cats prefer a particular type of cat food, but it is doubtful that every cat has been asked! The way facts are used is influenced by the writer's purpose and intention. They are used to make a text more believable.

Being as creative as you can, but using some 'facts', write a short statement to inform new students at your school about an aspect of school life.

⊃ Task

A checklist for analysing or writing non-fiction that you might find helpful is to think of an apple.

A **Audience** – who are you writing for?
P Purpose – why are you writing? What message is being conveyed?
P Presentation – what features, images or layout should this text type have?
L Language – what vocabulary and sentence structure suits it best?
E Effect – has the writing achieved the purpose for the audience?

Work with a partner to design your own checklist for the class to use throughout your GCSE course. Try to think of any everyday word where each letter indicates something you want to remember in English.

⊃ Taking it further

1 Use the **APPLE** checklist to write a plan for some writing that argues that school uniform should be compulsory.
2 Now write the **argument**. Remember that, unlike persuasion which may present only one view, an argument looks at both sides of a subject. To make sure you balance your argument well enough, copy and complete the table below before you start:

Arguments for school uniform	Arguments against school uniform

3 Share your writing with a partner and identify two positive features and one aspect that needs improvement.

The World of Texts

5

1.6 Spoken texts – style and register

You will learn about the terms 'style' and 'register'. You will practise using the correct style and register for different speaking situations.

⊃ For starters

Look at the **style** of these greetings:

> Good morning. I am most pleased to make your acquaintance. I do hope you are well.

> Hello. Very nice to meet you. How are you?

> Wotcha. 'kay?

What do you notice about the use of language in these greetings? What can you learn from this about language?

⊃ Task

1 Using the right level of formality, write a response to each greeting above in the correct style.

2 Practise the most formal example with a partner. It may feel very strange to start with!

Register refers to the language we would expect for a particular style or type of text, whether it is spoken or written. It is one of the ways examiners can spot when a student has copied work from the Internet as the register is suddenly different to their other writing.

3 Copy and complete the table on the right, suggesting some vocabulary to match the register for each situation.

4 Read this extract from a science textbook on the right. Identify five stylistic choices made by its writer that lead you to confidently believe it is from a science textbook.

ⓘ Concept bank

Style: the choices about words and sentences that a writer or speaker makes, such as the level of formality of a text.

Register: the way a text 'speaks to' and addresses its readers or listeners – the text's voice.

Situation	Language for the situation
Attending a job interview	
A teacher telling off a student	
Two 15-year-old girls gossiping	

The principal source of the noble gases is the atmosphere. Table 7.1 shows the nine most plentiful components of the atmosphere by mass. Over 98% is nitrogen and oxygen, but the noble gas argon comes third, making up over half the residue.

⊃ Taking it further

With a partner, write a script to perform, using an appropriate style and register for the situation. Choose one of these situations:

• trying to persuade a parent to let you go to a party
• reporting student views about lunches to the Headteacher
• complaining about a faulty MP3 player in a shop.

Learning aim

This unit will help you prepare for Section A of the English or English Language examination. In the exam you will be given non-fiction texts and asked questions on them. The questions will be designed to test how well you understand what you read, and how well you can analyse the texts.

2.1 Reading information texts

You will learn how to read information texts more efficiently, how to **analyse** them and how to judge their effectiveness.

ⓘ Concept bank

Analysis: in English, analysis is the careful investigation of language to see how it works. Hence we can analyse metaphors in a poem, or analyse the use of 'we' and 'you' in a political speech, to see what impact these uses of language have. We then explain how this impact is achieved.

⊃ For starters

Individuals and organisations write information texts to tell us things. We read them to find things out. We want to do this quickly and efficiently.

One 'trick of the trade' you can use to improve your reading of information texts is called **S3QR**. This is a tool to help you gain information from texts effectively. The idea is that you:

S	skim a text – you let your eyes travel quickly across it to get an idea of what the text is about
3Q	question a text – you come up with three questions that you want to answer when you look again at the text
R	read – you reread the text in order to get the answers to your questions.

Now apply the **S3QR** checklist to the Crufts text on the next page.

With practice, this approach to speed-reading really works and is a useful way to help you read more effectively inside or outside the exam room.

History of Crufts

How it all started: the development of Crufts Dog Show

Crufts is named after its founder, Charles Cruft. The young Charles, leaving college in 1876, had no desire to join the family jewellery business. Instead he took employment with James Spratt, who had set up a new venture in Holborn, London selling 'dog cakes'. Charles Cruft was ambitious and a relatively short apprenticeship as an office boy led to promotion to travelling salesman. This brought him into contact with large estates and sporting kennels. His next career move with Spratts saw him travelling to Europe and here in 1878 French dog breeders, perhaps seeing entrepreneurial talents in Cruft, invited him to organise the promotion of the canine section of the Paris Exhibition. He was still just two years out of college. Back in England in 1886 he took up the management of the Allied Terrier Club Show at the Royal Aquarium, Westminster.

The first Crufts show in that name was booked into the Royal Agricultural Hall, Islington in 1891. This was the first in a long series of shows there. During this era it was possible for individuals to run shows for personal profit, an aspect that appealed mightily to Charles Cruft, and he ran his shows with considerable profit to himself. Today there are no privately owned dog shows and permission to hold shows is granted by the Kennel Club, which licenses only non-commercial organisations.

In 1938 Charles Cruft died and his widow ran the 1939 show. Three years later Mrs Cruft felt the responsibility for running the show too demanding so, in order to perpetuate the name of the show her husband had made world famous, she asked the Kennel Club to take it over and it was sold to them; 1948 was the first show under the Kennel Club auspices. Held at Olympia, it proved an immediate success with both exhibitors and the public. Since then Crufts has increased in stature year by year.

In 1979 it was decided to change the venue from Olympia to Earls Court as the increasing entries had the show bursting at the seams. In 1982 the show ran for three days and in 1987 for four days to accommodate the increasing numbers of dogs and spectators. 1991 saw the Crufts Centenary Show being held at the Birmingham National Exhibition Centre, this being the first time the show had moved from London. 2010 will be the twentieth year that the show has been staged at the NEC.

⊃ Task

We read information texts to find things out. When we read them we want to trust what we are reading. We want to believe that what we are reading is accurate and comes from a reliable and expert source. Writers of information texts write in such a way as to create this sense of authority – to make their writing seem trustworthy and reliable. We should ask ourselves – what makes this text seem trustworthy and reliable? How can we best analyse it?

The mnemonic **FIFAT** will help you to analyse and judge an information text:

F How <u>factual</u> is it – how far is it full of **facts**, or is it full of unproven **opinions**?

I How <u>impersonal</u> is it – how far is the author standing back and trying to give a fair and objective view of the topic? Or is it very **personal**, full of 'my' and 'I', and very subjective?

F How <u>formal</u> is it – how far is the language distant and measured in tone, or is it colloquial and chatty?

A How <u>authoritative</u> is it – how much of an expert on the topic does the writer seem to be, or do they seem no more knowledgeable than the rest of us? How certain does the language sound?

T How <u>trustworthy</u> is it – how far does the language used create a sense of honesty and openness, or do you feel it is manipulating you?

1 Reread the Crufts text then use **FIFAT** to complete a table like the one below. Award a mark of 1–7 for each **FIFAT** question by placing a tick in the correct column.

	Very	1	2	3	4	5	6	7	**Very**
F	Factual								Opinionated
I	Impersonal								Personal
F	Formal								Informal
A	Authoritative								Unreliable
T	Trustworthy								Untrustworthy

2 Analyse the last paragraph of the Crufts text. Explain in writing how far it comes across as trustworthy and reliable. Include specific references to language used as evidence.

⊃ Taking it further

Harrison Holden is an expert at writing for the Internet. He gives people attending his lectures on effective web writing three 'kisses' of advice:

- **K**eep **I**t **S**traightforward – not complicated
- **K**eep **I**t **S**hort – never longer than it needs to be
- **K**eep **I**t **S**tructured – never in a random order.

These are Holden's 'golden rules' of writing for the Internet.

1 How well does the Crufts text follow Holden's 'golden rules'? Aim to write about 100–150 words.

2 Write an informative text of about 200 words on a completely imaginary famous person. You must make up every single fact in it! Nothing must be true, but you must write the text in a way that makes it come across as reliable and completely trustworthy. It should also stick to Holden's 'golden rules'.

3 In about 100 words, explain how you tried to make your text seem trustworthy. Give examples from your writing to support your explanation.

Reading Non-Fiction

2.2 Reading advice texts

You will learn how texts that give us advice work. You will learn some terms for describing and analysing advice texts.

➲ For starters

1 Think of something you do and that you know quite a lot about. It might be a sport, a leisure activity or hobby. Create a rough spidergram of ideas and information about this topic. For example, all the words and phrases that come to mind when you think about street dance.

   Use these notes to help you tell a partner about the topic. What is it? What is involved?

You have just *informed* your partner about your topic.

2 Now imagine your partner shares your interest in your topic. They do it, but not as well as you. Do another 'brainstorm' but this time jot down ideas and suggestions about what your partner should do to get better at this activity.

Then give them your *advice* on how to get better at the activity.

3 What difference was there between giving information and giving advice? (Think about what you said, but also how you said it.)

➲ Task

Here is an extract from a factsheet about looking after your dog if you visit the seaside:

Text A

If you do decide to take your dog away with you, there are many considerations that have to be made to ensure that your dog is safe and happy. We hope that this factsheet helps you to have a safe and enjoyable break with your best canine friend …

At the seaside

Unfortunately some coastal towns have banned dogs from their beaches in order to gain clean-beach awards and some may allow dogs only at certain times of the year (usually October to April).

- **Check with the local authority or tourism office before booking your holiday** to make sure that there will be a dog-friendly beach nearby.
- **Be careful of beaches with strong tides or undercurrents.** If there is a swimming ban or warning signs for human swimmers, then do not allow your dog to swim either.
- **Be careful if you are throwing a ball** for your dog to retrieve on sand, as he may ingest a large amount of sand and become ill.
- **Keep your dog under control** – especially in the presence of children. Always remember to pick up your dog's poop …

If you choose the right holiday for you and your dog, a great time can be had by all, with many happy memories to remember for months to come.

1 Look at the second bulleted piece of advice in Text A. Below it is rewritten as information – not advice.

> Some beaches have strong tides or undercurrents. There will be either a swimming ban or warning signs telling visitors not to swim at such beaches.

Now turn the third bulleted piece of advice back into the information it was based on.

2 Compare and contrast the two originals and the new versions. How is the language used in one version different to the other? What conclusions can you come to so far about how advice texts are written?

3 Here is part of an advice leaflet called *You and Your Dog in the Countryside*. Read it using **S3QR**. (Turn back to page 7 if you need to remind yourself what to do.)

Text B

You and Your Dog in the Countryside

> Hello! I'm John the sheepdog from the Countryside Code, and I just love the countryside. I'll guide you through this leaflet to help you have an enjoyable time by being responsible with your dog in the countryside, and help protect the landscape, wildlife and people that make it so special.

Whether ambling along leafy lanes, rambling through forests, or exploring new access land, the countryside is a great place for you and your dog to explore and enjoy. Here are six steps to worry-free 'walkies' by following the Countryside Code.

- By law, you must control your dog so that it does not scare or disturb farm animals or wildlife. On most areas of open country and common land, known as 'access land', you must keep your dog on a short lead between 1 March and 31 July – and all year round near farm animals.
- You do not have to put your dog on a lead on public paths, as long as it is under close control. But as a general rule, keep your dog on a lead if you can not rely on its obedience. By law, farmers are entitled to destroy a dog that injures or worries their animals.
- If a farm animal chases you and your dog, it is safer to let your dog off the lead – do not risk getting hurt by trying to protect it.

- Take particular care that your dog does not scare sheep and lambs, or wander where it might disturb birds that nest on the ground and other wildlife – eggs and young will soon die without protection from their parents.
- Everyone knows how unpleasant dog mess is and it can cause infections, so always clean up after your dog and get rid of the mess responsibly. Also, make sure your dog is wormed regularly to protect it, other animals and people.
- At certain times, dogs may not be allowed on some areas of access land or may need to be kept on a lead. Please follow any official signs.

You can also find out more about these rules from www.countrysideaccess.gov.uk, by emailing openaccess@naturalengland.gov.uk or calling **0845 100 3298**.

Wherever you go, following these steps will help keep your pet safe, protect the environment, and show you are a responsible dog owner.

Text B wants to influence how people who take their dogs into the countryside behave. It includes information. It also gives advice about what you should and should not do but without the reader feeling got at. It does this by using an appropriate **register**!

4 Which of these best describes the register of Text B:
   - authoritative and intimidating
   - firm but friendly
   - chatty and chummy?

   In your answer, include four specific references to or quotations from the text to support your choice.

5 Now be even more analytical and examine in detail the particular choices the writer has made. These choices create the register – that overall sense of the text having a 'voice'. Make notes as you will need them later. Apply a 'register detector' of six questions:

   - Word choice – How are words used? Identify six specific words or phrases that contribute to the register of the text.
   - Address – Is the reader acknowledged in the text? If so, how? Look for any pronouns.
   - Sentence types – Which sentence types are used (or not used)?
   - **Syntax** – How simple or complicated in structure are the sentences in the text?
   - Whole-text structure – Look again at the text as a whole. How has it been structured? How does it start and end, for example?
   - Presentational devices – How is the advice presented on the page? How is it made easier to read and more appealing?

6 You have now described the register of the text in question 4 and analysed aspects of it in question 5. Why do you think the writer chose to use this register in the text (remember what the purpose of the text is)?

⟳ Taking it further

Write a detailed analysis of the register of Text B. You might find it helpful to start by describing the text and its purpose, then work through each of the bulleted features, and then end with a paragraph where you conclude by saying what you feel the register of the text is.

2.3 Reading persuasive writing

You will learn how texts that aim to persuade us work. You will learn some terms for describing and exploring persuasive texts then produce a more detailed analysis of a persuasive text.

⊃ For starters

1 Write down six positive **facts** about your school or college and six positive **opinions** about it.

2 Write the advertising copy for a 20-second local radio advert that promotes your school or college to new students (and their parents). There is an Open Evening in three weeks. Below, the Head offers a starting point, but you don't have to use it:

> A new school year? A new start? How about [name of school/college]?

⊃ Task

Information texts tell us things. Advice texts influence how we behave by guiding us on how to do things. Persuasive texts also try to influence how we behave, but their writers assume that we might not easily be influenced to change our behaviour. That's why we have to be persuaded!

Psychologists say that our actions are influenced by our thoughts and feelings. These thoughts and feelings are what drive us to behave in particular ways. Thoughts are based on facts and information. Feelings are based on emotions. We give to charity because we know from evidence that the money will help homeless people, but also because the poster makes us feel sorry for them. Persuasive texts use these insights to influence us. They use facts to shape our thoughts; they use opinions and **emotive language** to work on our feelings.

Here is the opening text from a web page produced by a dog-food maker:

ⓘ Concept bank

Fact: a statement that can, at least in theory, be checked and confirmed as being true or false. Example: 'The writer of the last sentence is 37 years old.'

Opinion: one person's thoughts or feelings about something – other people may not agree. Example: 'The writer of the last sentence is remarkably handsome!'

Emotive language: words or phrases which describe the writer's emotions and/or make the reader feel a certain way. For example: 'breathtakingly boring'.

Our 8 Product Promises

For good healthy food

Making our products healthier and tastier is a never-ending job. We've put 60 years of research into our latest recipes so they have the right balance of vitamins, fibre and protein for healthier digestion. Dogs also find them more tail-thumpingly delicious than ever. But we believe that research alone isn't enough.

Something else that helps make our products naturally delicious are our eight product promises. They make sure that quality is always our first, second, third, fourth, fifth, sixth, seventh and eighth priority.

You will spot very quickly that this writing is trying to persuade you to buy their brand of dog food. But how?

1 In the text find examples of:
   - facts and opinions being used to persuade you
   - emotive language being used to persuade you.
2 How effectively are facts, opinions and emotive language used here?

Language that is crafted to be powerfully persuasive is sometimes called **rhetorical language**.

Here is part of a web-based advert trying to persuade dog owners to buy an MP3 audio guide on dog training:

Part Friend, Part Family
Taking Care of Your Dog Safely and Naturally

Are You Ready to Transform Your Dog Into an Obedient and Composed 'Poised Pooch' That Will Follow Your Every Command and Behave Under ANY Circumstances? If so, Then I've Got GREAT News ...

For the First Time Ever, The Impenetrable Canine Mind Has Been 'Cracked!' – Take This Exclusive Opportunity to Peek Inside It and Discover Expert Training Tactics and Techniques That Are Guaranteed to Tame Even the Rowdiest, Most Unruly Dog! Keep Reading to Learn How to Raise and Train a Dog From Any Age!

Dear friend,

Let's be honest with ourselves here, everyone obviously knows that dogs – however cute, lovable and playful they may be at times – can be (sometimes extremely!) difficult at others!

It doesn't matter whether you are trying to raise your puppy into a healthy dog ...

Or matter whether you've tried to train and discipline your dog so that it responds to your commands and learns the behaviours you want it to (and it won't!) ...

Or whether you are simply curious and want to learn everything there is to know about dogs – how to look after them, care for them, tend to their needs (and even how to understand 'dog language') the right way – like a true dog lover should ...

None of that really matters right now. That is, until you place yourself in the 'inner circle' of dog-training knowledge containing secrets and tricks that allow experts to charge CRAZY fees – for nothing more than implementing proven principles. You will learn all of that above and tons more.

And yes, you bet, the PROVEN principles I'll be talking about are the EXACT ones that you'll be learning today so ...

'... I Suggest You Cancel Your Next Appointment With Your Personal Dog Trainer IMMEDIATELY ...'

... because you certainly won't be needing him or her once you're 'in the know'.

And it's absolutely true – because that's what you will be learning – how to train your dog ... including every nitty gritty little detail the dog trainers know off by heart. Within the next couple of minutes, you WILL pick up on information that you probably thought would never be possible to obtain so easily.

You WILL learn a range of tips, tricks and techniques, so honed, and so fine-tuned, that even if you hired a personal dog trainer at $50–100 PER HOUR or more to stop that repetitive bad behaviour – he or she would NOT reveal them!

3 Read this persuasive text. Use **S3QR** – quickly skim it, then think of three questions to ask of it, then read it again.

4 Analyse the register of this text:
- How informal or formal is the writer trying to be? Evidence?
- How close to or distant from the reader is the writer trying to sound? Evidence?
- How emotionally involved with or detached from the advertised product is the writer trying to sound? Evidence?

5 Identify and comment on two uses of fact and two uses of opinion in this text.

6 This text uses rhetoric to influence you to buy the audio guide. Find the rhetorical devices listed below. For each one, give an example, and try to explain how it might work on the reader's thoughts and feelings.

> **Rhetorical devices:**
>
> - **rhetorical question**
> - alliteration
> - **hyperbole**
> - **contrasting pair**
> - **list of three**
> - **colloquialism**
> - simile
> - **personal address**
> - inclusive pronoun.

7 How straightforward, simple and structured is this text?

⊃ Taking it further

How are dog owners persuaded to buy the MP3 audio guide? You should write a paragraph on each bulleted item below, remembering to include examples:
- register
- fact and opinion
- language, including rhetorical devices.

ⓘ Concept bank

Rhetorical questions: are asked for dramatic effect and/or to make an audience think. They do not require an answer. Example: 'Do you really want to carry on wasting money on useless trinkets?'

Hyperbole: where an idea is exaggerated. Example: 'Bad hair day? Are split ends **ruining** your life?'

Contrasting pair: where two ideas opposite in meaning are held next to each other. Example: 'You might say give in, surrender, roll over! I say never submit to terrorism!'

List of three: where a writer repeats something three times to emphasise the point being made.

Colloquialism: informal words or phrases, including slang – deliberate use of a less formal register. Example: 'Listen, matey, that's not how to talk to a teacher!!'

Personal address: where a listener or reader is directly addressed as 'you'.

⊙ Grammar link

Inclusive pronouns draw readers or listeners into the writer's or speaker's position. Example: 'Pupils in Year 11, you know how important these exams are. *We* wouldn't want you to fail them, would *we*?'

2.4 Reading argument writing

You will learn how texts that argue work. You will use some methods for describing and analysing argument texts before producing a more detailed analysis of an argument text.

⊃ For starters

1 Brainstorm a set of notes to argue for or against the view that 'Dog owners who let their dogs stray should be very heavily fined'. Aim to make your case last at least a minute.

2 Use these notes to argue your case with a partner who takes the opposite view.

⊃ Task

1 Read the newspaper article below. Use **S3QR** – quickly **s**kim it, then think of **three q**uestions to ask of it, then **r**ead it again.

NIGHT-TIME NO-GO AREA

Our town centre is going to the dogs and the Council needs to act now, writes Mark Philips, a Middlesfield street cleaner who has had enough.

Have you been into the town centre of an evening? When the crowds have staggered home, the last bus has picked up its kebab-spattered yobs, and the police are chasing the car thieves? I have and it is not pleasant. You will not have seen me and the team. We are the ones driving those brush-trucks around Middlesfield cleaning up the day's mess. So what's the problem? More pay? Shorter hours? No. What we want is to do our jobs – doing other folks' dirty work – without fear for our safety. Too much to ask? Apparently so for this town council!

You in your office, do you look over your shoulder whilst checking the morning's accounts or sit less snug in your boardroom for fear that a pit bull will rip at your shins? In the last year, six street cleaners from Middlesfield have been attacked by stray dogs whilst carrying out their work. Next time you flit past your local street cleaners, Starbucks coffee in one hand, briefcase in the other, spare them a second glance. Look more closely and you might spot a limp, a pained expression, a bandaged wrist. Bad luck? No. The result of a council that asks its workers to battle through grime and garbage whilst being growled at by angry strays, and does nothing to protect us.

Since 2008, the number of dogs loose on the streets of Middlesfield has risen by 28%, according to RSPCA regional research. Middlesfield General Hospital reports that the number of patients treated for dog bites has more than doubled in the past year and no one will have missed recent reports documenting the case of Hannah Wishcombe, the Frinley girl savaged by a stray on her way home from school. After countless stitches and tetanus jabs, Hannah has made a remarkable recovery – but next time? The dozens of street cleaners forced to take to the streets every night without the protection of daylight or passers-by may not be quite so lucky. Middlesfield Council has yet to act decisively to stamp out this threat.

What can be done about it? It will cost more and those costs will have to come out of council tax. Fewer schools. Libraries closed. Old folk not cared for! Nonsense. Under the 1990 Environmental Protection Act, every council has the legal responsibility to 'deal with dogs straying on any land where the public have access'. We simply want tougher penalties for dog owners who fail to secure their pets, including hefty fines for the collection of dogs found straying by local authorities. Use the revenue raised to fund an increase in the number of dog control officers. If owners fail to collect their dogs or take responsibility for their behaviour then the animals should be confiscated permanently. Too drastic? Tell that to Steve Coombes, a 42-year-old Cranton street cleaner, still in hospital after an attack from a Rottweiler. Steve was clearing your streets of gum, litter and beer bottles.

How many more council workers will suffer before something is done? In a country happy to stump up millions for the 2012 Olympics, it is criminal to ask street cleaners to risk their wellbeing when there are easy and affordable solutions. It is nothing short of a scandal. **We** are leading a dog's life and it is driving **us** barking mad! Middlesfield Council, sort it.

Argument writing (or speaking) has been described as 'reasoning wrapped in rhetoric'. In other words, a set of linked ideas that make a case and present it in persuasive language. If we want to explain how an argument works, it is helpful to describe how the argument is put together. A typical argument structure might look like this:

- Introduction: where the writer's point of view or goal is stated.
- Development (1): where **anecdotes** or experiences are used as evidence.
- Development (2): where statistics and 'expert' witnesses are used as evidence.
- Counter-argument rebuttal: where the opposing view is mentioned but only to be dismissed.
- Conclusion: where the writer ends the argument with a 'punch'.

2 Look again at the newspaper article by Mark Philips. How far does it fit this typical argument structure? Use a table like the one below to decide if it does.

Argument structure element	Evidence: quotation from text
Introduction – point of view stated	
Development (1) – anecdote or experience	
Development (2) – statistics and expert witnesses	
Counter-argument rebuttal – opposing view dismissed	
Conclusion – ends with a 'punch'	

It is highly likely that one of the questions in your exam will ask you to summarise a piece of argument writing. When you do this, use the argument-structure approach to shape your answer. So, imagining you are summarising the Philips text, you might say:

Philips introduces his argument by stating … He then goes on to develop this by saying … A little later he develops this further by mentioning … and using statistics such as … to further … He then includes the opposing view by saying … before then … Finally, he ends his argument by …

3 Use this as a script frame for answering this question:
- How does Philips argue that the Council should do more to control stray dogs in Middlesfield?

⊃ Taking it further

Remember, argument writing is 'reasoning wrapped in rhetoric'.

1 Write four paragraphs in which you analyse Philips' use of language in the *Night-Time No-Go Area* article. Use these prompts to help you with each paragraph:

- Paragraph one: What is the purpose of Philips' article? Who might its target readership be?

- Paragraph two: Describe the register of the article. How formal or informal is the writing? How does Philips come across to you, the reader? Friendly? Detached? How often does Philips use emotive language?

- Paragraph three: Which rhetorical devices are used particularly effectively? Identify four instances where Philips wraps up his reasoning in rhetoric. Explain why these uses of language are effective.

- Paragraph four: Overall, how successfully does Philips argue in the article?

2 'Dog owners who let their dogs stray should be very heavily fined'. Argue for or against this view. Remember to use:

- an argument structure
- an appropriate register
- facts and opinions
- rhetorical devices
- emotive language.

Aim to write for about 30 minutes.

2.5 Exam practice for reading non-fiction

You will practise for the exams by answering some exam-style questions.

Exam practice

Time allowed: 45 minutes

1 Read Text A – *My Rottie, Henry*. It describes Joy Rogers' pet Rottweiler dog called Henry.
   What are Rogers' thoughts and feelings towards Henry? (8 marks)

2 Read Text B – *Why Are Dogs Man's Best Friend?* by S. Elliot. In it Elliott considers the relationship between dogs and humans. (You will find Text B on page 20.)
   According to Elliott, what is the relationship between dogs and humans? (8 marks)

3 Compare how language is used in Text A – *My Rottie, Henry* and Text B – *Why Are Dogs Man's Best Friend?* (16 marks)

! Examiner's tip

Remember to read the questions before you read the texts so that you know what you are looking for.

Text A

My Rottie, Henry

I didn't know much about rotties when I first got Henry, but he has helped me learn. He has been a little character since the day I brought him home in February 1991. He was happiest when we were out walking in the woods or playing ball or just lying on my lap playing with his toys. He was never one to get into the garbage or chew on furniture, but he loved to grab my socks and take off with them with that mischievous look in his eyes.

He potty trained easily and quickly, but he knew that whenever I was on the phone, my attention was elsewhere, and he would immediately squat while looking me square in the eye! He knew what he was doing, the little imp! I didn't know whether to yell at him or laugh. Now when I'm on the phone, he just leans against me to get his butt scratched.

He's always been a smart dog, one of the smartest I've ever had. He needs to be shown what I want only once or twice, and he catches on. Of course, he's taught me all about that rottie stubbornness, too. My mother used to try to tell me he was dumb, and I'd tell her, 'He's not dumb, he's stubborn. He knows darn good and well what you want.' He still steals socks if he thinks he's being neglected, and he still loves to lay on my lap and play with his toys (although at 105 pounds, it's no fun for me anymore!).

Henry is usually so sweet, cuddly, and calm, it's hard for me to accept that he can behave in a ferocious and aggressive manner, but he surely does. When the builder came to try to finish the decking, he had to quit because he thought Henry was going to break through the double-paned glass doors (we weren't home), but when he came back to do it when we were home, Henry greeted him like a long-lost friend.

When I first met Henry as a puppy, he was more interested in playing with his littermates than in being affectionate with a stranger, and I mistakenly thought this meant he would be aloof even to me. HA! He may not follow me from room to room all the time, but he will lie in a strategic location so that I (or anyone else) have to get by him to go in or out. And when I'm working in the yard, he assumes his watchdog role, lying near but always with eyes and ears alert to what's going on in the neighborhood. Although he loves my husband dearly (Henry was two when we started dating), it is clear that Henry's loyalty always will be with me first.

I have had many canine companions in my lifetime, but Henry tops them all. I wanted Henry for a friend and companion, and he has surpassed all my expectations. He is now five years old and beginning to grey slightly around the muzzle. We've had a lot of experiences together in those five years, and he helped me make it through some really rough times. No wonder he's getting grey.

Why Are Dogs Man's Best Friend?

The Relationship Between Humans and Dogs

The next time you look over at Fido and see him as a big mooch, you should remember that the origins of our relationship with dogs is one that is steeped in mystery.

Although no one knows exactly when dogs were domesticated, archaeologists do know that many cultures around the globe began treating dogs like members of the tribe around 14 000 years ago. This alliance with dogs was so profound that in many ancient cemeteries dogs have been discovered buried in the same graves as humans.

Why are Dogs So Much a Part of Human Society?

Dogs are team players. They take direction, naturally follow a social hierarchy, and easily accept humans as part of their pack. It is in the nature of dogs to be industrious and to try to please their pack-mates. This means that dogs can be taught to take direction and perform tasks that man is sometimes unwilling or unable to perform. These innate traits make dogs easily adaptable to human society.

With so many breeds, it's hard to imagine what the forerunners of the modern day canine might have been like. Through the centuries they have changed and adapted to better perform the tasks assigned to them. Again and again, they have been called upon to risk their lives in the service of their human allies. Every year there are newspaper stories and eyewitness accounts of dogs rescuing babies and young children, warning humans of impending danger, and finding lost loved ones over long and hazardous distances.

After such a successful partnership with man, their fate is inextricably linked to that of humans.

Man and Dogs – The Ties That Bind us Together

Dogs have the ability to feel deep affection and project unfailing good will. They are often good natured, accepting partners of our domestic circumstances. Dogs seldom complain, never threaten to leave us, and always forgive our failings. Their constancy can be a comforting presence as we manoeuvre our way through the obstacle course of modern life.

Fido may be a mooch, he may even steal a cookie off the coffee table now and then, but if he does, consider it payment for long and valued service.

Unit 3 Understanding Presentational Devices

Learning aim

In this unit you will prepare for the question in Section A of the English and English Language exam which asks you to look at the presentational devices used in a text, to comment on why and how they are used, and the effect they have. You will learn what presentational devices are and how to analyse their use.

(i) Concept bank

Presentational devices: features of presentation, design and organisation that help a text communicate its information, ideas and feelings. These features include choice of font, selection of images, columns, headings and use of colour.

3.1 Introducing presentational devices

You will look at how writers and text designers use presentational devices to make texts easier to read, navigate and understand.

↻ For starters

Look at this text from a leaflet for babysitters produced by Avon Fire Service.

Text A

Living safely. Safety advice for babysitters. When you are babysitting make sure you do not create any fire hazards. All fires should have a secure fireguard. Do not leave a child alone in a room where there is a fire. Don't let children play too close to fires as their clothing may catch light. Keep matches and lighters out of the sight and reach of children. Never leave children alone with lighted candles. If you have been given permission to smoke while babysitting always make sure that any cigarettes are out and cold before you empty the ashtray. Never leave smoker's materials where a child can reach them. Don't leave ashtrays on upholstered furniture. Never leave the kitchen when you have cooking on the stove. If you have to answer the door or phone turn the heat off or down. Make sure that children can't reach the saucepan handles. If the children in your care are in bed when you are in the house make sure that you know what the family's fire action plan is. (Ask the adults responsible for the children about this before they leave). Do you have an emergency contact telephone number? Is there a trusted family friend or neighbour you can contact? Do you know where the nearest telephone outside the house is? Do you know what the smoke alarm sounds like? If clothing catches fire: Stop – don't run the flames will get worse. Drop – get on the ground or floor. Roll – back and forward quickly until the flames are smothered. You can help by covering the casualty with clothing or blankets and patting to extinguish the flames. Make sure you protect your own hands before attempting this. If there is a fire: Raise the alarm – don't investigate, get everyone up and out of the building. If it's smoky, stay low, crawl if you have to. Once you are outside stay there! Call 999 – Stay calm and ask for the Fire Service. Website: www.avonfire.gov.uk e-mail: community.safety@avonfire.gov.uk tel: 0117 926 2061 in case of fire call 999 Avon fire & rescue preventing protecting responding

↻ Task

How easy or difficult did you find it to read and absorb the information and advice? Make some notes to explain your answer.

Text B

LIVING SAFELY

SAFETY ADVICE FOR BABYSITTERS

WHEN YOU ARE BABYSITTING MAKE SURE YOU DO NOT CREATE ANY FIRE HAZARDS.

All **fires** should have a secure fireguard. Do not leave a child alone in a room where there is a fire. Don't let children play too close to fires as their clothing may catch light.

Keep **matches** and **lighters** out of the sight and reach of children. Never leave children alone with lighted **candles**.

If you have been given permission to **smoke** while babysitting always make sure that any cigarettes are out and cold before you empty the **ashtray**. Never leave smoker's materials where a child can reach them. Don't leave ashtrays on upholstered furniture.

Never leave the kitchen when you have cooking on the stove. If you have to answer the door or 'phone, turn the heat off or down. Make sure that children can't reach the saucepan handles.

If the children in your care are in bed when you are in the house, make sure that you know what the family's **fire action plan** is. (Ask the adults responsible for the children about this before they leave).
  • Do you have an emergency contact telephone number?
  • Is there a trusted family friend or neighbour you can contact?
  • Do you know where the nearest telephone outside the house is?
  • Do you know what the **smoke alarm** sounds like?

If clothing catches fire:
STOP – don't run – the flames will get worse.
DROP – get on the ground or floor.
ROLL – back and forward quickly until the flames are smothered. You can help by covering the casualty with clothing or blankets and patting to extinguish the flames. Make sure you protect your own hands before attempting this.

IF THERE IS A FIRE:
  • Raise the alarm – don't investigate, get everyone up and out of the building.
  • If it's smoky, stay low, crawl if you have to.
  • Once you are outside stay there!
  • Call 999 – stay calm and ask for the Fire Service.

website: www.avonfire.gov.uk e-mail: community.safety@avonfire.gov.uk

TEL: 0117 926 2061
IN CASE OF FIRE CALL 999

AVON FIRE & RESCUE
PREVENTING PROTECTING RESPONDING

Text B uses the same text as Text A, but some text presentational devices have been added:

1 Find an example in Text B of each of the devices listed on the right.
2 Explain in detail why each device is used. Clue: think about how it might help the reader.

Text presentational devices

- Headings and subheadings
- CAPITAL letters where it isn't for sentence starts or proper nouns
- Different sizes of lettering: 6 point; 12 point; 18 point, and so on ...
- **Bold** or *italic* text
- Bulleted or numbered lists
- Different fonts:
  - Serif fonts (such as Times New Roman) and **sans-serif** fonts (such as Arial)
  - 'Gimmick' fonts such as *Old English*, CURLY or **BROADWAY**
  - Handwriting fonts.

Finally, here is the same text professionally designed for an Avon Fire Service leaflet. It contains further presentational devices. See if you can spot them!

Text C

LIVING SAFELY

SAFETY ADVICE FOR BABYSITTERS

WHEN YOU ARE BABYSITTING MAKE SURE YOU DO NOT CREATE ANY FIRE HAZARDS.

All **fires** should have a secure fireguard.
Do not leave a child alone in a room where there is a fire.
Don't let children play too close to fires as their clothing may catch light.

Keep **matches** and **lighters** out of the sight and reach of children.
Never leave children alone with lighted **candles.**

If you have been given permission to **smoke** while babysitting always make sure that any cigarettes are out and cold before you empty the ashtray. Never leave smoker's materials where a child can reach them. Don't leave **ashtrays** on upholstered furniture.

Never leave the kitchen when you have cooking on the stove. If you have to answer the door or 'phone turn the heat off or down. Make sure that children can't reach the saucepan handles.

If the children in your care are in bed when you are in the house make sure that you know what the family's **fire action plan** is. (Ask the adults responsible for the children about this before they leave).

• Do you have an emergency contact telephone number?
• Is there a trusted family friend or neighbour you can contact?
• Do you know where the nearest telephone outside the house is?
• Do you know what the **smoke alarm** sounds like?

If clothing catches fire:
STOP - don't run the flames will get worse.
DROP - get on the ground or floor.
ROLL - back and forward quickly until the flames are smothered. You can help by covering the casualty with clothing or blankets and patting to extinguish the flames. Make sure you protect your own hands before attempting this.

IF THERE IS A FIRE
• Raise the alarm - don't investigate, get everyone up and out of the building.
• If it's smoky, stay low, crawl if you have to.
• Once you are outside stay there!
• **Call 999** - Stay calm and ask for the Fire Service.

website: www.avonfire.gov.uk
e-mail: community.safety@avonfire.gov.uk

TEL: 0117 926 2061
IN CASE OF FIRE CALL 999

AVON FIRE & RESCUE
PREVENTING PROTECTING RESPONDING

3   Why is the background pink?
4   Why is a range of fonts used?
5   Why is italic lettering used?
6   Why is the logo used?
7   Overall, how far has the use of these additional presentational devices helped the text to fulfil its purpose? Or are they added for other reasons too? Write a paragraph to explain.

⟳ **Taking it further**

You have looked closely at the *rear* side of this leaflet so far. Your focus has very much been on how the presentation of written text helps readers to access the text, find what is most important in it and absorb the key information. Here is the cover of the *Advice for Babysitters* leaflet:

Look closely at the four written text elements on the cover:

- The 'Living Safely' heading in the top left
- The 'Safety Advice for Babysitters' title underneath
- The 'Avon Fire & Rescue' text that is part of the logo
- The three-word slogan 'Preventing Protecting Responding'.

You will see that each element is presented differently. The designer has chosen four quite different font styles.

1 In four short paragraphs, explain what the purpose of each of these text elements is and why you think it has been presented in the way that it has.
2 Would you change anything about how the text is presented on the cover or would you leave it as it is? Write a paragraph to explain your thinking.

3.2 Analysing visual devices

You will look at how presentational devices are used to help readers to understand the ideas and information communicated in a text. In particular, you will learn about how and why devices such as diagrams, graphics and pictures are used.

⟳ For starters

1 Take a sheet of paper and write the word 'PICTURES' in the middle. Spend two minutes doing a 'brainstorm' of the situations at school where diagrams, graphics and pictures are used.
2 Do these situations have anything in common? Are there situations where you use diagrams, graphics and pictures more often? Why is this?

⟳ Task

Below and on page 26 are four texts that contain pictures. Spend two minutes looking at the texts and ask yourself how the pictures are being used.

Text A

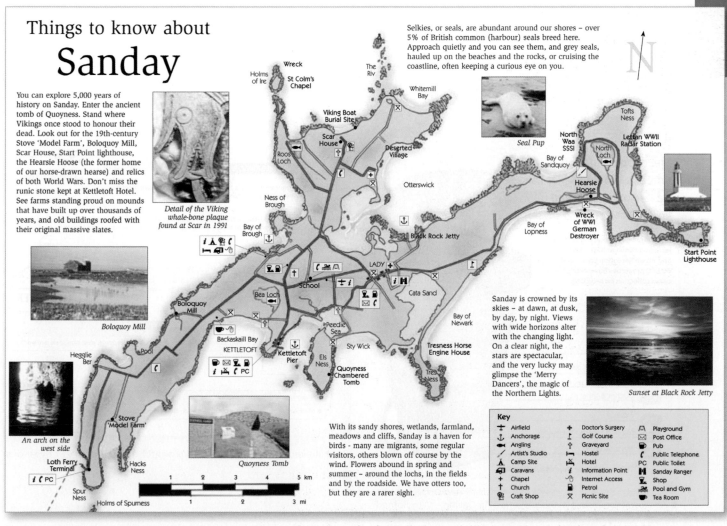

↑ A tourist leaflet about the island of Sanday

Text B

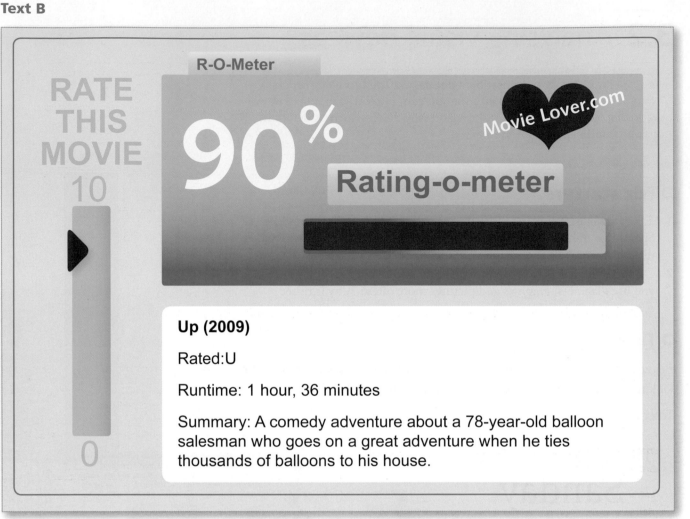

↟ *A review of the film* Up, *from a website*

Text C

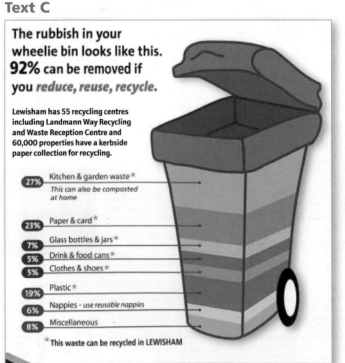

↟ *An illustration from a magazine article* Re-Cycling – Why Bother?

Text D

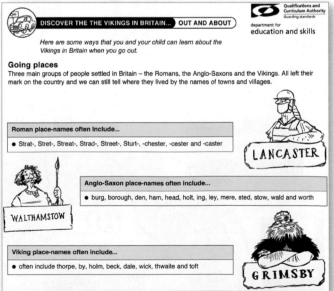

↟ *An information sheet on the Vikings for the parents of 7–11 year olds*

1 You will notice that different types of pictures are used in the texts. Use a
table like the one below to record which types are used in each text.

	Photo	Cartoon/drawing	Map	Graphic	Diagram	Logo
Text A						
Text B						
Text C						
Text D						

Different types of pictures can be used for different reasons in texts. If you
learn to describe these reasons more precisely, your analysis of them will
be better focused. The table below will build up your understanding and
vocabulary. Read it carefully as you will use what you learn later in the unit.

Uses of pictures in texts

Purpose	Vocabulary
Illustration: where a picture is used just to let us see what something the author has mentioned looks like.	'This *lets us see* what the actor looks like …'
Demonstration: where a picture is used to help the author make a point about something in the text.	'The picture *shows us* how …'
Explanation: where a picture is used to give a visual explanation, or a simplified version of something in the text.	'The diagram *helps us* understand how oxygen …'
Information: where a picture is used to present additional information (not in the written text) to the reader.	'The pie chart *tells us* that …'
Substantiation: where a picture is used to help convince us of a claim made or to prove something the writer is saying.	'This *supports* the claim that it …'

2 Look again at Texts A–D and the table you completed for task 1. Now
use a table like the one below to analyse each text in turn. An example has
been given for an imagined text to help you.

You are using the table to note:

- who the audience for the text might be
- the picture types used
- and an analysis of them.

Text	Audience	Pictures used	Analysis
Example (a page from a Geography textbook about the water cycle)	School students (11–13)	Photo of clouds over a mountain; and a diagram of the water cycle	The photo illustrates the topic (school students know what clouds and mountains look like!); the photo might actually be just to make the page less text heavy. The diagram is much more important because it simplifies the complex stages in the water cycle.
Text A			
Text B, etc.			

3 Choose the two texts that you feel use pictures most effectively. Explain your choices in three paragraphs. Use these headings to structure each paragraph:

- Purpose of the text
- Purpose of the picture(s) used
- Why the picture use is effective.

⊃ Taking it further

Here is a page from an American bicycle safety booklet called *Sprocket Man*.

Write two paragraphs about how pictures are used. Use this structure:

- Purpose and audience for the booklet
- Uses and effects of pictures (use words from the 'Uses of pictures in texts' table on page 27 if it helps).

3.3 Code-breaking

You will look at how text presentational devices influence the responses we have to the subject matter presented in the texts. You will learn about how pictures and other images do not just *show* us things, but can also create ideas, feelings or **connotations** in readers' minds. To help you do this, you will learn about codes and how they work in photographic images.

⊃ For starters

Look at these three photos of a lakeside tourist 'hotspot' in Austria called Hallstatt.

Photo B

Photo A

Photo C

Spend two minutes talking about the pictures:

- What are the similarities and differences between the photos? Don't just think about what they show. Look closely at the **shot** (type, framing and orientation, and use of colour) and the **editing**.

- Did you spot the 'trick' in one of the photos?
- Which would make the best postcard? Why?

Text A

↑ *An image used in a driving school's website*

Text B

↑ *The cover of a local magazine* Lewisham Life, *produced by Lewisham council*

Texts A and B show young people through pictures and other devices, but the connotations of each image are different. To understand how this happens, you need to analyse the images in detail. A starting point is to think about the **codes** at work in the photos. Photos featuring people use codes such as:

- facial expression
- eye contact
- gesture and body posture
- clothing, hair and make-up.

All texts – written, spoken, visual, non-verbal – use codes to communicate meaning. To analyse a text we can break it down into the codes it uses to communicate. In image analysis, we can look at codes such as facial expressions or people's clothing. These are non-verbal codes of communication used in many different images – although they feature in photographs they are not specific to photography. They are part of our everyday lives. We form a view of people based on their facial expressions; whether or how they look at us; the gestures they use and how they stand; the clothes they wear, or how they do their hair and make-up.

⊃ Task

1 Look again at the two people in Text A. Write a paragraph about the impressions you have of them because of their:
- facial expression
- eye contact
- gesture and body posture
- clothing, hair and make-up.

2 Now look closely at the group of young people presented in Text B. Again, write a paragraph about the impressions you have of them because of their:
- facial expression
- eye contact
- gesture and body posture
- clothing, hair and make-up.

3 Which of the two images (Text A or Text B) creates a more positive impression of the young people represented? Give *four* reasons.

Photographers make choices when they take photographs and then when they digitally edit them on their computers. These choices are the specific codes of photography. The effects of these choices are powerful in shaping the meanings and connotations of the images. Codes specific to photography include: shot type, shot angle, colour or black and white, degree of colour saturation, and image orientation (landscape or portrait).

4 Compare (or contrast) the *shot types* used in Texts A and B. Are they similar or different? What is the effect in each case of the choice of shot type? How do the choices shape your impressions of the young people? Write a paragraph.

5 Compare (or contrast) the *shot angles* used in Texts A and B. Are they similar or different? What is the effect in each case of the choice of shot angle? Why has that unusual angle been used in Text A? How do the choices shape your impressions of the young people? Write a paragraph.

Colours have a strong psychological effect on us. Designers use colours to create thoughts and feelings in the reader. Here are some connotations of different colours:

Red – sexy, dangerous, 'wicked', 'stop'

Purple (children's favourite colour) – excitement

Green – good, healthy, ecological, 'go'

Yellow – warm, happy, lively

White – pure, clean

Pink – 'girlie', cute

Brown – earthy, wholesome, traditional

Gold – luxurious

Orange – fun

Black – mysterious, forbidding

Blue and **grey** are neutral colours, often used simply to create a background.

6 Look closely at the use of colour in Texts A and B. Is it used similarly or differently? What is the effect in each case of the use of colour? How does colour shape your impressions of the young people? Look at that background to Text A. Write a paragraph.

7 Look closely at the lettering in Texts A and B. Is it used similarly or differently? What is the effect in each case of the use of colour, the font choice and point size? How do choices made by the designers here work with (or against) the impressions of the young people created by the images? Write a paragraph.

⊃ Taking it further

Which text on page 30 (Text A or Text B) uses codes most effectively to present its subject matter? Write four paragraphs about how it uses the codes. Use these questions as prompts for the four paragraphs:

- What overall meanings and connotations about these young people are suggested by the text? How do they come across?
- How does it use non-verbal codes to create these connotations?
- How does it use specific photographic codes to create these connotations?
- How does it use lettering colour, font choice and point size?

3.4 Exam practice for understanding presentational devices

You will look at how presentational devices work to strengthen and deepen the overall meanings and connotations of the text. You will complete an exam-style question.

➲ For starters

This poster is trying to persuade young people to use a scheme called CAF to help them deal with any worries they may have.

Do you think the poster would work? Think about:

- its use of language
- the central photo
- other presentational devices.

➲ Task

Here is a list of presentational devices and a list of reasons for presentational devices being used in a text.

Presentational devices		Reasons for use	
a	Bold lettering	1	… to reinforce the emotions presented in the text
b	Headings	2	… to help the reader access the text
c	Logo	3	… to give the reader a sense that the text's writers are dependable
d	Colour photographic images	4	… to give the text a contemporary feel
e	Photographic images that look up	5	… to create an emotional support for the ideas presented in the text
f	Font variations	6	….to create a sense that readers can trust the writer
g	Images of positive-looking people	7	… to give the text a sense of authority and status
h	Close-up photographic images	8	… to reinforce and back up the information presented in the text

i	Columns	9	… to give the text an informal tone
j	Eye-level photographic images	10	… to help the reader navigate through the information
k	Drawings	11	… to better indicate what the important parts of the text are
l	Images of sad people or situations	12	… to help put complicated information across
m	Graph/chart	13	….to make the reader feel that the text's writer knows their needs
n	Ordered design and use of space	14	… to create a friendly overall mood for the text
o	Overall colour scheme	15	… to help the reader understand how to do something
p	Bullets	16	… to shape the emotions of the reader so they act in a particular way
q	Text boxes and similar devices	17	… to make the reader feel supported by the text's writer
r	Letter capitalisation	18	… to make the reader share the thoughts and feelings of the writer
s	Cartoon/graphic images	19	… to make the intended meaning of the text less ambiguous
t	Maps or plans	20	… to make the reader feel this text is aimed at them
u	Plain background	21	… to reassure or calm the reader
v	Photographic images that look down	22	… to make the text more visually appealing and attention-grabbing
w	Diagrams	23	… to create a sympathy for or empathy with people in the text
x	Point size variations	24	… to make certain that the text's key messages will hit the reader
y	Images where people make eye contact	25	… to lessen the likelihood of the reader losing interest in the text
z	Italic lettering	26	… to draw attention to the text even from a distance

1 Look at the list of presentational devices. Choose *four* that you think are powerful in shaping the audience's response to the poster on page 32.

2 Now match your chosen four devices to *four* items from the 'Reasons for use' list. Present your decisions and ideas in a set of four sentences, starting, for example, like this: 'The poster uses bullets to …', then adding one of the 'Reasons for use' phrases. If you are writing, leave at least a two-line gap after each sentence. Here's an example (top right) on a different text.

3 Now you will add to each sentence by following it up with another that analyses the effect of the device being used. That is why you left the gap between each sentence if you were writing. For each one, think about what is gained in the text by its use of a specific presentational device. Here's an example (bottom right) of what we now have.

If you link four devices to four reasons, and then explain what the effect of each device is, you will have eight sentences of thoughtful analysis!

4 Now look again at the two tables and match the rest of the devices and reasons together.

➲ Taking it further

Find a text of your own that you think makes interesting use of presentational devices. Using the devices and reasons lists on page 32 and above, and your own ideas about the effects of the devices, write two paragraphs on it. Remember to structure your answer by using PADRE (see page 34).

> The leaflet advertising Chester Zoo uses a map to make the reader feel supported by the text's writer.

> The leaflet advertising Chester Zoo uses a map to make the reader feel supported by the text's writer. The effect of this is to make the potential visitor feel confident that they can find their way to the zoo, but it also creates a positive bond between the writer and the visitor; they really care for me there!

Time allowed: 15 minutes

This is a poster produced by Wyre Borough Council in the North of England. How does the poster use presentational devices?

Use PADRE to help you:

- **P**urpose of the poster and **A**udience for the poster
- **D**evices used, **R**easons for them and their **E**ffects (8 marks)

Don't forget **PEE** when writing about presentational devices. The examiner will reward you for making a **P**oint, for using **E**vidence to support what you are saying, and for **E**xplaining how the evidence supports the point.

If you'd like to help young people try something new and make a positive contribution to the local community then contact the Young Transformer Wyre Project on:

Telephone: 01234 567890
Email: YoungTransform@webaddress.org
Text: WYRE to 017345 567890

www.youngtransformerwyre.webaddress.org

Young Transformers

WHO DO YOU SEE?

Troublemaker, Thug, Hoody? or DJ, Stylist, Chef?

It all depends on your point of view doesn't it?

We see the potential that people have if they are given the chance.

That's where you can help.

The Young Transformer Wyre Project is providing grants of up to £2,500 for organisations to deliver training courses, classes and activities that can give young people aged between 7 to 25 years a chance to change their lives.

WYRE   Wyre Borough Council   Community Foundation

Unit 4

Changing Minds – Arguing and Persuading

Learning aim

This unit will help you to produce effective persuasive and argumentative work. You will be helped to write in a convincing, persuasive manner, to write an effective argument, and to give engaging persuasive and argumentative presentations.

4.1 Persuasive writing – adverts

You will explore advertising techniques and write your own effective advertisement.

➲ For starters

1 Where do you see persuasive writing on a daily basis? Write a list of six examples that you can think of.

2 When you read persuasive writing, how do you know it is trying to persuade you? Write a list of six language features that you typically find in persuasive writing.

➲ Task

1 Read the advertisement for Disneyland Paris on page 36. It is very rich in persuasive language.

2 Now look at the text in the box that begins **Disneyland ® Resort Paris is a magical destination ...** Identify three examples of **emotive language** and explain how each tries to get the reader to come to Disneyland (look out for adjectives).

3 Look at the text in the box that begins **Disneyland Resort Hotels**. How does it try to appeal to a variety of potential visitors? How does the text refer to potential visitors? (You should spot a change as you look for the answer.) What is the effect of this change?

4 Now look back at the writing in the box that begins **The Walt Disney Studios ®.**
How does the writer use contrasting sentence lengths and types to persuade readers to visit?

5 Overall, how successful do you think the language used in the advertisement is?

ⓘ Concept bank

Emotive language: words or phrases which describe the writer's emotions and/or make the reader feel a certain way: for example, to convince you a place is worth going to visit – 'a magical destination where dreams can come true'. Words like 'magical' and 'dreams' are very emotive and are used here to convince the reader that they want this experience.

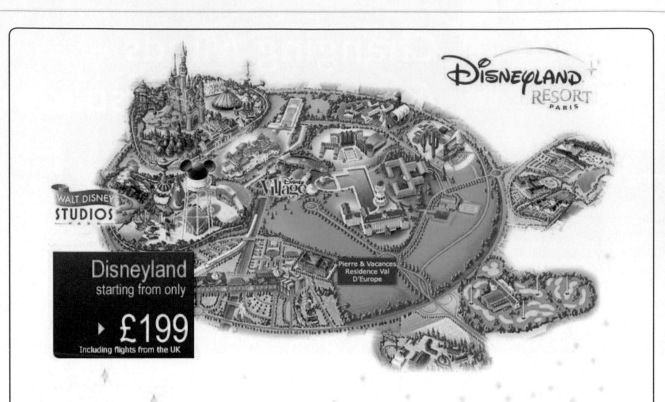

Disneyland ® Resort Paris is a magical destination where dreams can come true. All the family can meet and greet some of their favourite characters.

Disneyland ® Park

Disneyland ® Park offers a huge range of fabulous parades for kids of all ages.

Divided into 5 themed areas the park includes restaurants, shops and attractions from the exhilarating Space Mountain: Mission 2 to the wildest ride in the Wild West, Big Thunder Mountain. If you want to slow things down fly with Dumbo and Peter Pan in Fantasyland or gently cruise around the river of the far west on one of the elegant steam boats in Frontierland.

Meet all your favourite Disney characters. Get a photo on main street USA with some of your favourite Disney characters, then be taken "to infinity and beyond!" on Buzz Lightyear Lazer Blast (inspired by Disney-Pixar's *Toy Story 2*) in Discoveryland.

The Walt Disney Studios ®

Welcome to the Walt Disney Studios ® Park …

Where it's lights! Camera! Magic!

Everywhere! All the time!

Step through the Studio gates and let your imagination soar. Time to immerse yourself in the never-ending, always fascinating world of movies, animation and television.

Four production zones within the park featuring rides, shows and entertainment with one single focus: entertainment for the whole family.

Disneyland Resort Hotels

Choosing to stay at the resort can truly turn a weekend break into a magic experience. Thanks to the fact that there are hotels to suit every budget and taste – there is something for everyone. Each choice comes with its own magical experience.

Within the seven onsite hotels, guests will find numerous restaurants ranging from buffet style food courts to formal table service. In addition, each hotel has its own bar and gift shop.

But whether you choose to stay in a wild west town or a rustic hunting lodge, a big apple sky scraper or a Mexican Pueblo, you can be assured of one thing … Disney's outstanding quality and famous love for the magical details that will make your trip a truly unforgettable one.

⟳ Taking it further

In 200–300 words, write the advertising copy to accompany a picture of
a place of interest or tourist attraction in your area. This could be a tourist
attraction like Alton Towers, a local park, a youth club, a football stadium
or other place you enjoy going to. Use the Disneyland advert as an example
– but do not copy it!

Remember to use powerful and persuasive language which really grabs the
attention of the reader, such as 'fantastic place' or 'awe-inspiring location'.

Key language devices used in advertising include:

- You – using the word 'you' makes the advertisement appear to be talking
  directly to the reader.
- **Lists of three** – by listing ideas in threes, the advertiser makes their
  product sound more convincing.
- Slogans – often adverts have a slogan, which is an easily remembered
  phrase or word. Good slogans will help you remember why a product is
  worth buying.
- Straplines – are well-known second lines in adverts that come after the
  product or company name.
- Softened imperatives – imperatives are words telling you to do something.
  Softening them means they ask you to do something in a more gentle,
  polite manner.

ⓘ Concept bank

List of three: where a writer
repeats something three times to
emphasize the point being made.

🔗 Grammar link

Punctuation can also help add
emphasis to a point. For instance,
if you use exclamation marks it
shouts out to the reader that this
is a good idea – 'Come on this
holiday! You will love it!' This
technique is used in the Disney
advertisement.

4.2 Argument texts – newspaper articles

You will explore and analyse newspaper argumentative writing techniques then write your own argumentative piece.

○ For starters

1 Read these sentences:

It is a lie.   I can prove it.   Just let me.

2 The three sentences are short and make their point efficiently. Why might a writer use three short sentences like this? What is the effect?

3 Write three short sentences of your own. Remember to create a strong dramatic impact.

○ Task

1 Read the following article from *Media Week*. The article gives information on how the children's TV channel Nickelodeon has joined with the government on a scheme to promote healthy living. As you read it, think about what techniques the writer uses to put across a point of view.

Nickelodeon joins forces with the government to promote healthy living

LONDON – Nickelodeon, the ad-funded children's TV network, has joined forces with the British Government to help promote healthy living by dedicating free airtime and branding opportunities for the Department of Health's Change4Life movement.

The partnership was officially announced at the unveiling of Nickelodeon's autumn/winter programming schedule last night (8 July).

The second largest commercial kids' TV network in the UK will soon include Change4Life messages and branding in bespoke campaign spots.

The move complements the network's Nicktrition initiative, which it proactively launched in 2005 in response to growing concern about the health of children in the UK and subsequent Ofcom review of so-called junk food advertising.

Two new brand spots will air across the network from today (9 July) that endorse the importance of healthy, balanced eating and an active lifestyle.

Approximately 16 spots are expected to run on-air every day over the next 12 months, forecast to reach more than six million people within the first three months.

Howard Litton, managing director of Nickelodeon UK, called the initiative 'a natural fit' with the network's Nicktrition campaign and stressed corporate social responsibility played a 'core part of the brand'.

He added: 'We're in a great position to support the movement as we represent a unique and trusted voice among UK kids. We can use this voice to tackle issues in an effective and engaging way.'

Change4Life is a national movement to encourage kids to 'eat well, move more and live longer'. It already has support from more than 18 000 grass roots organisations, ranging from charities and supermarkets to commercial organisations.

Discuss the following in small groups and make notes on your thoughts.

2 What is the argument being put forward in this article? Write a summary.

3 What is the purpose of the summary under the main heading?
   - How effective is it?
   - What would happen if it was not included?

4 This argument makes use of **facts** and **opinions**, which are a very common feature of argumentative writing.
   - Pick out two facts from the article and explain their effect.
   - Pick out two opinions from the article and explain their effect.

5 Why are we given this information: 'The second largest commercial kids' TV network in the UK'?

6 Look at the quotations that are used in the article. Who made each comment and why have these quotations been used?

7 The language used is very definite and makes it very hard to argue against what Change4life are doing. For example:

> 'Two new brand spots will air across the network from today.'

Find two more examples of language which is very definite, saying something is definitely happening, and explain the effect.

> ### ⓘ Concept bank
>
> **Fact:** a statement that can, at least in theory, be checked and confirmed as being true or false.
>
> **Opinion:** one person's thoughts or feelings about something – other people may not agree.

➲ Taking it further

Write a 300–400 word article for a school magazine putting forward your views on advertising for children. You could discuss advertising for children generally, or look at a specific area, such as:
- music or DVDs
- food or drink
- clothes
- beauty products
- computer games.

Include some of the argument techniques covered in this unit so far:
- quotations from other people
- facts and opinions
- persuasive language.

4.3 Writing and performing speeches

You will learn how to use speech devices to create a strong and convincing argument for an audience. You will then be able to write and deliver an argumentative speech to an audience.

⊃ For starters

By 4 June 1940, the Second World War had been going on for nearly a year. The Prime Minister of the time, Winston Churchill, gave a speech on the radio to try to get the listeners to believe that Britain could win the war. This speech is famous as it was very successful in making people want to fight to defeat Germany.

1 Read the speech, imagining you are on the radio and that you are trying really hard to make your audience believe in what you are saying.

> I have, myself, full confidence that if all do their duty, if nothing is neglected, and if the best arrangements are made, as they are being made, we shall prove ourselves once again able to defend our Island home, to ride out the storm of war, and to outlive the menace of tyranny, if necessary for years, if necessary alone …
>
> Even though large tracts of Europe and many old and famous States have fallen or may fall into the grip of the Gestapo and all the odious apparatus of Nazi rule, we shall not flag or fail.
>
> We shall go on to the end, we shall fight in France, we shall fight on the seas and oceans, we shall fight with growing confidence and growing strength in the air, we shall defend our Island, whatever the cost may be, we shall fight on the beaches, we shall fight on the landing grounds, we shall fight in the fields and in the streets, we shall fight in the hills;
>
> we shall never surrender, and even if, which I do not for a moment believe, this Island or a large part of it were subjugated and starving, then our Empire beyond the seas, armed and guarded by the British Fleet, would carry on the struggle, until, in God's good time, the New World, with all its power and might, steps forth to the rescue and the liberation of the old.

2 The speech had a powerfully persuasive effect at that time. Would it be as persuasive today? Explain why or why not.

→ *Winston Churchill*

⊃ Task

A typical exam question might ask you to analyse the language used in a piece of persuasive speaking or writing. You are going to investigate what makes this speech effective as a piece of persuasion.

1 The speech includes a range of persuasive techniques:
   - What is the effect of the repetition of 'we shall fight' in the speech?
   - Churchill uses a lot of listing. For example: places where 'we' shall fight, how 'we' shall fight. What is the effect of this listing?
   - Why does Churchill address the audience as 'we'? What would the impact have been if he had used 'you' instead?
   - Most of the phrases used here are short. Why has Churchill chosen to use short phrases rather than long, complicated ones?
   - How does he answer the question: 'When will we surrender?'

2 How do the techniques discussed above make the speech more persuasive? See below for an example of how personal pronouns are used in the speech.

> *Churchill opens the speech speaking about himself directly to the audience –*
> *'I have, myself, full confidence' – which makes the message more personal both to Churchill himself and to those he is directly speaking to.*

3 Using about 20–30 words from the speech, and a few of your own, write the text for a poster to be displayed throughout Britain in June of 1940.

⊕ Grammar link

Pronouns are often used in speeches to involve the audience. Pronouns are words such as: 'we', 'you', 'I', 'us'.

⊃ Taking it further

Write your own speech that could be delivered to the class on the topic: 'Is all advertising for children based on lies?'

You will need to plan what you are going to write so that your speech takes at least one minute to deliver. Think about points for and against the title. Try to include some of the following key speech techniques:
- **lists of three**
- **rhetorical questions**
- voice or style of address
- involving the audience
- balance of material
- effective openings and conclusions.

Remember when you deliver your speech:
- speak with a loud, clear voice
- do not rush
- look at your audience
- do not hide your face behind your notes
- keep still
- sound like you mean what you are saying.

ⓘ Concept bank

Lists of three: where a speaker repeats something three times to emphasise the point being made. Politicians are very good at using lists of three in their speeches to persuade their audience that what they are saying is right: 'we must pick ourselves up, dust ourselves off, and begin again the work of remaking America' (from Barack Obama's inauguration speech).

Rhetorical questions: are asked for dramatic effect and/or to make an audience think (but not to shout out their answers!). They do not require an answer. For example: 'Would you jump off the edge of a cliff just because someone asked you to?'

4.4 Persuasive writing – making a sales pitch

You will learn how to write and deliver a sales pitch.

↪ For starters

If you invented a new product for children, what would it be?

- A new music-playing device?
- A new phone with an original twist?
- A machine that does homework?

Brainstorm ideas in a small group and come up with a few suggestions for a product from which you can then select one idea to develop further.

↪ Task

You are going to appear on the programme *Fab New Ideas*. This allows you to put new ideas to a small panel of experts who will then decide if your product is good enough to be developed and put into shops.

You have to prepare a four-minute sales **pitch** for the panel. In your sales pitch you will need to give some basic details:

- your name and your company's name – something interesting and snappy that people will remember
- what your product is called – something catchy so everyone will know what it is and remember it
- what it does – think about what your product or invention can do for people in their daily lives
- what it looks like – a rough drawing may help here
- how much it will cost to produce – think about how much the materials will cost and how much time will be spent making it
- how much people will pay for it – make the price something that will attract people to buy the product. If it is too expensive it will put people off. If it is too cheap people will think it is rubbish. Perhaps you need to research similar products to see how much they cost and come up with a similar price.
- how many you will sell in each of the first three years – you need to think through how many people are likely to buy your product in each of the first three years and why
- why the panel should invest in your product – you need to be able to persuade the panel to part with their money to help you develop and build your product. What can you say to convince them? Come up with something special to say about your product which will satisfy them.

ⓘ Concept bank

Pitch: a short speech where you attempt to persuade someone to buy a product. Often given to a group of people from businesses.

FAB NEW IDEAS

You will need to be persuasive to make sure that the panel is convinced by your idea. Think of the persuasive writing techniques that you have looked at so far in this unit and try to use some of them here.

Think of words and phrases that you can use to make your product seem more amazing. For example:

- fantastic
- brilliant
- superb
- completely unique
- excellent value
- extremely popular.

Include things in your pitch that will make you sound authoritative – you know what you are talking about! For example, try to include:

- facts and figures
- examples of research undertaken
- specialist vocabulary.

Make sure that you:

- are polite and friendly
- are well-rehearsed
- make good eye contact with the panel
- use appropriate body language to show you are keen and trustworthy
- are very clear what your product does and why it is worth investing money in
- try to anticipate questions that may be asked by the panel.

Grammar link

Try to use abstract nouns in your presentation. These are nouns (names) that you cannot actually see, feel, touch, hear or taste. They are concepts. For example: 'Who does not love and want **freedom**?' or 'Which of us here in this room says no to **justice**?' 'Freedom' and 'justice' are the abstract nouns here.

⊃ Taking it further

In class, present your sales pitch to a small panel of students (as well as the rest of your class). The panel will listen to your pitch and ask you questions about your product before deciding whether to invest in it. Each member of the panel will then get a chance to say why they will or will not invest in your product.

Everyone in the class should have a chance to be on the panel and be able to present their own product.

4.5 Letters of persuasion and argument

You will explore and analyse the devices used in letters for persuasion and argument.

↪ For starters

Look at the poster on the right. It is designed to persuade people to watch what they are eating.

How effective is the campaign poster? Write brief notes to help you feed ideas back to others.

↪ Task

1   Read the letter below from the Minister for the Olympics and for London, Tessa Jowell, to MP David Currie. A typical exam question might ask you to look at the letter and to examine how Jowell uses language and form to argue her case. As you read the letter, think about what she is writing about and what she is trying to achieve with the letter.

Please note that:

- **OFCOM** is a body responsible to the government which checks that TV, radio and all other communication networks are providing reliable information to the public.

hands up who wants our kids to live longer?

We all do! But if we carry on living as we are, 9 out of 10 kids are set to grow up with dangerous levels of fat in their bodies. This can cause life-threatening diseases like cancer, diabetes and heart disease. So it's really important that we all get together and do something about it – now!

Change4Life is a nationwide movement which aims to help us all, but especially our kids, eat well, move more and live longer.

Get involved today! ✆ Search for Change4Life or call 📱 0300 123 4567*

change 4 life

Eat well   Move more   Live longer

*Calls to 03 numbers should cost no more than geographic 01 or 02 UK-wide calls, and may be part of inclusive minutes subject to your provider and your call package. Our offices are open from 9am to 6.30pm, Monday to Friday.

50% recycled

CODE ON THE ADVERTISING OF FOOD PRODUCTS TO CHILDREN

We recently spoke about this. I am now writing to OFCOM to consider proposals for strengthening the existing code on advertising food to children.

This reform is but one part of the developing programme to tackle childhood obesity, which is currently under close scrutiny by the Food Standards Agency, the Department of Health and the Health Select Committee.

Although I am well aware that there are many factors involved in the increase in levels of childhood obesity – and Government is committed to halting and reversing the decline in levels of physical activity in particular, not least through our work to boost PE and school sport and to encourage physical activity more generally – I take the issue of food advertising very seriously. I believe the current code of conduct governing the advertising of food and drink products to children to be inadequate and in need of review.

I know that you will want to take into account the conclusions of the FSA Report, the Department of Health's Food and Health Action Plan and the Health Select Committee's inquiry into obesity. I also know that industry is willing to work with us, and this is welcome because a package of solutions is required. I will be exploring further with the food and drink manufacturers how they can partner with Government to promote healthy eating and active lifestyles.

I also believe that the problem of childhood obesity highlights the importance of OFCOM's statutory duty to promote media literacy among children. In addition to understanding the need for a balanced diet and regular exercise, children and young people need to understand that companies advertising any product (not just food and drink) to them are doing so for commercial reasons and want them to spend more of their money on the products of those advertisers.

I look forward to hearing what plans you have to conduct research, review regulation and strengthen the code in this area, and to promote greater media literacy among children.

2 Look carefully at how the letter is structured. Why has the first line been put in capital letters?

3 Jowell uses several language features:
   • How does Jowell use emotive language when she writes: 'I take the issue of food advertising very seriously'?
   • Find and comment on the effectiveness of a list that Jowell uses in her letter.
   • What is the effect of using the personal pronoun 'I' in 'I believe'?

4 In the second to last paragraph, what does Tessa Jowell state must be done now? What must children be told?

5 How does she conclude the letter? Find and comment on Jowell's use of a list of three in the last paragraph.

6 Why has she chosen to end with the words she has used?

7 Write a paragraph in which you explain whether you think this letter is effective or not.

⊃ Taking it further

Write your own letter to the Health Minister presenting your views on either the Healthy Eating Campaign or the Anti-Smoking Campaign. (You can find an anti-smoking poster on page 46.)

Remember to use persuasive writing techniques:
• emotive language
• short and long sentences
• lists of three
• repetition
• structural devices
• pronouns and other ways of addressing the reader
• rhetorical questions.

Grammar link

Personal pronouns represent particular people or things. They can be singular – 'I', 'you', 'he', 'she' – or plural – 'we', 'you', 'they'.

Grammar link

Using the appropriate register of voice is crucial when letter writing. If you are writing a formal letter to someone who you do not know, you will normally end 'Yours faithfully'. If you are writing to someone who you have met, you will end 'Yours sincerely'.

4.6 Role-play and exam practice

You will use your skills of persuasion and argument in a public meeting scenario and answer an exam-style question.

⊃ For starters

1 This advert, which aims to stop people smoking, has been criticised by some people. Discuss in pairs what you think of the advert and why.

2 Look in more detail at the advert. Why might people be troubled by it and why might others think it is really good? Think about:

• what it says

• the presentation and picture.

↪ Task

You are going to use your skills of persuasion in a scenario based on the following events:

> Some parents hear that the advert is being displayed in their child's secondary school. They see it, then write a letter to the Headteacher explaining why they object to it.
>
> The Headteacher tracks down the staff member responsible for placing the advert around the school – the Head of Health Education. The Head of Health Education defends it.
>
> The Headteacher also asks the school council to consider the advert. Two students with opposing views reply (in writing) – one says it reminds him of a dying relative, the other says the advert is not hard hitting enough.

You are going to role-play a group meeting to discuss the advert and whether it should be allowed to stay up. There will be five people in each group. Each person will play one of these roles:

- the Headteacher, who will be chairperson
- the complaining parent
- the Head of Health Education
- the two students with opposing views.

Whichever character you are, remember that you will have to use particular language to suit the character and their views.

You will have the opportunity to present your views to the meeting so prepare the points you will be making. Plan what you are going to say. Remember to include the key elements of argumentative writing when preparing your material. For example, you could include a list of three or repetition to get across your views.

↪ Taking it further

Once you have planned and prepared what you are going to say, you will be given the chance to put forward your views during the meeting and will have the chance to discuss other people's views.

At the end a vote will be taken to decide whether the advert stays or goes. Your teacher will guide what is to happen in the debate.

Writing an argument text

Plan and write the answer to the exam-style question on the right.

Plan your essay by first of all deciding which side of the argument you will be on: for or against a ban on advertising to children.

Then think up several good reasons that support your side of the argument.

First, write a short introductory paragraph explaining why you are writing the letter.

Next, write three paragraphs in which you present your side of the argument. Start each paragraph with a topic sentence making the point, and then support your point with evidence and a developed explanation.

Next, write a paragraph in which you reject the counter-argument. Start it by writing: 'Some people might say that …' and outline their point. But in the middle of your paragraph, write: 'However, …' and explain why you disagree with this.

Finish with a paragraph in which you make a direct appeal to the Minister to ban children's advertising. Start with the word: 'Therefore …' and use lots of emotive language.

Exam practice

Time allowed: 35 minutes

Some people think that advertising products to young children on television is a bad thing and should be banned.

Write a letter to the government minister responsible for broadcasting, arguing *either* that advertising to children should be banned *or* that it should be allowed to continue. Begin the letter: 'Dear Minister'. (24 marks)

Good writing techniques

Your writing should include:
- Clear discourse markers, both at the start of a paragraph ('Firstly, …' 'Secondly, …') and also within a paragraph ('Also, …' 'However, …').
- Some complex sentences, with a number of clauses, joined by connectives, especially 'because', 'which' and 'although'.
- Short sentences to give excitement and pace.
- A blunt fragment.
- All the senses (see, hear, smell, taste, touch).
- Adjectives.
- Adverbs (-ly words).
- Specialist words.
- The appropriate person ('I', 'You', 'we', 'they').

If appropriate, somewhere in your essay, use:
- A range of punctuation: .,?!:;()""
- One list of details, separated by commas.
- Direct speech, "correctly punctuated".
- At least one rhetorical question.
- Repetition of a key phrase.
- A list of three.
- At least one simile ('like …'/ 'as … as …').
- A colloquialism.
- A hyperbole.

! Examiner's tip

Remember to:
- begin your letter clearly and concisely, stating your views
- give several reasons to back up your argument
- use paragraphs
- keep your writing tone appropriate
- try to anticipate questions and answer them here
- use some statistics and facts to back up your argument.

Tell Me About It – Explaining, Advising and Informing

Learning aim

In this unit you will learn explaining, advising and informing skills so that you are confident in writing in the exams at the end of your course. Speaking uses many of the same rules as writing, so you will also use explaining, advising and informing skills in speaking and listening activities. The presentation and the role-play will be assessed and the marks will go towards your final GCSE grade.

5.1 Speaking to communicate

> By the end of this section, you will know the main features of speaking to inform: the 5Ws and 1H (who, what, when, where, why and how).

↻ For starters

Speaking and listening marks are worth 20 per cent of your overall grade. This could mean the difference between a Grade A and a Grade C!

Spend three or four minutes thinking about speaking and listening activities you have done in the past. Note down your strengths and the areas you need to improve. Share your list with a partner and see if you can offer one another any advice.

↻ Task

Later you will be giving a short presentation to inform your class about a topic you feel confident about. The GCSE specification gives you the objective on the left.

Speak to communicate clearly and purposefully; structure and sustain talk, adapting it to different situations and audiences; use Standard English and a variety of techniques as appropriate.

The objective can be split into four parts:
- speak to communicate clearly and purposefully
- structure and sustain talk
- adapt to different situations and audiences
- use **Standard English** and a variety of techniques as appropriate.

'Speak to communicate clearly and purposefully' means that you need to get your information across, make yourself heard and speak with an appropriate pace.

ⓘ Concept bank

Standard English: a non-regional English dialect that is often used in formal contexts, such as education and serious media.

1. Think about the three other parts of the objective. What is each one asking you to do? Read the requirement carefully and look up any words you are not sure about.

2. Read these examples where someone is providing information for another person. With a partner, work out what was bought, when and from where. Then decide which speaker seems to be communicating clearly and purposefully.

   - Well, it was like Tuesday but it could have been like Monday. No it was Tuesday 'cos I was with Shania and I like got it from like Tesco.
   - I bought the CD from Tesco last Tuesday.
   - I beg to inform you that I purchased the digitally reproduced audio performance from the supermarket shortly after the commencement of last week.

↑ *Speak clearly and purposefully so your audience does not get bored.*

When you are speaking to inform, even if you need to be quite formal and use Standard English, there is no need to use extra long words and sentences to gain good marks. Adapt what you say to different audiences and purposes, just like when you are writing.

Structuring your presentation is really important. You need to plan what you are going to say and the order in which you will say it.

3. Rewrite this student's plan to inform someone how to make a mug of coffee.

   Pour boiled water onto coffee in mug.

   Stir in sugar to taste.

   Boil water in kettle.

   Add milk to taste.

   Drink.

   Place one spoon of coffee in mug.

   Measure a mug of water into kettle.

   Then, consider what information the student could have included in the instructions to make the information more helpful and specific, and make the improvements.

4. Write a set of instructions to inform someone how to do something. It could be how to tie a knot, tie shoelaces, make a sandwich or a process of your own choice. Read your instructions to a partner and get them to give you feedback on how effective they were. Note down some of your successes and how you could adapt your instructions to make them more successful.

When you have to listen to information, what helps you concentrate on what the speaker is saying?

5. Think about the need to use 'a variety of techniques'. What else could you do to make the information about making a mug of coffee, or tying a shoelace or tie, or whatever you chose, more interesting and clearer to your audience?

6 Look at the leaflet below giving information on drug driving. Note down exactly what information is provided. See if you can answer these questions:

- Who is the leaflet aimed at?
- What information are they given?
- When might someone be given this leaflet?
- Where might the leaflet be available from?
- Why would a person need this leaflet?
- How is the leaflet presented so that it helps to give information?

How could this leaflet have given information in a more effective way?

COCAINE

Cocaine leads to a sense of over confidence and this is reflected in their driving style. Users typically perform higher risk, more aggressive manoeuvres at greater speeds, which is obviously dangerous.

The specific effects of driving on cocaine are:

- Aggressive manoeuvres
- Speeding
- Poor control of the vehicle
- Erratic driving
- Over-confident, high risk behaviour

The following effects are likely to occur once someone has stopped taking the drug and are related to the fatigue that results from cocaine use:

- Inattentive driving
- Distraction and drowsiness
- Falling asleep at the wheel

ECSTASY

Although it's not a drug that makes people violent, it is extremely dangerous to drive on ecstasy because it results in:

- Distorted vision
- Heightened sounds
- Increased fatigue and tiredness
- Affected perception and judgement of risks

ECSTASY (continued)

- A more aggressive attitude
- Day-after effects similar to cocaine, leading to distraction, drowsiness and inattentive driving

USING MORE THAN ONE DRUG

People often take more than one drug or mix drugs with alcohol. For example – a stimulant like cocaine to 'sharpen up' after having alcohol or cannabis. In fact, combining drugs can have a dramatic and unpredictable effect on the user's state and driving.

WHAT ABOUT LEGAL DRUGS?

Medicine is obtained either on prescription or over the counter because people need to take it for their health. Medicines should always be taken properly. Advice about this is provided on the packaging and in the patient information leaflet supplied and packed in with the medicine. Advice can also be obtained from a doctor who has prescribed the medicine or pharmacist who dispenses it.

If you want more information on drug driving, please visit **www.dft.gov.uk/think/drugdrive**

For confidential drugs information and advice, please visit **www.talktofrank.com**

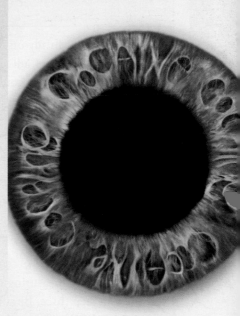

DRUG DRIVING.
YOUR EYES WILL GIVE YOU AWAY.

7 Sum up the information in five sentences to tell a partner.

8 Now inform your partner about the leaflet's content.

⊃ Taking it further

Think back on what you have learned in this section. Now produce a list of 'Six Tips for Giving Information'.

5.2 Presenting information

You will learn how to present information in a way that suits your audience and purpose for a formal speaking and listening assessment.

⊃ For starters

Look at these step-by-step instructions informing an audience how to measure their shoe size. What makes this informative text successful? What needs improving? Use technical vocabulary in your answer.

All you will need to get your proper foot measurement at home is: • a piece of paper larger than your foot • a pencil and a ruler or measuring tape.	
Sit with your foot firmly on the floor, and your leg bent slightly forward so that your shin is slightly in front of your ankle. Trace the outline of your foot. Measure your foot without shoes, but with socks like those you'll be wearing with the shoes you are buying. Hold the pencil upright and not at an angle. Make sure the pencil is resting snugly against your foot as you draw around it.	
Use your pencil to draw straight lines touching the outermost points at the top, bottom, and both sides of the outline.	
Use your ruler or measuring tape to measure the length from the bottom line to the top line that you drew in step three. Be sure to hold the measuring tape straight, and find the closest mark that you can (for inches, use the closest 16th mark) – don't round up or down.	
Many people will need a narrow or wide shoe. This step will help you to find the width of your foot. Measure the width of your foot by using your measuring tape or ruler to measure from the line on one side of your tracing, to the line on the other side. Again, be certain to find the closest mark that you can (for inches, use the closest 16th mark). Write this number down.	
Repeat these steps for your other foot, and use the larger of the two. After you have your numbers written down, take away $\frac{3}{16}$ of an inch from the numbers. These final numbers are your actual foot measurements.	

↻ Task

Many information presentations need images, sound or other **visual aids** to help engage the audience.

1 Read the extract below from *A Kestrel For A Knave* by Barry Hines, where Billy is explaining to his classmates how to train a goshawk to fly and return to its keeper. Then answer these questions:

- What facts is he telling his classmates?
- How clearly has he got his information across?

Again, use technical vocabulary in your answer.

> Jesses are little leather straps that you fasten round its legs as soon as you get it. She wears these all t'time, and you get hold of 'em when she sits on your glove …
>
> Then you get your swivel, like a swivel on a dog lead, press both jesses together, and thread 'em through t'top ring of it. T'jesses have little slits in 'em near t'bottom, like buttonholes in braces, and when you've got t'jesses through t'top ring o' t'swivel, you open these slits with your finger, and push t'bottom ring through, just like fastening a button.

2 Using the mark scheme for speaking and listening you looked at with your teacher, decide with a partner what mark you would give to Billy and why. Be ready to tell the class.

3 Look at this version of Billy's information as a PowerPoint presentation. What are the faults with this presentation? How would you improve it so that it provides clear information for an audience of students aged 15 or 16?

4 Produce a ten-point checklist of 'The Do's and Don'ts of PowerPoint'.

5 Imagine you are going to provide the same information as Billy gives to your class. Create a storyboard for a PowerPoint presentation with five to eight slides. Be prepared to justify the choices you have made.

↻ Taking it further

Use a planning grid to help you create a successful information presentation for your class on a subject of your choice. You might inform them about a hobby or keeping an animal. Perhaps you play an instrument, have a Saturday job or are in a sports team. You could inform your audience about any aspect, but you will be more successful if you are interested in the information yourself!

You will be formally assessed on your presentation as part of your GCSE.

5.3 Presenting explanations

You will learn that a good explanation speech must include a variety of facts, reasons, adjectives, verbs and adverbs. You will be able to use them for effect in your own talk.

⊃ For starters

Look back over the information presentation you made as an individual in the last section. Decide on two aspects that you will try to improve in your next speaking and listening assessment so that you get into the next mark band.

Now you are going to undertake a different kind of speaking and listening: role-play.

⊃ Task

To take part successfully in a role-play, you need to understand the difference between facts and explanation. The newspaper article on the right, about the proposed building of a new sports centre, will help you to do this.

1 Read the newspaper article and write an analysis of it, showing how it contains features of both information and explanation.
2 Read this information about road traffic accidents:
   • Every day, eight people die on British roads.
   • In 2007, 2946 people were killed on Britain's roads.
   • In 2007, nearly one in three deaths (891) were young people and children under the age of 25.
   • One in 200 people die on roads.
   • You are 10 000 times more likely to die or be injured in a car journey than in a plane.

Explanation texts make facts clear and give reasons for them. The facts above do not have reasons to help explain them.

Write a paragraph, using the facts, that explains the effects of these facts on the families of those killed or why the figures are so shocking or important.

3 Now, read what the charity Brake has to say about the effects of traffic accidents:

> Deaths and serious injuries on roads are violent and sudden, ripping apart families and devastating communities. They result in serious mental conditions, such as Post Traumatic Stress Disorder and depression as well as devastating grief and social consequences, such as loss of work.

Compare your writing with what Brake says. Which do you find the most effective explanation and why?

⊂⊃ Grammar link

Adjectives (words that describe a noun) can be used in an explanation text to help explain the effect something has.

Verbs (words that say what something does) can also be used in an explanation text to help explain the effect something has.

> After three years of wrangling, the Crowson Court Sports Centre has finally got the go-ahead. Public consultation meant that the £2.75 million project was delayed as contractors fought to allay fears over damage to the environment and danger to children through increased traffic. Project manager Steve Hill said, 'This is a thumbs up for common sense because the local community will have a resource that improves the quality of life for everyone.'

ⓘ Concept bank

Explanation texts: often contain facts and figures like information texts, but they can also be subjective and biased.

4 You are going to take part in a role-play debate about the proposed building of a new sports centre in a small town. Read the information extract below. The information was provided by the building constructors who want to build the centre. Identify the factual information and any aspects that provide explanation. You will need these points to develop your role-play later.

> The site is close to the Eastgate Court sheltered accommodation for the elderly and some two miles from both the primary and secondary schools. It backs onto the Spinney Woods nature reserve and is next to a mixed housing development of local authority and private housing for some 16 000 people.
>
> The proposed development will provide a range of facilities including a play area, swimming pool, sports field, bowling alley and a cafeteria with Internet access.
>
> Building is estimated to take 14 months to complete. During this time, access to two main local roads will be restricted.
>
> It is anticipated that the Crowson Sports Centre will improve a run-down area and provide a facility for all ages to use.

5 You will be allocated a role to play in a public meeting about whether the proposed sports centre should go ahead. The roles are members of these groups or organisations:

- the developers
- the local nature conservation society
- residents of the local houses
- local schools
- elderly people living in the sheltered accommodation
- teenagers

Make sure that your group is ready for the public meeting. Remember that you will be expected to play the role you have been given. Your group should:

- prepare a list of questions to ask the developers (or questions to expect, if you are role-playing the developers)
- prepare a set of views about the development for your group and explanations for these views
- think about the explanations that others might put forward for their views and be prepared to oppose them
- think about the questions others might have about your group's explanations and be prepared to defend your group's point of view.

6 Play your role in the public meeting.

↻ Taking it further

Reflect on your performance in the role-play. Look back at the notes you made at the beginning of this section. Have you managed to improve? If so, how? If not, what do you need to do next time?

5.4 Linking speaking and listening with writing

> You will understand the links between speaking and listening and writing. You will learn some features of how to write to advise.

↻ For starters

You will soon be considering choices about work, sixth form or college. List where you would go to get advice about your choices and the different texts you might expect the advice to be found in.

↻ Task

1 Think about the options facing you at the end of your GCSE course. Write one paragraph that gives advice to a Year 11 student about careers.

2 Working with a partner, listen to each other's paragraph and check if you have included who, what, where, when, why and how features. Now revise your paragraph and add any missing aspects. Ask yourself if what you are writing sounds right for your purpose and audience.

3 Turn your improved paragraph into a question-answer structured piece of writing. For example:
   • Question: Where might I get advice about 16+ options?
   • Answer: There are several people you could talk to at school. You could start with your form tutor, or you could book an interview with the careers advisor in the school.

   Write at least five question-answer pairings.

4 Here is the reply given to a parent who has asked a magazine for advice on what she can do about her son's drinking problem. Read what the mother is advised to do.

DRINKING becomes a problem

First let me say what a lucky person your son is to have you so concerned about him. If you can find an appropriate time, you should talk to your son and tell him how worried you are. Drinking becomes a problem when it starts to change how well we cope with life and affects our relationships. As alcohol can be very dangerous to health, you do need to get help. There are many places where you can get advice about alcohol. If you log on to the Internet www.nhs.uk has some helpful advice. You could also ring Frank (0800 77 66 00) and talk through your problems with a trained person.

- The mother is advised to do several things. What are they?
- Look again at the reply. How does the writer use language that would help the mother feel more confident about the situation, and what she might do about it? Include several examples of language use.

5 One language feature you might have spotted is the writer's use of modal verbs ('can', 'should', 'could'). Why are they used here? What is the effect of their use?

6 Read these two letters to a teenage magazine's 'agony uncle' and 'agony aunt', Bill and Jane.

Dear Bill,

There is a girl I really like at school but she is two years older than me. Do you think I should ask her out? How can I get to talk to her?

Dear Jane,

I have to do a Saturday job and work three evenings a week to help out with money at home, but I'm always in trouble at school for not doing my coursework on time. What should I do?

In each case, discuss with a partner what you think the advice should be:

- What challenges might the letter writers face in acting on your advice?
- How might they overcome these challenges?

⊃ Taking it further

Choose one of the scenarios in the letters above. Write a response as though you were the newspaper's agony aunt or agony uncle:

- Start with a sentence or two reassuring the worried person.
- Write one or two sentences about the problem in general terms.
- In a new paragraph, move on to some specific advice – remember to use modal verbs such as 'might' and 'could', and to include developed explanations.
- Then, in a final paragraph, finish by suggesting places they might go to get extra help.

> **Grammar link**
>
> Modal verbs are used to suggest ideas about possibility, intention, obligation or necessity. For example: can, could, will, would, shall, should, may, might, must.

5.5 Writing to advise

You will learn more about writing to advise.

⊃ For starters

Read these two sentences:

- Do your coursework on time.
- You should do your coursework on time because you may have less stress in trying to balance a workload and you might have more time to review your writing and get a higher grade.

The first sentence instructs, the second advises. What are the differences between them? Remember to use technical vocabulary in your response.

⊃ Task

When you write to advise, you will need to use words that prompt the reader to do something.

1 Write four sentences that give advice to someone who is falling behind with their school work, using one of these words in each sentence: 'could', 'should', 'might', 'may'. Also include a connective in each sentence to create **cohesion**.

2 Extend and explain your sentences by adding a clause after the connectives 'because', 'which' or 'although'.

3 Now write advice text for one of the following situations:
   - someone going rock climbing (to keep them safe)
   - someone who has fallen out with their boyfriend or girlfriend
   - someone who wants to do something nice for Mother's or Father's Day.

4 Swap your work with a partner and check each other's sentences carefully. Have you both used modal verbs and connectives? Have you included capital letters and full stops? Are all the spellings correct? Have you used other types of punctuation such as a semicolon?

5 Read the notes below that a student has made for writing a letter of advice to a friend who has recently moved to another part of the country and is finding it hard to make new friends. Then write the letter, using a separate paragraph for each of these pieces of advice, and giving clear reasons for them. Think carefully about how you will link the paragraphs and the order they should be in. Remember to use the right language for your target and audience – this is a friend so be quite personal.

> *Tell parents*
>
> *Join school club*
>
> *Talk to teachers (other students might be better)*
>
> *Go to local youth club*
>
> *Bullying?*

ⓘ Concept bank

Cohesion: the means by which we make links within and through a text, such as through connectives.

⚭ Grammar link

A clause is a part of a sentence. A clause may give extra information. Connectives are linking words such as 'because', 'which' or 'although'.

⚭ Grammar link

A semicolon is a piece of punctuation that looks like this ; . It can join two sentences together when they are about the same topic.

⊃ Taking it further

Look at this advice taken from a leaflet. It sets out to advise people about what to do in the event of a flood.

BEFORE the Floods

△ Know what the flood warning codes mean

△ On receiving a flood warning, inform your neighbours

△ Plan to allow time to protect your valuables and important documents.

△ Find out whether your Local Council supplies sandbags

△ Consider it may be dark before the flooding arrives - so keep a torch handy

△ Know how to turn off gas and electricity

△ If evacuated, try to tell friends and relatives where you are going

△ Take medication with you along with any food for special dietary needs (such as baby foods)

△ Co-operate with any requests to evacuate your premises

△ If you are evacuated, domestic pets will be cared for by the RSPCA while you are at the rest centre

DURING the Floods

△ Do not return to your property until you have been informed that it is safe

△ Be aware that flooding may not have reached its peak, or may be predicted to return

△ When driving in a flooded area, obey 'Road Closed' signs

△ If driving in a flooded area, drive slowly to avoid making waves which may put rescue workers in danger

△ Respond to the instructions from Police Officers - they have your safety in mind

△ Avoid unnecessary contact with water, it maybe contaminated

△ Pets which are normally kept in tanks or cages should, wherever possible, be left where they are or moved upstairs

AFTER the Floods

△ Gas and electricity should only be restored after consultation with an approved contractor

△ Throw away food that has come into contact with contaminated water - even sealed or tinned food

△ Take photographs or video footage of all flood damage to your property and personal possessions

△ Wear protective clothing when handling debris it may have come into contact with contaminated water

△ Good ventilation is essential to dry your property - remember to lock and secure your property when unoccupied

△ Obtain several quotations before any repairs are undertaken. Consider using locally known and recommended companies

Flooding

Floodline 0845 988 1188

Be prepared for flooding.

1 Identify and coment on eight features of language use and presentation that help to make the advice-giving successful here.

2 Write the text for a leaflet that advises young people on how best to cope if they have to move to another part of the country, and find making new friends difficult.

Try to include the following:

- advice organised into lists of suggestions and statements
- formal, impersonal register
- facts and specialist words to make it sound authoritative
- direct address – 'you'
- verbs of command and instruction
- short, powerful sentences
- prominent helpline phone number (the Childline number is 0800 1111) or other places to get help (for example, the school counsellor)
- a good slogan.

5.6 Writing advice – exam practice

You will work out exactly what you are going to write in a mock exam answer giving advice.

⟳ For starters

1 Look at the list of techniques (on the right) on how to advise which you have learned in this unit. Read it and try to memorise them. Now cover over this box and no peeking!

2 Working with a partner, take turns to advise each other on how to write advice texts successfully.

3 Uncover the box on the right. Did you include all of the techniques?

⟳ Task

Choose one of the exam questions to do from the *Taking it further* section below. Use the **APPLE** checklist (see right) to help you think about how you might approach the question.

Note down all the ideas for advice you can think of to include in your essay; you will need about five different points. For each point you think of, include a reason why they need to do that; this will be useful when you come to explain your points.

Then, **write a short introductory paragraph** explaining why you are writing.

Then, organise your points into the best order to present them to your reader and write them up as a **series of paragraphs**. Start each paragraph with a topic sentence making the point, and then support your point with evidence and a developed explanation.

Finish with a paragraph suggesting **where they could go for further help**.

⟳ Taking it further

Exam practice

Time allowed: 25 minutes

Choose one of the following:

1 Write a letter to a friend giving them advice on how to stop smoking.

2 Write a help sheet advising Year 9 students about how to organise a school disco.

3 Write an article for a school magazine advising Year 7 students on how to survive their first day in secondary school.

(16 marks)

Writing advice techniques:

- Appropriate register, including modal and instructional verbs
- Direct address
- Clear explanations, including connectives, facts and specialist words
- Reassurance
- Specific suggestions or instructions
- Where to find further help.

Plan your essay so that it:
- suits the **A**udience
- achieves its **P**urpose
- has good **P**resentation
- uses the right **L**anguage
- has a powerful **E**ffect.

! Examiner's tip

Use the 'Good writing techniques' listed on page 48.

5.7 Writing explanations – exam practice

> By the end of this section, you will know exactly what you are going to write in a mock exam answer that explains.

Writing explanations:
- Giving clear reasons
- Facts and specialist words
- Connectives (especially 'because' and 'therefore').

⟳ For starters

1 Think of your favourite TV programme or film and the reasons you like it so much. This is likely to be a list of 'because ... because ... because'.

2 Now work with a partner. Explain to them what your favourite film or TV programme is, but get them to ask you 'Why?' every time you offer a reason. Each time this happens you are likely to be developing and deepening your explanation.

3 Swap over to let your partner practise giving explanations.

⟳ Task

1 Look at how this student has planned an answer to a question on how to make the most of your time at school. What is good about this plan?

Writing to explain so quite formal

→ *Explain how to make the most of your time at school* ←

Audience – school so 11–16 year olds

Make the most – paragraph for each:
Lessons and exams
Sports
Clubs, trips, etc.
Friends
The future

Use the **APPLE** checklist (see right) to help you think about what the student has not included in this essay plan. What else might have been included to deepen and develop the explanation?

2 Choose one of the exam questions from the *Taking it further* section below and plan your essay using the **APPLE** checklist.

3 Write down all the reasons you can think of to include in your essay; you will need about five different points.

4 Write up your points as a series of paragraphs. Start each paragraph with a topic sentence making the point, and then support your point with evidence and a developed explanation, using facts and connectives.

Plan your essay so that it:

- suits the **A**udience
- achieves its **P**urpose
- has good **P**resentation
- uses the right **L**anguage
- has a powerful **E**ffect.

⟳ Taking it further

Exam practice

Time allowed: 25 minutes

Choose one of the following:
1 Explain why you enjoy a particular hobby or activity.
2 Explain why staying on at school at 16+ is a good idea. (16 marks)

! Examiner's tip

Use the 'Good writing techniques' listed on page 48.

5.8 Looking back, looking forward

> You will reflect upon what you do well and what you need to improve when you write to inform, explain or advise.

⊃ For starters

Review the work you have done in this unit. Be prepared to explain to the class one thing you have improved in your informing, explaining and advising work and how you know:

- It might be that you can structure your writing better.
- It might be that you know what you need to do when you write in an exam.
- It might be that you know what makes a successful presentation.

Whatever you feel you have improved, be prepared to say how you know and give an example from your work.

⊃ Task

1   Look again at the mark schemes you have worked with in this unit and see what is written next to the marks you got for your latest answer in exam conditions.

   Discuss your work with a partner, analysing what you need to do to get into the next mark band when you write to advise, explain or inform in the future.

2   Now write yourself a ten-point checklist for future writing.

3   Choose one of the written tasks you have completed and rewrite at least three paragraphs, improving them so that you could be awarded a higher mark. Some aspects you might consider are:
   - have a clear topic sentence at the beginning
   - use of modal verbs and connectives
   - use of different sentence lengths
   - make vocabulary more, or less, formal to fit the task and audience.

⊃ Taking it further

Make sure you keep collecting examples of different types of texts that inform, explain and advise.

Plan different answers using the titles, questions and ideas in this unit. Practise writing the answers in exam conditions. Give yourself about five minutes to plan and 25 minutes to write.

Practice makes perfect!

Learning aim

This unit will help you prepare for Section A of the Poetry across Time exam paper in English Literature. For Section A in the exam, you will be asked to compare **two** poems from **one** of the poetry clusters in the AQA Anthology. In this unit you will be introduced to checklists to help you write about poems and compare them.

6.1 'The Charge of the Light Brigade'

You will examine a long poem from the literary heritage and learn to compare it with other poems. You will start to practise using the **WRITER** checklist.

In this section you will need a copy of 'The Charge of the Light Brigade' by Tennyson from your Anthology.

'The Charge of the Light Brigade' was written in 1854 in response to the Battle of Balaclava. The battle took place on 25 October that same year, during the Crimean War, fought between England and Russia. The Light Brigade followed a misguided command to ride to the end of a valley and attack the enemy, even though they were outnumbered and outgunned.

↻ For starters

A way of remembering how to write about poems is simply to think of **WRITER**:

W   **What** is happening in the poem? **Who** is speaking?
R   Rhyme, rhythm and structure
I   Imagery
T   Tone
E   Effects
R   Response

To practise using the checklist, you need a copy of the poem and six coloured pencils, one for each letter of **WRITER**.

ↄ Task

Use a different coloured pencil to do the highlighting in each of the sections below.

What?

1 Find and highlight the two lines in stanza 2 which tell you that the charge was unsuccessful. Comment on the 'odds' of the battle.
2 Find and highlight the line in stanza 4 which tells you that the Light Brigade turned back after attacking the Russian guns. Was this a retreat? Or a return after a job well done? Highlight phrases to support your comments.
3 Highlight the lines in stanza 4 and stanza 5 which tell you how many returned. What effect does this realisation have on the reader?

Who?

Tennyson wrote this poem to celebrate the bravery of the Light Brigade, despite their defeat. He was a well-known public figure and published the poem in a newspaper.

4 Why do you think he did this? What did he want his readers to feel about what was, after all, a defeat? Highlight lines from the poem which support your comments.

Rhyme and structure

5 Highlight all the words in the poem which rhyme with 'hundred'. Comment on why these words are important.
6 What do the rhymes with 'shell' in stanza 3 tell you about the bravery of the soldiers? The words are repeated in stanza 5. This time another rhyming word is added. Why?
7 What do the rhyming words 'reply', 'why' and 'die' emphasise about the soldiers' situation? What do the rhyming words 'bare', 'air' and 'there' tell you about what the soldiers were doing with their sabres? In the same stanza, there is another set of three rhyming words. How does this let you know how well the soldiers were attacking the enemy?

The rhythm (one long stressed syllable followed by two short) creates the sound of horses galloping as the soldiers ride into and then out of the valley.

8 Why does the rhythm change at the beginning of stanza 2?
9 What about the next two lines? When does the galloping rhythm get going again?
10 Look at stanza 6. Why does the galloping rhythm stop here?
11 The stanzas are different lengths. Explain why.
12 There is a great deal of repetition in the poem. Find three examples and explain how it builds up the atmosphere of the poem.
13 The turning point in both the charge and the poem occurs at line 37: 'but not/Not the six hundred'. How does the mood of the poem change now?

Imagery

Two metaphors are used to describe the valley into which the soldiers are riding: 'The valley of Death' and 'The jaws of Death'.

14 Look at the medieval image of the mouth of hell on the right. How effective are these metaphors?

Tone

15 What does Tennyson think about the actions of the soldiers and the commanding officers of the Light Brigade?

16 The poet uses the phrase 'all the world wonderer'd' twice. Do you think it means the same both times? ('Wonder' can mean to think about something, to worry. It can also mean to be in awe of something, to be impressed.)

Effects

This is where you explain how the techniques which you have found in the poem contribute to the overall effect. For example:

> The strong rhythm creates the effect of the cavalry galloping bravely into the valley and then returning. The change in the rhythm when the officer orders the charge creates an exciting and dramatic pause – we wonder if the men will obey. The change in the rhythm at the end, when Tennyson wonders when their glory will fade and asks the reader to 'honour' the brigade, makes us pause and think about his message.

17 Now you try. Copy and complete these sentences:

1. The repetition of the words 'six hundred' makes the reader realise that …
2. The words 'flash'd', 'sabring', 'charging' and 'plunged' create the effect that …
3. The words 'reel'd', 'shatter'd' and 'sunder'd' suggest that …
4. The image of the entrance to the valley being like 'the mouth of Hell' creates the effect that …
5. The image of the entrance to the valley being like the 'jaws of Death' makes the reader realise that …

⤴ Taking it further

Response

English Literature is one of the few exams you will take where you will be asked what you think! What is your own, personal response to this poem?

- What did it make you think about?
- How did it make you feel?
- How relevant is it to you today?
- How might different people respond to it?

Here is an example:

> 'The Charge of the Light Brigade', because it is about a real historical event and was written soon after it, had a great deal of impact at the time. Some people then – as now – might have thought it inappropriate to criticise military decisions. The Crimean War was the first to be reported on by war correspondents. Nowadays we expect to be informed about every stage of the war in Iraq or Afghanistan through 24-hour news media. The poem still has impact today, because the story of blundering leadership and brave soldiers is sadly one we are very familiar with, especially after the First World War. My lasting response to the poem is one of admiration and sadness for the unquestioning bravery of the soldiers.

Now write a paragraph of your own and be ready to share it with others.

⬆ Augustus Butler's engraving of the charge of the Light Brigade

6.2 Comparing 'Flag' with 'The Charge of the Light Brigade'

> You will examine a contemporary poem from the Conflict cluster and compare it with 'The Charge of the Light Brigade'. You will apply the **WRITER** checklist again and use another checklist (**IF-DISCS**) to compare the poems.

In this section you will need a copy of 'The Charge of the Light Brigade' by Tennyson and 'Flag' by John Agard from your Anthology.

⊃ For starters

1 Here are the flags of six countries. Can you identify them?
2 Why do flags mean so much to people? What do they symbolise?
3 In the USA, some schoolchildren have to take an oath of allegiance to the American flag. What are your views on this?
4 You might have seen news stories on TV where people were filmed burning the flags of other countries. Why were they doing this?

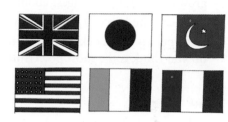

⊃ Task

You are going to use the **WRITER** checklist to explore the poem 'Flag' and to compare it with 'The Charge of the Light Brigade'.

Who?

1 Read the poem 'Flag' aloud in pairs with one person reading the first line in each stanza, the other person reading the next two. How many voices can you hear in the poem?
2 Now try reading it in different ways with different numbers of voices.
3 Which way of reading seemed to work best, and why?

In these two questions you start to compare the two poems:

4 Tennyson asks two **rhetorical questions** in his poem. John Agard asks five direct questions and also provides the answers. What do you think about the answers?
5 What do you think the poets want the reader to think about?

> **ⓘ Concept bank**
>
> **Rhetorical questions:** are asked for dramatic effect and/or to make an audience think. They do not require an answer.

What?

6 What sort of flag, in what sorts of situations, is being described in 'Flag'? Is John Agard being specific or universal here?
7 Why is the word 'flag' – the title – not used in the poem until the last stanza? How is it referred to until then? What do you think is the significance of this?

'The Charge of the Light Brigade' was written in response to a specific battle on a specific date in a specific place, whereas 'Flag' seems to be about war or conflict in general. The loyalty and obedience of the soldiers in the Light Brigade – 'Theirs not to reason why, Theirs but to do and die' – is perhaps like the loyalty to their country's flag, which makes people fight.

8 How similar and how different are the poets' attitudes to patriotism?

Rhyme, rhythm and structure

9 The ABA **rhyme scheme** of the first three stanzas of 'Flag' disappears in stanza 4 and changes to a final rhyming **couplet** in stanza 5. Can you explain why?

10 The rhythm of the poem is 4 beats, then 3, then 4. What does this do to the second line of each stanza?

11 How does the repeated line change in the last stanza? Which word stays the same? What is John Agard trying to make us realise about flags?

12 Both poems contain repetition of important words. Both poems use rhyme. Both poems use rhythm. Can you see any differences, though?

Imagery

13 What do the metaphors 'brings a nation to its knees' and 'the guts of men grow bold' in 'Flag' suggest about the effects of flag-waving patriotism?

14 How can the 'piece of cloth' outlive the spilled blood which it causes?

15 Both poems use shocking images to communicate ideas. Which of them do you think is the most powerful/memorable? Why?

Tone

16 What is John Agard's attitude to flags?

17 What happens when people take loyalty to a flag/country seriously, in Agard's view?

18 Is John Agard more critical of patriotism and obedience than Tennyson? Does he admire soldiers in the same way?

Effects

Look at 'fluttering', 'unfurling' and 'rising'. The **-ing** endings suggest that this is happening now, in the present tense.

19 'The Charge of the Light Brigade' is about a specific event in history, and is therefore mostly in the past tense. It changes at the end when Tennyson is telling the reader what to do now. Agard ends with an instruction too: 'Just ask for a flag, my friend.' Do you think he means the word 'friend'?

Response

20 What is your response to 'Flag'? What did it make you think about? How relevant is it to you today? How did it make you feel? How might different people respond to it?

21 Look back at your paragraph responding to 'The Charge of the Light Brigade' and then write a paragraph where you compare your responses to the two poems. Which did you prefer, and why?

↻ Taking it further

Use the **IF-DISCS** checklist on the right to write an eight–paragraph response to:

Compare how Tennyson in 'The Charge of the Light Brigade' and Agard in 'Flag' present their thoughts and feelings in their poems.

Write a paragraph for each letter of **IF-DISCS**, comparing each time, and then finish with an eighth paragraph where you say which poem you think is the more effective and why.

ⓘ Concept bank

Rhyme scheme: a regular pattern for end rhymes which can be represented by letters, each standing for one rhyme position, e.g. ABAB, where first line rhymes with third and second with fourth.

Couplet: a pair of lines which belong together in some way, often rhyming.

IF-DISCS

You may find another checklist, **IF-DISCS**, a helpful way to organise your comparison of two poems. It provides a useable and memorable way to write a response to the pair of poems.

The typical Higher-tier question stem is: *Compare how x is presented in poems x and y.* Obviously x and y are the titles of poems, but x can be a particular theme or idea. So we might get a question like the one in *Taking it further*.

Using **IF-DISCS** works because it lets you systematically compare the 'what' (**IF**) and 'how' (**DISCS**) of a poem, using the seven letters to make a comparison of each element:

I The **i**deas and thoughts presented in the poems.

F The **f**eelings presented in the poems.

D The **d**iction used by the poets.

I The **i**magery used.

S The **s**ounds used in the poems (rhythm, alliteration, rhyme, onomatopoeia).

C The **c**omparisons used by the poets – similes and metaphors.

S The way the poets **s**tructure the poems.

6.3 Comparing 'Bayonet Charge' with 'The Charge of the Light Brigade'

You will examine another poem from the Conflict cluster, using the **WRITER** checklist, and compare it with 'The Charge of the Light Brigade'.

In this section you will need a copy of 'The Charge of the Light Brigade' by Tennyson and 'Bayonet Charge' by Ted Hughes from your Anthology.

⊃ For starters

- My country – right or wrong.
- For Queen and Country.
- Patriotism is the last refuge of the scoundrel.

Talk to your partner about the meanings of the statements above.

⊃ Task

Who? What?

1 On your copy of 'Bayonet Charge', highlight all the words which are to do with war or soldiers. Annotate the poem with any ideas about when and where this event might have taken place. Unlike Tennyson in 'The Charge of the Light Brigade', Hughes is not specific about the battle or even the war. Why do you think this might be?

2 Now highlight all the words in the poem which are to do with nature. How is the fighting changing the landscape?

Ted Hughes was born in Yorkshire in 1930. His poems are often about nature, but he was also very interested in the First World War, in which his father and his uncle had fought. His father, William, was one of only 17 survivors of a whole regiment of the Lancashire Fusiliers killed at Gallipoli.

Hint: You may wish to take the idea of war and nature further by reading 'Mametz Wood' and 'Falling Leaves' in your Anthology. Both these poems are about the First World War and its effects.

Rhyme, rhythm and structure

3 How many sentences are there in 'Bayonet Charge'? How do they fit into the three stanzas? What do varied sentence length and **enjambement** suggest about the soldier's movement? What word(s) would describe it?

4 Highlight the dashes and present participles (*-ing* words) in the poem. How do these also contribute to the effect of the soldier's movement?

5 Find the question mark where the action seems to stop for a moment. Why does time seem to stand still for the soldier here?

Imagery

6 Why is the simile 'numb as a smashed arm' an appropriate way to describe the way the soldier is carrying his rifle?

7 The soldier's 'patriotic tear' is now 'Sweating like molten iron from the centre of his chest'. How have his feelings changed between joining up and finding himself in this battle?

8 Images of stillness in stanza 2 seem to suggest that time is standing still or slowing down for the soldier. Find an example and try to explain it.

9 What do the images of warfare – 'molten iron', 'shot-slashed', 'flame', 'dynamite' – emphasise?

10 Why is the word 'luxuries' used in line 21?

Tone

11 'King, honour, human dignity, etcetera / Dropped like luxuries …'. What does the word 'etcetera' tell us about what the soldier feels about patriotism now?

12 Find a quotation from 'The Charge of the Light Brigade' which gives a different perspective on loyalty and patriotism.

Effects

13 Three colours are used in 'Bayonet Charge'. Which colours are associated with nature and which with battle?

14 What happens to the hedge, the ploughed field and the hare during the battle?

15 The battle is 'unnatural' and terrifying. Which words or phrases create this effect the best, in your opinion?

Response

16 What is your own, personal response to 'Bayonet Charge'?
- What did it make you think about?
- How did it make you feel?
- How relevant is it to you today?
- How might different people respond to it?

Write a paragraph describing your response.

17 Look back at your paragraph responding to 'The Charge of the Light Brigade' and/or 'Flag'. Write a paragraph comparing 'Bayonet Charge' with either 'The Charge of the Light Brigade' or 'Flag'.

⟳ Taking it further

Use the **IF-DISCS** checklist (see page 68) to make notes in which you compare 'Bayonet Charge' with the other poem.

> **ⓘ Concept bank**
>
> **Enjambement:** the carry-over of a phrase or sentence into the next line or stanza.

6.4 'You have picked me out …'

You will examine a poem written in response to an event where ordinary people were caught up in a terrorist attack. You will use the **WRITER** checklist and images of the attack.

In this section you will need a copy of 'You have picked me out …' by Simon Armitage from your Anthology. This is a section of a longer poem called 'Out of the Blue' written for a TV programme five years after the destruction of the Twin Towers in New York on 11 September 2001.

⊃ For starters

1 In pairs, look at the images from 9/11 above. Choose one and write a title or caption for it. Share your choice with another pair.
2 In fours, do the same with another image. Share your ideas with the rest of the class.

⊃ Task

What? Who?

1 If you did not know already what the poem is about, what evidence could you find that it is about someone trapped in a burning skyscraper? Highlight the words or phrases and choose those you think are the most memorable.
2 Simon Armitage is writing in the first person as if he is one of the victims of 9/11, creating a **persona**. Who is the 'you' the persona is talking to?

Rhyme, rhythm and structure

3 Present participles are used throughout the poem and some are repeated. What effect does this have? Annotate your copy of the poem.
4 Most stanzas begin with a short sentence followed by a longer one. Read the beginning sentences – do they tell the story? What further details are given by the longer sentences? Why do you think the sentences get shorter towards the end?

ⓘ Concept bank

Persona: where poets write as if they are characters, not themselves. We should be careful of always thinking that the 'I' in a poem is the poet.

5 There are five questions in the poem – are they all directed to the same person? The last one does not have a question mark – is the speaker expecting an answer?

6 There is rhyme in the poem but it does not follow a regular pattern – why? Which pair of rhyming words do you think is the most effective?

Imagery

7 'You have picked me out. Through a distant shot …' – the man is aware that his loved one may be watching the incident on TV. Images of 'seeing' and 'noticing' appear throughout the poem. Find some examples. How do these support the idea of him 'waving'?

8 In line 15 the trapped man says 'the white of surrender is not yet flying'. Remembering that to wave a white flag is the traditional way of surrendering or giving up in a battle, what do you think he means by this? What are the 'others like me' doing?

9 Look at line 4 'a white cotton shirt is twirling' and line 28 'I am flagging'. The image of the white flag runs through the whole poem. How does John Agard in 'Flag' use the idea of flags differently to Simon Armitage?

Tone

10 The tone of the poem is very personal and we share the persona's emotions as we – and he – realise that he will not be saved and he needs to jump if he does not want to be burned to death. Not much of a choice. 'You have picked me out' could mean 'you have picked out my face in the crowd' or 'you have picked me out as a partner' – could it be both? Similarly, 'flagging' could mean beginning to give up or trying to signal something by waving a flag or waving a white flag of surrender. Which do you think it is?

11 What are your thoughts about a poet imagining himself to be in such a terrible situation? Could he ever really understand it? Is there a sense that he is exploiting suffering? Or is he doing an important thing by reminding us and making us think? Discuss your ideas.

Effects

12 There is a lot of alliteration (when two or more words have the same first letters) in the poem. Which do you find most effective?

13 In stanza 1, 'shot' and 'shirt' are linked by sound and by their position in the line. Why are these words so important?

14 What short sentence in stanza 5 makes it clear how high up the man is? What other words or images in the poem add to this effect?

Response

15 What is your own, personal response to this poem?
- What did it make you think about?
- How did it make you feel?
- How relevant is it to you today
- How might different people respond to it?

Write a paragraph describing your response.

↺ Taking it further

1 Think about the images of the Twin Towers which you looked at on page 71. Choose a line or phrase from the poem to caption them.

2 Find or design an image of 9/11 to illustrate the poem. Write a paragraph explaining why you chose the image. Present your image to the rest of the group.

6.5 Comparing 'The Right Word' with 'You have picked me out …'

> You will examine another contemporary poem from the Conflict cluster, using the **WRITER** checklist, and compare it with 'You have picked me out …'.

In this section you will need a copy of 'The Right Word' by Imtiaz Dharker and 'You have picked me out …' by Simon Armitage from your Anthology.

⊃ For starters

1 What is the difference between a terrorist and a freedom fighter?
2 Read the poem 'The Right Word'. With a partner, explore the situation that Dharker presents in the poem.

⊃ Task

What? Who?

Imtiaz Dharker was born in Pakistan, brought up in Scotland, and now lives between India, London, and Wales. She regards herself as cross-cultural.

1 From what viewpoint is the poem written – first person internal or third person external? Highlight two pieces of evidence. What is the effect of this choice of perspective? How does this compare with 'You have picked me out …'?
2 Who is the person 'outside the door'? Explain your thinking.
3 Who is 'you' that the speaker addresses towards the end of the poem? How is this similar or different to 'You have picked me out …'?
4 List five words or phrases that best describe the poem's speaker. What is the experience that the speaker is talking about?

Rhyme, rhythm and structure

5 What tense is the poem written in, past ('this was') or present ('this is')? Highlight two examples. What is the effect for the reader? How does this compare to 'You have picked me out …'?
6 There is no obvious rhyme or rhythm.
   • Why has the poet written the poem like this?
   • What is the effect for the reader?
   • How does this compare to 'You have picked me out …'?
7 The poet has structured the poem into stanzas, instead of one long piece of writing. Look at how each new stanza begins. What pattern can you spot for why Dharker starts a new stanza?
8 Two questions are asked in the poem.
   • Who are they addressed to?
   • How does this compare to 'You have picked me out …'?

Imagery

9   One key image in this poem is 'shadow'. It has a literal meaning, and a metaphorical meaning. Highlight the six times in the poem where the person outside is described as being, literally, 'in the shadows'.

- What is a 'shadowy' character? How else is the person 'shadowy' as well as literally being there?
- What else is Dharker trying to say when she tells us that the person outside the door is 'in the shadows'?

10 The second key image is that of 'outside'. Again, the person is literally 'outside' the door.

- How else is he 'outside' our society?
- How does the speaker treat the person by the end? Why?

Tone

11 Underline the words used by the speaker to label the person in each stanza; for example, 'terrorist' in the first stanza. What do you notice about how the words change?

12 What is Dharker trying to say about her thoughts and feelings towards the 'terrorist' by the end of the poem?

13 How are these thoughts and feelings different to those of the speaker in 'You have picked me out …'?

Effects

14 Copy out the opening sentences of stanzas 2–7. Each of these sentences seems to be about how the speaker is trying to find the 'right word' to talk about the person at the door. Does the speaker ever find the 'right word'? Explain your answer.

15 Look at that word 'carefully' in the final stanza? Why is it used? Why does the 'child' take his shoes off?

16 How effective do you feel the ending of the poem is?

Response

17 What is the 'message' of Dharker's poem? What would a relative of the man who jumped to his death in 'You have picked me out …' think about that message?

18 Think again about the difference between a terrorist and a freedom fighter. What might Dharker think about this?

↪ Taking it further

1   A GCSE student describes 'The Right Word' and 'You have picked me out …' as 'poems about terrorism'. How far is she correct? Explain your thinking.

2   Which other poem in the Conflict cluster might these two poems be compared to? Why?

Exam practice

Time allowed: 45 minutes

Plan and write the answer to the exam-style question below.

Compare how attitudes to conflict are shown in 'You have picked me out …' and one other poem from the Conflict cluster. (36 marks)

You might find it helpful to structure your answer using the **IF-DISCS** checklist.

Unit 7 Poetry – Unseen

Learning aim

This unit will help you prepare for Section B of the Poetry across Time exam paper in English Literature. In Section B of the exam, you will be asked to respond to an unseen poem. In this unit you will develop your confidence and knowledge of how to approach any poem. You will practise using the **WRITER** checklist to respond to poems.

7.1 One writer – Simon Armitage

You will read poems by Simon Armitage and use the **WRITER** checklist to write about them.

↺ For starters

We all have our own ways of remembering important information, especially what we need to know for exams.

Share with a partner any mnemonics – words or phrases to help remember key information – you use at school or in general.

A good way to write about a poem is to always remember the **WRITER** checklist:

W **What** is happening in the poem? **Who** is speaking?
R Rhyme, rhythm and structure
I Imagery
T Tone
E Effects
R Response

⊃ Task

1   Read the poem 'It Ain't What You Do It's What It Does to You' by Simon Armitage:

I have not bummed across America
with only a dollar to spare, one pair
of busted Levi's and a bowie knife.
I have lived with thieves in Manchester.

I have not padded through the Taj Mahal,
barefoot, listening to the space between
each footfall picking up and putting down
its print against the marble floor. But I

skimmed flat stones across Black Moss on a day
so still I could hear each set of ripples
as they crossed. I felt each stone's inertia
spend itself against the water; then sink.

I have not toyed with a parachute cord
while perched on the lip of a light aircraft;
but I held the wobbly head of a boy
at the day centre, and stroked his fat hands.

And I guess that the tightness in the throat
and the tiny cascading sensation
somewhere inside us are both part of that
sense of something else. That feeling, I mean.

2   In pairs, use the **WRITER** checklist to explore and respond to this poem. Spend 20 minutes maximum on this.

Here is a student's response to the poem. She is answering this question:

> What do you think the poet is saying about what is important in life and how does he present his ideas?

The speaker is reflecting on what he <u>has not</u> done in his life and what he <u>has</u> done. He has not done adventurous things like hitchhiking across America, visiting India or jumping from a parachute but he has lived with thieves in Manchester, skimmed stones across a lake and worked with a disabled boy. He seems to be saying that all these activities have equal value and impact. Living with thieves in Manchester (perhaps as a social worker type of job?) could be just as dangerous as hitchhiking across the USA. He might not have been to exotic places like the Taj Mahal, but he has had peaceful times just skimming stones across a lake at home (if Black Moss is a lake, and is in the UK, I've never heard of it). Sky diving might be exciting but comforting a boy with a 'wobbly head' at a 'day centre' is more useful.

There is rhyme in the poem but it is not a strict rhyme scheme. In line 2 'spare' and 'pair' rhyme within the line to emphasise that the hitcher only has one spare dollar and one pair of jeans. In the third stanza, 'inertia' and 'water' rhyme, which works well because the stone's lack of movement, 'inertia', is followed by a fall into the 'water'; the poem slows right down here as the semicolon separates off 'then sink'. The rhythm is not regular but seems a bit jerky. 'I have not' sounds definite, but then the 'but' part is always separated by a full stop or semicolon, as if the speaker is trying to organise his thoughts. 'I guess' and 'I mean' in the last stanza show how uncertain he is. The regular stanza structure of four lines each at first suggests that each one will deal with an 'I have' and an 'I have not', but the pattern is broken with the sentence which runs on from the second to the third stanza (enjambement). This is about the speaker skimming stones and perhaps the run-on line suggests the movement of this.

The word 'bummed' conjures a picture of an American 'bum', hobo or tramp, someone who doesn't have anything. The image of listening for spaces between footfalls at the Taj Mahal sounds magical and almost religious, as does the idea of feeling 'stone's inertia'. The image of toying with a parachute cord sounds playful, not serious in contrast to holding a 'wobbly head' and stroking 'fat hands'. I'm not sure if the 'tightness in the throat' and the 'tiny cascading sensation' are meant to be metaphors or real. It sounds a bit to me like that 'butterflies' feeling we all get when doing something special. The tone of the poem is quite personal and moving.

Sound effects such as alliteration are used effectively. For example, 'bummed', 'busted' and 'bowie' remind us how few things the hitchhiker has with him. The plosive 'p' sounds which suggest the careful picking up and putting down of feet on a marble floor are almost said in a whisper, which emphasises the special nature of the Taj Mahal. However, the sibilance of the skimming stones across Black Moss suggests the sssss sound of water, which is just as effective as the 'p' sounds.

The overall effect of the poem is the contrast between ordinary, boring real life and fantasy life. Once I'd thought about this contrast, I thought about the title. Perhaps what Simon Armitage is saying is that it's not important what you do in life; what is important is the effect it has on you as a person. I think I agree with this as you can be well travelled but know nothing about how to get on with people.

3 The student is using the **WRITER** checklist. Identify where she is following it.

4 Compare this very good response with your own notes on the poem. Has the student missed out anything? Hint: excellent responses at A/A* often 'say a lot about a little'. That is, the student explains an effect in detail, rather than writing everything they can think of about the whole poem. Is there anywhere you could develop the student's points?

⊃ Taking it further

Choose one of these Simon Armitage poems from your Anthology:

- 'The Clown Punk'
- 'Give'
- 'A Vision'
- 'The Manhunt'
- 'Harmonium'

Read it carefully then apply the **WRITER** checklist to the poem. Write at least six paragraphs. Try to find at least one point where you 'say a lot about a little'.

7.2 Forming opinions on poetry

You will explore two Simon Armitage poems using the **WRITER** checklist. You will also present an argument for keeping one of these poems in the Anthology.

⊃ For starters

1 With a partner, make a list of five poems you have looked at since being at secondary school. Which one is your favourite?

2 What criteria did you use to decide? Or, in other words, what factors did you consider when making your choice?

⊃ Task

1 Form five groups and each take one of these Simon Armitage poems from your Anthology:
   - 'The Clown Punk'
   - 'Give'
   - 'A Vision'
   - 'The Manhunt'
   - 'Harmonium'

2 Read your poem together in your group then use the **WRITER** checklist to organise and jot down your ideas about it.

3 Once you have talked about the poem, think about this question: 'Is this a good poem for GCSE students to study?' Share your answer with the group, explaining your reasons.

Your task is now to persuade the rest of the class that your poem *is* a good one for GCSE students to study, and that it should stay in the Anthology.

4 Read your poem to the other groups and present your reasons for keeping it in the Anthology.

5 After all the groups have presented their poem, the class votes on which poem to keep. Each student has one vote. You do not have to vote for the poem you presented, if another group has done a good job of convincing you about their poem.
   The poem with the fewest votes will be 'thrown out' of the Anthology.

6 Write a letter to AQA explaining why that poem should be taken out of the Anthology.

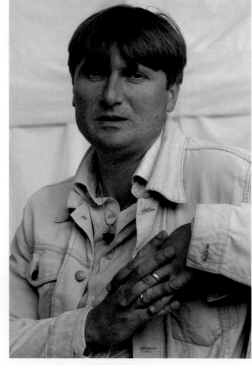

↑ *The poet Simon Armitage*

⊃ Taking it further

Choose one of the four poems presented by other groups – it could be the one which was 'thrown out' if you like. Use the **WRITER** checklist to make notes on this chosen poem.

7.3 Poetry stories

You will read two very different, but powerful, poems and think about how to respond to their images. You will use another checklist (**IF-DISCS**) to direct your analysis.

⊃ For starters

In groups of four, discuss these questions:
* What should poetry be about?
* Are there any topics which should be 'off limits' for poets? For example: child prostitution, war, injustice, sex, murder, child labour, poverty, death?
* Would you welcome any of these topics being dealt with in a poem?

⊃ Task

1 Read the poem 'London' by William Blake, written in the 19th century:

> I wander thro' each chartered street,
> Near where the chartered Thames does flow,
> And mark in every face I meet
> Marks of weakness, marks of woe.
>
> In every cry of every man,
> In every infant's cry of fear,
> In every voice, in every ban
> The mind-forged manacles I hear.
>
> How the chimney-sweeper's cry
> Every blackening church appals;
> And the hapless soldier's sigh
> Runs in blood down palace walls.
>
> But most thro' midnight streets I hear
> How the youthful harlot's curse
> Blasts the new-born infant's tear,
> And blights with plagues the marriage hearse.

William Blake uses the walk through London to comment on social conditions of the time.

2 In groups of two to four, create six still images or tableaux to illustrate the poem. When you present your images or tableaux, other groups should try to give each one a line from the poem as a title.

3 Now use the **IF-DISCS** checklist (below) to make notes on the poem.

> **I** **I**deas presented in the poem
> **F** **F**eelings presented in the poem
> **D** **D**iction – the speaker's choice of words
> **I** **I**magery – the speaker's vivid pictures created out of language
> **S** **S**ound – the way the poem uses sound to create effects
> **C** **C**omparison – the use of metaphor and simile
> **S** **S**tructure – how the content is shaped and organised

4 Critics often praise Blake's use of **oxymoron** in the last stanza of this poem. For example, 'marriage hearse'. How does this make the poem even more effective?

ⓘ Concept bank

Oxymoron: combining contradictory terms to create an expressive or amusing phrase such as 'same difference' or 'extremely average'.

5 Now read the poem 'Medusa' by Carol Ann Duffy:

A suspicion, a doubt, a jealousy
grew in my mind,
which turned the hairs on my head to filthy snakes
as though my thoughts
hissed and spat on my scalp.

My bride's breath soured, stank
in the grey bags of my lungs.
I'm foul mouthed now, foul tongued,
yellow fanged.
There are bullet tears in my eyes.
Are you terrified?

Be terrified.
It's you I love,
perfect man, Greek God, my own;
but I know you'll go, betray me, stray
from home.
So better by far for me if you were stone.

I glanced at a buzzing bee,
a dull grey pebble fell
to the ground.
I glanced at a singing bird,
a handful of dusty gravel
spattered down

I looked at a ginger cat,
a housebrick
shattered a bowl of milk.
I looked at a snuffling pig,
a boulder rolled
in a heap of shit.

I stared in the mirror.
Love gone bad
showed me a Gorgon.
I stared at a dragon.
Fire spewed
from the mouth of a mountain.

And here you come
with a shield for a heart
and a sword for a tongue
and your girls, your girls.
Wasn't I beautiful
Wasn't I fragrant and young?

Look at me now.

Carol Ann Duffy uses the Greek myth of Medusa, the Gorgon, whose glance turns things to stone, to think about jealousy and aging.

6 In groups of four, create six still images or tableaux to illustrate the poem. When you present your tableaux or image, other groups should try to give each one a title from the poem.

7 Use the **IF-DISCS** checklist to make notes on the poem (see page 79).

○ Taking it further

Using all the ideas you have talked about for both poems, design a poster entitled 'Powerful Poetry'. You may draw or use computer-generated images to illustrate the poems but you should also use quotations and comments from your notes on the poems.

7.4 Writing a response to an unseen poem

This section shows you in detail how to use the **WRITER** checklist to analyse an unseen poem. You will then analyse a poem yourself.

⟳ For starters

Beat the clock!

In 60 seconds, jot down everything you can remember about a poem you have studied recently.
Compare notes with someone else.

What sorts of things did you remember? Interesting images? The story? The rhyme? What did your partner remember?

Different people are affected by poems in different ways, which is why the final **R** of **WRITER** is so important. It is your **response** that the examiner is interested in.

⟳ Task

1   Read the poem 'Belfast Confetti' by Ciaran Carson:

> Suddenly as the riot squad moved in, it was raining
>   exclamation marks,
> Nuts, bolts, nails, car-keys. A fount of broken type. And the
>   explosion.
> Itself – an asterisk on the map. This hyphenated line, a burst
>   of rapid fire …
> I was trying to complete a sentence in my head but it kept
>   stuttering,
> All the alleyways and side streets blocked with stops and
>   colons.
>
> I know this labyrinth so well – Balaclava, Raglan, Inkerman,
>   Odessa Street –
> Why can't I escape? Every move is punctuated. Crimea
>   Street. Dead end again.
> A Saracen, Kremlin-2 mesh, Makrolon face-shields. Walkie-
>   talkies. What is
> My name? Where am I coming from? Where am I going? A
>   fusillade of question marks.

2 The questions in the table below support the **WRITER** framework. Look at the questions and the responses to the poem 'Belfast Confetti' which answer these questions.

WRITER framework	Questions	Responses to 'Belfast Confetti'
W Who is speaking?	• First person or third? • Is it the poet speaking or a persona created by the poet? • Is there a 'you' addressed in the poem?	• The poet writes in the first person, describing a scene as if he was there. • At the end there is clearly a voice asking him questions, which he repeats.
W What is happening?	• What happens in the poem? • When do the events take place? • What has happened previously? • What will happen next?	• This is a 'riot' in Belfast where people are throwing objects; there is an explosion and gunfire; the army is blocking off roads. • This must have happened during the Troubles in Northern Ireland. • The speaker is caught up in the riot and is asked by a soldier to explain himself.
R Rhyme	• Is there a regular rhyme scheme? • Is there internal rhyme, or **half rhyme**? • What is the significance of this?	• There is no rhyme scheme used, perhaps to reflect the chaos of the disordered situation. • There is assonance in places – 'r<u>ai</u>ning'/'exclam<u>a</u>tion'/'n<u>ai</u>ls' – which emphasises what is raining down. • 'l<u>i</u>ne'/'f<u>i</u>re' – this assonance makes you realise he is in the line of fire.
R Rhythm	• Read the poem to yourself, noticing the number of stressed syllables in each line. Is there a pattern? • Does the rhythm make you read the poem quickly or slowly, or a mixture?	• There is no regular rhythm, again to reflect the confusion of the event. • When you read the poem aloud you are forced to stop and start, which shows how the speaker is stopping and starting as he tries to get away from the riot.
R … and Structure	• Do the stanzas each deal with something different? • How many sentences are there? Do any of them run on? • Are short – or long – sentences used for effect?	• The first stanza explains the situation and ends with a definite full stop to show the road block; the second shows the speaker trying to get away but then being stopped and questioned. • There is a variety of sentences. Some run-on lines suggest movement: 'raining / exclamation marks' (the hail of small objects being thrown), 'it kept / stuttering' (the speaker running). Others suggest speech: 'What is / My name?' The fact that 'Walkie- / talkies' is separated onto different lines emphasises the jerkiness of speaking and walking at the same time in such a tense situation. • Long and short sentences are used to create the effect of movement: 'This hyphenated line …' suggests running up and down streets; 'Dead end again.' suggests stopping. Dashes and **ellipsis** are used to create dramatic pauses. The first short question – 'Why can't I escape?' – shows the speaker's panic. The final three questions show the soldier interrogating the speaker.

WRITER framework	Questions	Responses to 'Belfast Confetti'
I Imagery	• What are the most striking images? • Are there any similes? • Are there any metaphors? • What is the effect of the imagery used?	• The main metaphor in the poem is of punctuation. The objects thrown are described as 'exclamation marks' and 'broken type'. The army blocks the roads just as a full stop or colon ends a statement. 'Every move is punctuated.' • Questions are important in the last stanza and those the soldier asks are referred to as a 'fusillade' – a sustained burst of gunfire – suggesting that he is not waiting for an answer but just bombarding the speaker with questions. • Images of water – 'raining' and 'fount' – suggest that the nails, etc., are everywhere, but could also suggest burst water pipes, which often result from explosions.
T Tone	• What mood does the poem create in the reader? • What is the attitude of the speaker or poet? • Is the poem emotive or detached? Ambiguous or clear?	• The fear and uncertainty felt by the speaker are shared by the reader. The idea of being trapped in a 'labyrinth' and unable to escape is frightening. • The attitude of the speaker to the riot squad is that they are faceless, identified only by their tanks and protective gear – which are ironically given their proper names, 'Kremlin-2 mesh', etc.
E Effects	• Are there any sound effects such as alliteration, **onomatopoeia** or assonance? • Any other effects?	• 'Burst', 'stuttering' and 'fusillade' suggest the sounds of the riot. • It is interesting that the street names are of British battles, warships and generals. This suggests a Protestant area of Belfast.
R Response	• How did you respond to this poem? • How do you think the poet wanted you to respond? • Was the poet successful in your view?	• The sense of panic at being caught up in a violent disturbance is very real. • Ciaran Carson wants us to understand what life was like for ordinary people during the Troubles. • He uses punctuation both to create effects and as a central metaphor, which I think is very clever.

⊃ Taking it further

Using this analysis of 'Belfast Confetti' as a model, select another poem that you have not read before from the Anthology. Use the **WRITER** checklist to analyse the poem, answering all the questions in the Questions column of the table on these pages.

ⓘ Concept bank

Half rhyme: rhymes in which the last consonant(s) are the only things that rhyme, the vowels do not, e.g. little/scuttle.

Ellipsis: dots showing where words have been omitted.

Onomatopoeia: where words sound like what they are describing, such as 'squelch' or 'boom'.

7.5 Exam practice for poetry – unseen

You will practise the skills you have developed in analysing unseen poetry in 'mock' exam conditions. Once you have attempted the question yourself, you will look at some other answers and think about their marks.

⊃ For starters

Remind yourself of all the techniques you have learnt for writing about unseen poetry in this unit.

⊃ Task

In Section B of the Poetry across Time exam paper in English Literature, you will respond to an unseen poem. You will be tested on how well you:

- respond to a poem critically and imaginatively, selecting and evaluating relevant textual detail to illustrate and support your interpretation
- explain how language, structure and form contribute to the writer's presentation of ideas, themes and settings.

Spend 30 minutes answering the exam-type question on 'My Pen Has Ink Enough' by Vernon Scannell:

> My pen has ink enough; I'm going to start
> A piece of verse, but suddenly my heart
> and something in my head jerks in reverse.
>
> I can't go on – I did, with switch in tense,
> And here's the bleak, accusing evidence;
> I don't know why, or even what I seek.
>
> This thought jabbed hard: how insolent to make
> These blurred attempts when Shakespeare, Donne, and Blake
> Have done what they have done. And yet it tempts,
>
> This longing to make wicks of words, light lamps
> However frail and dim. And hell, why not?
> I've had six children yet more casually got.

Exam practice

Time allowed: 30 minutes

What do you think the poet is saying about the difficulties of writing poetry and how does he present his ideas?

(18 marks)

! Examiner's tip

This section of the exam tests your ability to:

- respond to a poem, using details to support your points
- explain how the writer is presenting ideas by using language in a particular way.

⊃ Taking it further

Exchange exam answers with a partner and make notes about how each other's answer could be improved.

8 Creating a Personal Voice

Learning aim

This unit will help you prepare for the Creative Writing Controlled Assessment Task. You will learn how to use a range of language devices to add shape and style to your writing. You will write in an interesting way about people, places and events from your life.

8.1 Introducing personal writing

You will learn how to write about yourself and others in a creative and engaging way. You will learn to identify and make use of a range of devices to enhance the style of your personal writing.

⊃ For starters

1 People have always enjoyed writing and talking about themselves and their experiences. Explore these questions:
   • Why do you think we enjoy writing and talking about ourselves? What are the benefits?
   • What methods did people use to communicate information about themselves to others in the past?
   • How have the media and technology changed the way we communicate to others about ourselves?
   Spend three minutes discussing your thoughts with a partner.
2 Why are social networking sites and reality TV programmes so popular today? What needs do they meet?

⊃ Task

1 Find out eight facts about a class partner and list them.

2   Add detail and description to each fact and turn them into an interesting paragraph which introduces your partner.

See how:

> Natalie is 14.
> She attends St Mary's School.

can become:

> Natalie is a friendly and popular 14-year-old student at St Mary's School.

3   Now, introduce your partner to the class using your paragraph.

⊃ Taking it further

Your Controlled Assessment Task will require you to demonstrate your ability to write 'clearly, effectively and imaginatively' to 'engage the reader'. The following set of tasks will help you develop these skills.

1   Read the following Internet blog an up-and-coming popstar.

Grammar link

Using a wide range of punctuation can help to make your writing more precise, lively and engaging.

> Hi Guys,
>
> I've spent what feels like the past 24 hours on the set of my new (and first!) music video. It's the video for my single 'Out of This World' which will be released in about a month's time. The director's idea was to make it a futuristic, space-age love story so we were all dressed in super-shiny silver suits. But, rather than feeling like a sexy astronaut, I just felt like I should have been a contestant on **'Hole in the Wall'**! Sad, eh? To make it even worse, we were filming in the middle of a snow storm! Very bizarre … Do they even have snow on the moon?! It was such a long day but now I'm just really excited to see the final, finished product. Everyone I worked with was so experienced and professional, I just know they'll make it look fantastic; it'll be amazing when I see it on MTV, I just can't believe how far I've come in such a short space of time. Listen out for the song next month and keep those eyes peeled for my shiny suit on the music channels – you really can't miss it!
>
> Catch ya later!

'Hole in the Wall': a television game show where they dress in silver suits

2   Identify the different language devices used by the writer. Look for things such as **colloquialisms**, **emotive language** and **imperatives**.

3   What effect does each device have on the reader? Why do these devices work particularly well for this format of writing?

4   Write 5–10 sentences about something you have done recently:
   • introduce the activity or event
   • if relevant, write about the weather, what you wore and the people you experienced it with
   • explain how you felt at the time and why.

5   Rewrite your sentences as a blog entry of 100–150 words. Add a range of the language devices we have identified: for example, you could use an imperative to address your reader directly at the end.

ⓘ Concept bank

Colloquialism: informal words or phrases, including slang.

Emotive language: words or phrases which describe the writer's emotions and/or make the reader feel a certain way.

Imperative: a sentence which commands the reader to do something.

8.2 Writing about people

You will identify some devices used to describe people and consider the effects created. You will use these devices in your own writing.

⊃ For starters

1 We all have inspirational and important people in our lives. Which friends, family members, teachers or others have made the biggest impact on your life so far?
2 Discuss with a partner the most influential people in your life. Why are they so important to you?

⊃ Task

An autobiography is a written account of your life. In autobiographies, people tend to write about memorable places they have been to or situations and events they have encountered. They also write a lot about the people who have helped to shape their lives and personalities.

1 Read the extract below, taken from Roald Dahl's autobiography *Boy*. Here, Dahl writes about Captain Hardcastle, a teacher from his boarding school.

We called them masters in those days, not teachers, and at St Peter's the one I feared most of all, apart from the Headmaster, was Captain Hardcastle.

This man was slim and wiry and he played football. On the football field he wore white running shorts and white gymshoes and short white socks. His legs were as hard and thin as ram's legs and the skin around his calves was almost exactly the colour of mutton fat. The hair on his head was not ginger. It was a brilliant dark vermilion, like a ripe orange, and it was plastered back with immense quantities of brilliantine in the same fashion as the Headmaster's. The parting in his hair was a white line straight down the middle of the scalp, so straight it could only have been made with a ruler. On either side of the parting you could see the comb tracks running back through the greasy orange hair like little tramlines.

Captain Hardcastle sported a moustache that was the same colour as his hair, and oh what a moustache it was! A truly terrifying sight, a thick orange hedge that sprouted and flourished between his nose and his upper lip and ran clear across his face from the middle of one cheek to the middle of the other. But this was not one of those nailbrush moustaches, all short and clipped and bristly. Nor was it long and droopy in the walrus style. Instead, it was curled most splendidly upwards all the way along

as though it had had a permanent wave put into it or possibly curling tongs heated in the mornings over a tiny flame of methylated spirits. The only other way he could have achieved this curling effect, we boys decided, was by prolonged upward brushing with a hard toothbrush in front of the looking-glass every morning.

Behind the moustache there lived an inflamed and savage face with a deeply corrugated brow that indicated a very limited intelligence. 'Life is a puzzlement,' the corrugated brow seemed to be saying, 'and the world is a dangerous place. All men are enemies and small boys are insects that will turn and bite you if you don't get them first and squash them hard.'

Captain Hardcastle was never still. His orange head twitched and jerked perpetually from side to side in the most alarming fashion, and each twitch was accompanied by a little grunt that came out of the nostrils. He had been a soldier in the army in the Great War and that, of course, was how he had received his title. But even small insects like us knew that 'Captain' was not a very exalted rank and only a man with little else to boast about would hang on to it in civilian life. It was bad enough to keep calling yourself 'Major' after it was all over, but 'Captain' was the bottoms.

2   Notice how Dahl uses **figurative language** to enhance
his description of Captain Hardcastle. Complete the following
sentence: Dahl uses the metaphor 'thick orange hedge' to describe
Captain Hardcastle's moustache; this gives the impression that … What
other examples of figurative language can you find? What impression does
each one create?

3   Identify Dahl's use of **emotive language**. What impression does it create?
Begin by discussing the word 'savage' in the fourth paragraph; what
feelings does it suggest that Dahl has towards the teacher? How does the
word make you react to him?

4   Identify Dahl's use of humour. What effect does it have?

5   In what other ways does Dahl use language for effect? Identify and
consider the effect of the adjectives, verbs and sentence structures
he uses.

⊃ Taking it further

In your Controlled Assessment Task, you may be asked to write descriptively
about a person who is important to you. The following tasks will help you
practise the planning and drafting process necessary to shape and develop a
successful piece of writing.

1   Choose a person from your own life who is important or memorable
to you.

2   Write down at least 10 details about this person. Use the different senses to
help you:
  • What do they sound like when they talk? When they eat? Do they sigh
    or grunt in a funny or annoying way?
  • How do they look? Consider their height, hair colour, what they
    wear, etc.
  • Do you associate any smells with this person? Does their house
    always smell of apple pie? Do they wear terrible aftershave or smoke
    a cigar?
  • What is their personality like? Are they clever, kind, funny?
  • Do they have any particular skills or hobbies?

3   Now, shape each detail into a sentence, using a range of figurative language
to add detail and description.

See how:

> My cousin Chris has spiky hair.

can become:

> My cousin Chris' **hair jumps** out in all directions; his **scary
> hedgehog spikes** are as **sharp as needles**!

4   Turn your sentences into a paragraph of writing introducing your person
in no less than 150 words. Play around with the order of your sentences,
and use humour and emotive language to engage the reader.

> ### Concept bank
>
> **Figurative language**: descriptions
> in which one thing is compared
> with another to create interesting
> or powerful images. Examples
> include similes, metaphors and
> personification.
>
> **Emotive language**: words or
> phrases which describe the
> writer's emotions and/or make
> the reader feel a certain way.

> Here *hair jumps*
> is personification, *scary* is
> emotive language, *hedgehog
> spikes* is a metaphor and *as
> sharp as needles*
> is a simile.

8.3 Writing about place

You will identify and comment on the devices used by writers to describe place and to engage a reader. You will learn to make greater use of a range of devices in your own writing.

⊃ For starters

1 We all have places which are special or memorable to us. Consider a place which really stands out in your memory – perhaps your home town, a place from your childhood or a favourite holiday destination.

2 Discuss your thoughts with your partner. Ask them questions to find out more details about their special or memorable places.

3 What places have you visited that really stand out in your memory? Why do they stand out?

⊃ Task

Travel writing allows people to share their experiences of different places, people and cultures with others. Travel writing describes places in a lot of detail so that the reader can imagine being there. In this format, writers may also use a range of different techniques to engage and sustain the reader's interest.

1 Read the extract below taken from Bill Bryson's *Notes from a Small Island*. In this piece of travel writing, Bryson discusses his experience of visiting Liverpool.

> I took a train to Liverpool. They were having a festival of litter when I arrived. Citizens had taken time off from their busy activities to add crisp packets, empty cigarette boxes, and carrier-bags to the otherwise bland and neglected landscape. They fluttered gaily in the bushes and brought colour and texture to pavements and gutters. And to think that elsewhere we stick these objects in rubbish bags …
>
> Here's a piece of advice for you. Don't go on the **Mersey** ferry unless you are prepared to have the famous song by **Gerry and the Pacemakers** running through your head for about eleven days afterwards. They play it when you board the ferry and they play it when you get off and for quite a lot of time in between. I went on it the following morning thinking a bit of a sitdown and a cruise on the water would be just the way to ease myself out of a killer hangover, but in fact the inescapable sound of 'Ferry 'cross the Mersey' only worsened my cranial plight. Apart from that, it must be said that the Mersey ferry is an agreeable, if decidedly breezy, way of passing a morning. It's a bit like the Sydney Harbour cruise, but without Sydney.

… continued on page 90

Mersey: a river in Liverpool; you can travel on the river Mersey on a ferry.

Gerry and the Pacemakers: a 1960s rock-and-roll group from Liverpool; they sang a song about the ferry across the river Mersey.

When they weren't playing 'Ferry 'cross the Mersey', they played a soundtrack outlining the famous sights from the deck, but the acoustics were terrible and 80 per cent of whatever was said was instantly blown away on the wind. All I could hear were snatches of things like '3 million' and 'world's biggest' but whether they were talking about oil refinery capacity or **Derek Hatton's** suits I couldn't say. But the gist of it was that this was once a great city and now it's Liverpool.

Now don't get me wrong. I'm exceedingly fond of Liverpool. It's probably my favourite English city. But it does rather feel like a place with more past than future. Leaning on a deck rail gazing out on miles of motionless waterfront, it was impossible to believe that until quite recently – and for two hundred proud and prosperous years before that – Liverpool's 10 miles of docks and shipyards provided employment for 100,000 people, directly or indirectly.

What impression of Liverpool is created and how?

How does Bryson influence the reader's opinion?

What language devices can you identify?

How are sentences used to create impact and effect?

Derek Hatton: a local politician.

2   Discuss with a partner your thoughts on each of the questions beside the extract.

3   Answer in writing: how successful do you feel Bryson's piece of writing is here? Give an opinion or two about Bryson's success. Remember to include some evidence from the passage, and explain it.

⊃ Taking it further

The following activities will once again guide you through the planning and drafting process that is vital when producing a piece of writing. This is a really important skill to practise and develop in preparation for your Controlled Assessment Task.

1   Choose a place you know well or that means a lot to you.

2   Make notes on all the different things you can remember about this place:
   • What can you see there? Consider the weather, the landscape and scenery, and how busy the place is.
   • What sounds fill the air? Think carefully about all the different noises, even the really quiet ones.
   • What can you smell? Food? Fresh air? Sweat? Petrol?
   • Use the sense of touch – is it hot or cold? Can you feel the sun, or wind or rain?
   • How do you feel in this place – excited, scared, lonely, happy? Try to say why.

3   Turn your notes into a series of paragraphs introducing this place in no less than 200 words. Add detail and description to your writing using the checklist of devices for travel writing to help you.

4   Band 4 of the Controlled Assessment mark scheme states that your writing should:
   • demonstrate 'confident control and crafting of language', using words deliberately for effect
   • use 'organisational devices to navigate readers through the writing'
   • make accurate use of a 'range of punctuation marks'.

Use these assessment criteria to help you edit and improve your piece of writing.

Checklist for travel writing:

✓ metaphor

✓ personal pronouns

✓ emotive language

✓ fact

✓ opinion

✓ imperative

✓ humour

✓ exaggeration.

⊂⊃ Grammar link

Using a range of sentence types and sentence structures can help make your writing fresh, lively and engaging.

8.4 Writing about events

You will learn how to better organise your thoughts and memories into a structured piece of writing. You will learn to use better a range of language devices to add style and interest to your writing.

⟳ For starters

1 What happy events from your life stand out in your memory? Have any situations helped to shape you into the person you are today? Have there been any special occasions you have shared with friends or family?

2 Spend a few minutes sharing your thoughts with a partner.

3 There are many important milestones in our lives which help shape our personalities. Discuss one such milestone in your life.

⟳ Task

Let's take a major event which we have all encountered: the first day at secondary school.

1 Begin by writing down all the things you remember about this day, using the questions below to prompt you. Your ideas do not need to be in any particular order; you will look at shaping your writing later.

Who did you share the day with?

What did you hear?

What did you see?

Did you meet anyone new?

What were you thinking about?

How did you feel?

How did you look?

What smells and tastes did you come across?

2 Complete a flowchart with at least six stages to organise your memories about the day into a logical and consecutive order.

3 For each stage, add three to five specific details.

4 Add at least one descriptive phrase to each detail; use adjectives, similes, metaphors and emotive language.

⊃ Taking it further

You have had lots of practice at planning a piece of writing in preparation for your Controlled Assessment Task. You are now going to focus on adding detail and description to your notes. The following activities will help you to shape your writing, and add powerful description through including a wide range of the devices you have looked at in this unit.

1   Read the following passage. Here a student remembers the moment that she first walked through the school doors.

> Nervously, I reached for the cold, grey handle. My palms felt clammy. Pulling the heavy door open allowed a loud, threatening wave of sound to wash over me. Looking around, I could see boys and girls scurrying in all directions like ants trying to escape from the foot of an enormous elephant! They all seemed to know someone else, or at least where they were going; I felt completely alone. Suddenly, I was jolted forward by a boy who towered over me like a giant.
>
> 'Shove it, squirt!' he yelled aggressively at me.
>
> 'Aw, leave her, she's only a little year 7 – you were like that once,' his heavily made-up girlfriend teased. Then, laughing manically, they disappeared into the sea of faces in front of me.

Checklist for personal writing:

✓ adjectives

✓ adverbs

✓ verbs

✓ similes

✓ metaphor

✓ personification

✓ emotive language

✓ personal pronouns.

🔗 Grammar link

Direct speech is a great way to introduce or develop character in a piece of personal writing. One way you can do this is through varying the verb from 'said' and by adding adverbs before or after the verb to reveal more about the character: 'he retorted gruffly' or 'she whispered viciously'.

2   Identify examples of the different language devices used in this writing. Use the checklist for personal writing to help you.

3   Choose one of the boxes from your flowchart about one of your memories from the first day at secondary school.

4   Write a paragraph or two about this memory. Remember to use a range of devices from the checklist.

   Challenge! Add a short passage of direct speech to help you introduce or develop character.

9

Creating Characters, Mood and Atmosphere

Learning aim

In this unit you will prepare for the Controlled Assessment Task by looking at a variety of skills you will need to write creatively and descriptively. You will learn to create a specific mood and atmosphere in your writing, create effective characters in your writing, and to use language techniques effectively when writing creatively.

9.1 Effective description

> You will learn how to use specific words and ideas to build up mood and atmosphere in your writing.

⊃ For starters

When you are creating a mood or atmosphere in your writing you are building up a specific feeling: for instance, you may want your writing to appear sad, happy or to be full of tension.

In pairs, read the following extracts. What mood or atmosphere do you think is created in each one? How does each writer create the mood and atmosphere?

> The water was warm and inviting, a well earned bath at the end of a hard day. I swam amongst the gentle waves, relaxed and at peace with the world. The sun smiled down on my face, kissing my forehead and making the droplets of water glisten in its golden rays.

> The heat was oppressive. It crushed me as I staggered through the dense foliage, with no idea of how soon I would reach the edge of the jungle. Sweat was pouring off every part of my body as I clawed my way through the ever darkening, hellish landscape.

> The wood was deep and dark. All around me were trees, oppressive and threatening, bearing down on me like bullies. Suddenly, a bird flew out of the branches above my head, shrieking in the deadly silence, cutting through it like a knife.

↻ Task

In your writing you need to create and sustain interest for your readers. A lot of this will depend on how you create a suitable mood and atmosphere for your reader.

1   Read the following extracts. Which are the most convincing and least convincing at gaining and keeping the reader's attention? Why did you put them in the order you chose? When making your decision think about:
   • what mood and atmosphere is created
   • how the writer goes about using language to build tension.

A

It was a cold, dark night and I could hear the owls shrieking in the distance. The moon had vanished behind a large, black cloud.

B

They were on my tail, but I had to keep moving. I ran through the streets, past the fish and chip shop and turned down a narrow alleyway. Suddenly it was much darker and I couldn't see as clearly. I could hear my heart pounding in my chest and it felt as if it would explode at any moment.

C

The summer breeze blew gently over the field, brushing the grass, almost caressing it like a mother's hand.

D

The traffic roared in every direction. It seemed almost impossible to cross this busy road.

E

I could hear the hissing sound all around me. I looked down and could see hundreds of snakes writhing around my feet, slipping over my shoes and leaving a slimy feeling over my feet.

2   The way in which a writer uses **adjectives** is very important in creating an appropriate mood and atmosphere.
   • When creating mood and atmosphere in your own writing, use effective adjectives in your work. Look at this sentence:

   > The *tall* man walked down the *long* street.

   • There are two adjectives, 'tall' and 'long', but these are rather dull examples. Make them more interesting like this:

   > The *elongated, creepy* man walked down the *never-ending* street.

   • Why is this a more interesting example?
   • Write two sentences of your own, each with two versions: one version with dull adjectives and the other with more vivid and exciting adjectives. Be prepared to justify your ideas to the rest of your class.

3   When you write, it is a good idea to vary the type of sentences you use. If you use too many simple sentences your writing can seem disjointed and simplistic.

   Write two simple, two compound and two complex sentences of your own that describe the room you are in.

ⓘ Concept bank

Adjective: a word which describes a noun (a thing, object or person). Examples are 'brilliant', 'massive', 'awesome'.

⊡ Grammar link

A simple sentence is a sentence which contains a subject and a verb and expresses a complete thought or idea.

A compound sentence is a sentence which has two independent clauses joined together by a coordinator such as: 'yet', 'and', 'for', 'so' and 'but'.

A complex sentence is a sentence which has an independent clause that is joined by a dependent clause. A complex clause always has a subordinator, e.g. 'because', 'although', 'when' or a relative pronoun such as 'which', 'who' or 'that'.

⮎ Taking it further

Write about 200 words creating a clear mood and atmosphere. You can choose to continue any one of the effective examples in this section or to write something completely original. If you select one of the examples in the book, remember to continue the story from that point and to build the mood and atmosphere in an appropriate manner. Think about:

• what mood has been created so far
• what words you might use to build this mood.

Use appropriate and interesting adjectives and a mixture of simple, compound and complex sentences. Think more about creating the mood and atmosphere and less about developing a plot.

9.2 Creating mood and atmosphere

> You will explore atmospheric description and apply it to your own writing.

⮎ For starters

When writers create a mood or atmosphere in their writing, they often have a visual picture in their mind of a specific scene or event. Look at the two photographs below. What mood and atmosphere do these pictures create for you?

List 10 words for each photograph. Share your ideas with the rest of your class.

⊃ Task

Frankenstein is a well-known horror story about a man who creates his own creature from the body parts of the dead and then brings it to life. The extract here is the moment when the monster comes to life for the first time, and the reaction of Frankenstein to the monster that he has created. The writer, Mary Shelley, has deliberately created an unpleasant mood and an atmosphere of horror throughout this passage:

> It was on a dreary night of November that I beheld the accomplishment of my toils. With an anxiety that amounted almost to agony, I collected the instruments of life around me, that I might infuse a spark of being into the lifeless thing that lay at my feet. It was already one in the morning; the rain pattered dismally against the panes, and my candle was nearly burnt out, when, by the glimmer of the half-extinguished light, I saw the dull yellow eye of the creature open; it breathed hard, and a **convulsive** motion agitate its limbs.
>
> How can I describe my emotions at this catastrophe, or how **delineate** the wretch whom with such infinite pains and care I had endeavoured to form. His limbs were in proportion, and I had selected his features as beautiful. Beautiful! – Great God! His yellow skin scarcely covered the work of muscles and arteries beneath; his hair was of a **lustrous** black, and flowing; his teeth of a pearly whiteness; but these **luxuriances** only formed a more horrid contrast with his watery eyes, that seemed almost of the same colour as the dun white sockets in which they were set, his shrivelled complexion and straight black lips.

Convulsive: sudden, jerky movement.

Delineate: describe.

Lustrous: bright, shiny.

Luxuriances: rare and delightful qualities.

What is important about when the moment is set: 'on a dreary night of November'? Why not in June or July or a clear, sunny day? This is an example of **pathetic fallacy**.

1   Shelley uses many negative words throughout the passage to show how horrifying the scene is, for example: 'anxiety', 'agony' and 'breathless horror'.

- What other negative words and phrases are used in the passage to build this up?
- Make a list of four examples and explain clearly what effect these words have on building up the horrifying nature of the scene. For example: 'breathless horror' – the scene is so horrible it makes Frankenstein breathless with shock.
- How is the monster described in this extract?
- How does this description add to the mood of horror in this passage?

ⓘ Concept bank

Pathetic fallacy: where the weather or surrounding landscape reflects the mood of the scene.

Writers often use pathetic fallacy, as Shelley did in *Frankenstein*. Here is an example from Chapter 2 of *Jane Eyre* by Charlotte Brontë:

> Daylight began to forsake the red-room; it was past four o'clock, and the beclouded afternoon was tending to drear twilight. I heard the rain still beating continuously on the staircase window, and the wind howling in the grove behind the hall …

2   The gloomy atmosphere of wind and rain and the cloudy skies reflect Jane's dark mood and sadness at living in Gateshead Hall where no one seems to love or care for her. What other words and phrases from the first paragraph add to the pathetic fallacy created?

Writers often use **similes** or **metaphors** in their work to help create the mood and atmosphere. For example, Frankenstein describes himself as an evil being to show how he feels responsible for creating the monster and for all the terrible things the monster has done: 'I wandered like an evil spirit' (simile). Shelley compares the monster's teeth to a pearl as they are so white: 'his teeth of a pearly whiteness' (metaphor). It makes the teeth seem almost unreal or unnatural, which reflects the fact that the monster is unnatural.

3   The sentences in the table below are either similes or metaphors. Identify which they are and then explain the effect of them. The first is done for you.

> **(i) Concept bank**
>
> **Similes:** compare one thing with another using 'as' or 'like'.
>
> **Metaphors:** much more direct comparison between two things.

Example	Simile or metaphor	Explanation of effect
'his teeth of a pearly whiteness'	Metaphor	The writer compares the monster's teeth to a pearl as they are so white. It makes the teeth seem almost unreal or unnatural, which reflects the fact that the monster is unnatural.
'He stood there looking at me like the devil.'		
'The mountains lay before me as if they were a masterpiece painted by the greatest painter alive.'		
'For some time I sat upon the rock that overlooks the sea of ice.'		

4   In pairs, brainstorm words that you might use if trying to create a mood or atmosphere of unpleasantness or horror in your writing. Try to come up with about 10 examples.

5   Explain, in detail, why these words are effective and appropriate.

6   Write two similes and two metaphors which could also add to the mood of unpleasantness or horror. Explain their effect.

➲ Taking it further

You have decided to enter a short story competition for your local newspaper. You have been given the following guidelines:

- Write a descriptive piece that creates an unpleasant mood or atmosphere.
- You can write about anything that you choose and you should write no more than 1000 words.
- Make your characters interesting and ensure that you have an effective ending. As this is a descriptive piece, keep the dialogue to a minimum.
- Use some of the examples you have come up with earlier, including pathetic fallacy, similes and metaphors to enhance your writing.

9.3 Creating characters

> You will explore how a writer uses words to create a character and apply this to your own writing.

➲ For starters

Read the three extracts below and at the top of page 99. Each is a description of a character in a novel. In pairs, discuss which is the most effective character description and why. Think about:

- what we are told about each character
- what adjectives are used to describe the characters
- the effect of the chosen adjectives.

Place them in a rank order, the best one first, the one you think is least effective last. Be prepared to justify your order to the rest of your class.

> Inside the floating cloak he was tall, thin, and bony: and his hair was red beneath the black cap. His face was crumpled and freckled, and ugly without silliness. Out of his face stared two light blue eyes, frustrated now, and turning, or ready to turn, to anger.
>
> (A description of Jack from William Golding's *Lord of the Flies*, page 16)

> Big Joe doesn't have to go to school and I don't think that's fair at all. He's much older than me. He's even older than Charlie and he's never been to school. He stays at home with Mother, and sits up in his tree singing Oranges and Lemons and laughing. Big Joe is always happy, always laughing. I wish I could be happy like him. I wish I could be at home like him. I don't want to go with Charlie. I don't want to go to school.
>
> (A description of Big Joe from Michael Morpurgo's *Private Peaceful*, page 8)

Gran hadn't changed much; her face looked just the same as I remembered it. The skin was soft and withered, bent into a thousand tiny creases that clung gently to the bone underneath. Like a dried apricot, but with a puff of thick white hair standing out in a cloud around it.

(A description of Gran from Stephenie Meyer's *New Moon*, page 3)

⊃ Task

Read this extract from *Great Expectations* by Charles Dickens. A young boy called Pip has met a prisoner on the run in a graveyard.

'Hold your noise!' cried a terrible voice, as a man started up from among the graves at the side of the church porch. 'Keep still, you little devil, or I'll cut your throat!'

A fearful man, all in coarse grey, with a great iron on his leg. A man with no hat, and with broken shoes, and with an old rag tied round his head. A man who had been soaked in water, and smothered in mud, and lamed by stones, and cut by flints, and stung by nettles, and torn by briars; who limped and shivered, and glared and growled; and whose teeth chattered in his head as he seized me by the chin.

'O! Don't cut my throat sir,' I pleaded in terror. 'Pray don't do it, sir.'

'Tell us your name' said the man. 'Quick!'

'Pip, sir.'

'Once more,' said the man, staring at me. 'Give it mouth!'

'Pip. Pip, sir.'

Sentence length can have an important impact on the creation of mood and atmosphere in a piece of writing. Long, flowing sentences can make a scene much more gentle and sweeping, whilst short sentences can make a passage much more tense.

1 Notice how Dickens uses a lot of short, sharp sentences throughout the passage. Pick out three examples of a short sentence in this passage. How does this help build up the tension of the scene?

2 Read again the dialogue between the two characters, Pip and the man (Magwitch). We are told Magwitch speaks with a terrible voice. List eight other details we are told about the characters.

3 What a character says helps the reader to find out a lot more about them. What does Pip say which tells us about his character?

4 What a character does also gives us a clear message about them. What does Magwitch do which also adds information about the characters?

⊃ Taking it further

Create a piece of writing which involves two characters and make sure there is a mood of tension between them. Use some of the examples in this unit to help you with your description. Think about how you can describe each character and how you can use *dialogue* to build up each character and create the tension. Use *short sentences* to help create the tension in places.

Remember to use a specific *narrative perspective*. It will depend on what you wish to do with your piece, but it can be more effective to use first person if you want a one-sided or personal view of something. Consider the following examples:

* I felt terrible and knew it was my fault.
* John felt terrible and knew that it was his fault.

The first example is more appropriate if you wish to show someone's own viewpoint.

9.4 Developing description and characters

> In this section you will learn how to develop more descriptive and effective character writing.

⊃ For starters

1. When writing, writers often use their senses to help create the scene. The five senses are sight, sound, taste, touch and smell. Which sense does each of the following examples use?

A

The ball hit her hard on the head and immediately she felt a dull throbbing of pain where the impact had been.

B

He was guided by the welcoming scent of fish and chips, as if nothing else mattered in the world anymore.

C

The scene in front of them was magnificent. There were trees made of chocolate, marzipan bushes and flowers of every colour you could imagine.

D

The curry was far too strong for him. As he put the first piece of chicken in his mouth he felt as if his whole head would explode as the surge of spices and herbs hammered at his every fibre.

E

The tremendous thud, thud, thud of the bass seemed to get louder every night and it was not long before Mr Johnson went round next door to complain about the ridiculous music playing into the night.

2 For each example look at the descriptive words used to bring the sentence to life. How could they be improved further? Look at this example:

A

> The ball hit her hard on the head and immediately she felt a dull throbbing of pain where the impact had been.

The descriptive words here are 'dull throbbing', describing how the pain hurts the character's head. This is a noun phrase as the female 'her' is the key character and the sentence is about what she feels after the ball has hit her. You could develop the sentence so that it reads:

> The *tennis* ball hit her *extremely* hard on the head and immediately she felt a *horrific* dull throbbing of pain where the impact had been.

By adding three further words, the sentence has become more vivid and clear. Add extra words to the other four examples to make them more interesting.

3 Write your own descriptive sentences using each of the five senses. Think of something rich in sensory detail. For example, a school dining room or town market place.

> **Grammar link**
>
> A noun phrase is where a noun is the key word. Most sentences contain several noun phrases.
>
> An adjectival phrase expands a noun phrase or completes a verb. For example, 'the strange, dark forest'. The adjective 'dark' is modified by the adjective 'strange' to form the adjectival phrase. This expands the noun phrase 'the forest'.
>
> Using such phrases effectively in your work will make it more interesting and increase your marks.

↻ Task

At the very beginning of Barry Hines' *A Kestrel for a Knave*, the writer introduces the central character, Billy Casper through description of what he does and where he lives rather than by what he says:

> There were no curtains up. The window was a hard-edged block the colour of the night sky. Inside the bedroom the darkness was of gritty texture. The wardrobe and bed were blurred shapes in the darkness. Silence.
>
> Billy moved over, towards the outside of the bed. Jud moved with him, leaving one half of the bed empty. He snorted and rubbed his nose. Billy whimpered. They settled. Wind whipped the window and swept along the wall outside.
>
> Billy turned over. Jud followed him and cough-coughed into his neck. Billy pulled the blankets up round his ears and wiped his neck with them. Most of the bed was now empty, and the unoccupied space quickly cooled. Silence. Then the alarm rang. The noise brought Billy upright, feeling for it in the darkness, eyes tight shut. Jud groaned and hutched back across the cold sheet. He reached down the side of the bed and knocked the clock over, grabbed for it, and knocked it farther away.

The atmosphere of where Billy lives is created very clearly by Hines. This gives us some key information about Billy's life and is an important part of his character development. We are told a lot about where he lives.

1 Look closely at the first paragraph in the extract. What does each of the five sentences tell us about where Billy lives? How does Hines build up his description of the scene to create the mood or atmosphere?

2 Now read the rest of the extract. How is Billy introduced here? Look at how his movement is described. Pick out words that show how Billy is made to seem: vulnerable; uncomfortable; resentful; alarmed.

3 How are any of the senses – sight, sound, taste, touch and smell – used in the passage?

⊃ Taking it further

1 You are now going to build up an interesting character of your own. You can either use any of the good ideas you have seen in this unit so far, or come up with something new and original. You will need to make several important decisions about your character. The pictures below of interesting looking people may help you.

2 Now write a description of a character appearing for the first time in a story. Think how you will describe this person to your reader to make it interesting for them. You may use similes to describe the person, for example:

- He was as skinny as a rake.
- He was as thin as a slithering snake.

Of these two examples, which is the most effective and why?

Try to make your writing as interesting and unusual as possible and avoid **clichés** if you can.

> ### ⓘ Concept bank
>
> **Cliché:** a tired or worn-out phrase or saying. They are not original and should be avoided.

10

Re-creations

Learning aim

This unit will help you prepare for the Controlled Assessment Task for Creative Writing called 'Re-creations'. You will transform one text into another. This unit will help you understand the choices you make about **form** and **style**.

ⓘ Concept bank

Form: the way in which subject matter is presented; for example, as a letter, story or newspaper article.

Style: the choices about words and sentences that a writer or speaker makes.

10.1 Playing with texts

You will explore ways in which one text can be transformed into another.

⊃ For starters

On the left is an illustration of the nursery rhyme 'Humpty Dumpty'. How closely does it match your idea of what the event might look like?

At the heart of this story is one important question: a question of life and death. What *actually* happened to Humpty Dumpty? There are four possible answers:

- Death by misadventure – he fell off by accident.
- Death from natural causes – he just died.
- Murder – someone pushed him.
- Sport incident – he jumped off deliberately.

1 Choose one of these four options. Create a story about Humpty Dumpty that ends with your choice. Remember the basic ingredients of any story, and make sure you can answer each as it fits your story: Who? What? When? Why? Where? How?

2 Tell your story, either in writing or to a partner in your class. You have just recreated a text!

↻ Task

You will now develop your thinking about text re-creation. Here are the openings of six different forms in which the original rhyme can be recreated.

A

LOCAL MAN DIES IN TRAGIC ACCIDENT

Tamptown residents could only stand in shock at 11.30 pm last Tuesday evening as they watched the King's cavalry men fail to resuscitate popular local baker Mr Humpty Dumpty following a fall from his garden wall. It is believed he was seeking to aid a bird with a broken wing …

B

Dear Mother,

I thought I would write to let you know how I am getting along on holiday. Remember how you were saying I should try and come out of my shell a bit? Well, you will be glad to know I have been trying out Extreme Sports this week! Tomorrow I am BASE jumping, which is leaping off a high wall with a parachute … It should be fun …

C

Born in 1960 to proud parents John and Lily Dumpty, Mr Humpty Dumpty of Tamptown will be best remembered for his outstanding contribution to the world of confectionery. Mr Dumpty, known affectionately as 'Hummer' due to his jolly demeanour and love of karaoke, was a much admired and respected resident of the Surrey village of Tamptown, where …

D

'Help!' A bloodcurdling scream pierced the still night air, jolting the sleeping residents of Tamptown from their untroubled slumber. Mrs Gloria Peacock stumbled from her once-elegant townhouse, wearing a crumpled silk dressing gown and gazed out fearfully into the thick, heavy darkness. Silence. Nothing. Eyes adjusted to the ink-black night, she could make out a …

E

At exactly 11:32 pm we received a call from a distressed Tamptown resident. The lady, a Mrs Claudia Fennelworth, was requesting our assistance, alongside that of the local ambulance service, in the matter of an accident in the vicinity of her home, 24 Scargill Vistas. She claimed that a local shopkeeper, a Mr Humpty Dumpty, had …

F

Here at *Estelle* we're all fond of celeb gossip and juicy scandals and no man has provided more shocking news than rapper 'Humpty Dumpty', real name Shaun Wesley. From his shock engagement to socialite Paris Ritz to his alleged secret baldness, Humpty Dumpty's death from a heart attack yesterday has stunned the world. The heart attack happened during a performance from the top of Tamptown wall …

1 What form of writing is each of the openings A–F? Think about the content and style of writing.

2 Each extract presents Humpty Dumpty's 'great fall' and the reason for it in a particular form. Choose one and continue writing it from the point where the extract stops. Add another 100 words or more. Keep thinking about the style of writing in the original.

3 Look back at the original nursery rhyme. How is your new version different in terms of form and style?

↻ Taking it further

Think of another nursery rhyme that you could transform into another text.

1 Which rhyme would it be?

2 What form would you transform it into?

3 Explain why you think this would work.

4 Write the first 100 words exactly and then stop!

10.2 Honour the charge they made

You will see how one of the most famous poems in the English language is a re-creation of another text. You will look at how the poet transformed the original by changing its form and style to create a new text.

➲ For starters

Look closely at this picture of a famous military attack, the charge of the Light Brigade. It is of a cavalry charge made at the battle of Balaclava in 1854.

Describe in detail what the picture shows you. Give the picture a title that says something about its mood as well as its content.

➲ Task

The charge of British cavalrymen against their Russian enemy shown in the picture above happened on 25 October 1854, but it wasn't until three weeks later that the event was reported by the British press. In the absence of 21st century technology, it took longer than today for news events to be gathered and presented. On 14 November 1854, the journalist William Howard Russell published his article 'The Cavalry Action at Balaclava 25 October' in *The Times* newspaper. You can find part of the article on page 106.

At ten past eleven our Light Cavalry Brigade rushed to the front ... As they passed toward the front the Russians opened on them with guns from…. the right, with volleys of musketry and rifles. They swept proudly past, glittering in the morning sun in all the pride and splendour of war. We could hardly believe the evidence of our senses. Surely that handful of men were not going to charge an army in position? Alas! It was but too true – their desperate valour knew no bounds, and far indeed was it removed from its so-called better part – discretion. They advanced in two lines, quickening the pace as they closed towards the enemy. A more fearful spectacle was never witnessed than by those who, without the power to aid, beheld their heroic countrymen rushing to the arms of sudden death. At the distance of 1200 yards the whole line of the enemy belched forth, from thirty iron mouths, a flood of smoke and flame through which hissed the deadly balls. Their flight was marked by instant gaps in our ranks, the dead men and horses, by steeds flying wounded or riderless across the plain. The first line was broken – it was joined by the second, they never halted or checked their speed an instant. With diminished ranks, thinned by those thirty guns, which the Russians had laid with the most deadly accuracy, with a halo of flashing steel above their heads, and with a cheer which was many a noble fellow's death cry, they flew into the smoke of the batteries; but ere they were lost from view, the plain was strewed with their bodies and with the carcasses of horses. They were exposed to an oblique fire from the batteries on the hills on both sides, as well as to a direct fire of musketry.

Through the clouds of smoke we could see their sabres flashing as they rode up to the guns and dashed between them, cutting down the gunners as they stood. The blaze of their steel, like an officer standing near me said, 'was like the turn of a shoal of mackerel.' We saw them riding through the guns, as I have said; to our delight, we saw them returning, after breaking through a column of Russian infantry and scattering them like chaff, when the flank fire of the battery on the hill swept them down, scattered and broken as they were. Wounded men and dismounted troopers flying towards us told the sad tale – demigods could not have done what they had failed to do. At the very moment when they were about to retreat, a regiment of lancers was hurled upon their flank. Colonel Shewell, of the 8th Hussars, saw the danger and rode his men straight at them, cutting his way through with fearful loss. The other regiments turned and engaged in a desperate encounter. With courage too great almost for credence, they were breaking their way through the columns which enveloped them, when there took place an act of atrocity without parallel in modern warfare of civilized nation. The Russian gunners, when the storm of cavalry passed, returned to their guns. They saw their own cavalry mingled with the troopers who had just ridden over them, and to the eternal disgrace of the Russian name, the miscreants poured a murderous volley of grape and canister on the mass of struggling men and horses, mingling friend and foe in one common ruin. It was as much as our Heavy Cavalry Brigade could do to cover the retreat of the miserable remnants of that band of heroes as they returned to the place they had so lately quitted in all the pride of life.

At twenty-five to twelve not a British soldier, except the dead and dying, was left in front of these bloody Muscovite guns. Our loss, as far as it could be ascertained in killed, wounded, and missing at two o'clock today, was as follows: Went into action 607 strong. Returned from action 198. Loss 409.

The Times, 14 November 1854

Although powerful journalism, it is likely that the event would hardly be known today but for one other event – the publishing by Tennyson a few weeks later of his poem, 'The Charge of the Light Brigade'. Tennyson transformed the article into a text of his own (see page 107).

Half a league half a league,
Half a league onward,
All in the valley of Death
Rode the six hundred.
'Forward, the Light Brigade!
Charge for the guns' he said:
Into the valley of Death
Rode the six hundred.

'Forward, the Light Brigade!'
Was there a man dismay'd?
Not tho' the soldier knew
Someone had blunder'd:
Theirs not to make reply,
Theirs not to reason why,
Theirs but to do and die:
Into the valley of Death
Rode the six hundred.

Cannon to right of them,
Cannon to left of them,
Cannon in front of them
Volley'd and thunder'd;
Storm'd at with shot and shell,
Boldly they rode and well,
Into the jaws of Death,
Into the mouth of Hell
Rode the six hundred.

Flash'd all their sabres bare,
Flash'd as they turn'd in air
Sabring the gunners there,
Charging an army while
All the world wonder'd:
Plunged in the battery-smoke
Right thro' the line they broke;
Cossack and Russian
Reel'd from the sabre-stroke,
Shatter'd and sunder'd.
Then they rode back, but not
Not the six hundred.

Cannon to right of them,
Cannon to left of them,
Cannon behind them
Volley'd and thunder'd;
Storm'd at with shot and shell,
While horse and hero fell,
They that had fought so well
Came thro' the jaws of Death,
Back from the mouth of Hell,
All that was left of them,
Left of six hundred.

When can their glory fade?
O the wild charge they made!
All the world wonder'd.
Honour the charge they made,
Honour the Light Brigade,
Noble six hundred.

Russell presents the charge as a newspaper article. Tennyson presents the charge in the form of a poem. Journalism has been transformed into poetry.

1 Which version gives us the most *factual* information about the event?

2 Which presents the event in the *most* detail? Give examples.

3 Find a verse from Tennyson which links to a section of the news article through its content. Look at the *language* used by Tennyson and Russell and think about their use of description, **figurative language** and **emotive language**. Which version do you think uses language most effectively?

4 Tennyson presents the events in ways we think of as 'poetic'. He exploits repetition of sound through rhythm and rhyme, and uses repetition of words and phrases. Look at a verse from Tennyson and comment on the effect of rhyme, rhythm and repetition of words and phrases.

5 Tennyson uses verses to organise his writing. Russell uses paragraphs. What difference does this make?

6 Which presentation of the events do you find the more effective – the article or the poem? Why? Include your thoughts about:
   • what you think each writer was trying to achieve in his text
   • what the news article tells us that the poem does not
   • whether the poem includes anything not in the news article
   • whether you prefer Russell or Tennyson's style and why.

> *i* **Concept bank**
>
> **Figurative language:** descriptions in which one thing is compared with another to create interesting or powerful images. Examples include similes, metaphors and personification.
>
> **Emotive language:** words or phrases which describe the writer's emotions and/or make the reader feel a certain way.

⊃ Taking it further

Look again at the Russell text. There are details that Tennyson does not use in his poem. In the style of Tennyson, write an extra verse based on these details that could be fitted into the poem or added at the beginning or the end.

10.3 Out of the valley of Death …

You will produce your own piece of writing, recreating the poem 'The Charge of the Light Brigade'. You will think about form and style.

⊃ For starters

Which of these phrases that Tennyson uses would be the best title for this painting? Why?

- The valley of Death
- Storm'd at with shot and shell
- The mouth of Hell
- Flash'd all their sabres bare

⊃ Task

Look at the cavalryman at the centre of the painting above. You are going to *imagine yourself as him* in the scene shown. You are in the midst of battle, with the roar of cannons all around you – death never more than a sabre's length away. As you answer these questions, remember you are the cavalryman, so use 'I'. You survive the charge when so many of your friends do not.

1 Describe the Russian cavalryman to your left. Give lots of detail – this might be the last thing you see before you die!
2 What are you thinking at this point?
3 Describe what you can smell (all those things around you that would create a terrible stench).
4 There are all sorts of noises. Write about four different things you hear.
5 You are seconds away from capturing the enemy cannon. Look how close you are to the Russian guns! How do you feel exactly at this point? You might well be feeling several emotions at the same time. Describe them.

6   You have your sabre raised, as does your Russian enemy. Describe what happens to you both next. (Remember, you do not die!)

7   You have survived! Finish this sentence, 'It was almost as if God wanted …' Then add two more sentences about your feelings at this point.

8   You are feet away from the Russian cannon when there is a huge explosion. As you fall from your horse, describe what is going on around you and what you see and hear.

9   In the last seconds before you black out, you see your dear friend, Thomas – he's the one in the picture (on page 108) standing over his badly injured horse. What happens to Thomas? What do you see and hear?

And then black-out. Nothing. Darkness.

↑ *This lithograph shows Florence Nightingale talking with an army officer at the Barracks Hospital in Scutari.*

You regain consciousness, and raise your bandaged head to see the scene depicted above. A man in the bed next to you, with much of his chest wrapped in thickly blood-stained bandages, whispers between groans, 'We're at Scutari … Scutari … she's an angel … an angel … Nurse Nightingale … light in the dark … '

Take in the scene as the haze and pain of your head injury recede.

10 Look at what you see. Let your eyes scan from left to right, moving slowly; there's that man being helped on the left, and then that empty bed to the right. What else? Describe what you see in as much detail as these few minutes allow.

Things start to come back to you; who you are and what happened. Look again at either the Russell article or the Tennyson poem. The details, or some of the details, of that horrendous day return.

11 The woman in the long black dress notices you are awake. Coming to your bedside, she says, 'Good afternoon, Captain Hobbs, the 11th Hussars, I believe. We've been tending to your wounds the past weeks. I'm Nurse Nightingale.' She asks the question you have been dreading: 'Can you tell me what happened, Captain Hobbs?' Details are hazy. Relive the details by looking at the notes you made in tasks 1–9, and then tell her. It doesn't matter if you stumble over your words; Florence Nightingale will understand.

Night time. Scutari military hospital in Turkey. About 350 miles across the Black Sea from the Russian Crimea and that valley of horror. It's 3.30 am. Something has woken you – possibly the screams of a cavalryman to your left, but more likely a dream, a nightmare, or an overwhelming desire to write to your betrothed, Emily, who you last saw in London, all those months ago. You are now going to begin the process of producing a piece of writing. This writing will draw upon all that you have learnt in recent lessons about form and style.

You will write either Captain Hobbs' nightmare or Captain Hobbs' letter to Emily. Although based on the same material, these pieces of writing should be quite different.

Consider these questions before you plan your writing:

- What would the content of Hobbs' nightmare be?
- What content might you find in the letter to Emily?
- Why might the content be similar, and why might it be different?
- You want to present events as if experienced in a nightmare. How would you craft words and phrases to make it seem like a nightmare? What would writing 'in the *style* of a nightmare' be like? William James coined the term 'stream of consciousness' to describe how our thoughts flow and move as we think. In dreams, our thoughts can be even more chaotic and unstructured. How might you represent a nightmare in writing?
- Now think about Hobbs writing to his fiancée, Emily, back in England. How would the *style* of writing be influenced by the fact he is writing to his betrothed? What kind of language might be used?
- Why might the voices be different in these two pieces of writing? Remember, in each case you are writing from the point of view of Hobbs.

12 Now produce the first 150–250 words of either Captain Hobbs' nightmare or his letter to Emily. If you need help starting, you could begin:

The nightmare:

That face ... that face ... haunting me ...

The letter:

Dearest Emily

My thoughts and heart are forever with you, and it is with deep hope for when we are together once more, that I begin this letter ...

○ Taking it further

1 Complete the writing you have started. Write a further 300–400 words.
2 You are Emily Hester, Captain William Hobbs' betrothed. William returns from the Crimea scarred by the horror he has lived through. Write a letter to Alfred Lord Tennyson expressing your thoughts and feelings about his poem, and the way it presents the events William barely survived.

Linking Words and Images

Learning aim

In this unit you will develop the skills and understanding needed to write a review for a 'Moving Images' Creative Writing Controlled Assessment Task. You will learn about the features of a typical **review**.

ⓘ Concept bank

Review: a critical report and evaluation of a film, book, play, performance or concert, often found in newspapers, in magazines or on the Internet.

11.1 What is a review?

> You will learn about what a review is, and its typical content.

➲ For starters

1 Think of a narrative film you have seen and know well. Write its name in the middle of a piece of paper and for two minutes produce a 'brainstorm' of facts about it and your opinions of it.

2 Using your notes, tell a partner about this film, then swap over so they tell you about theirs. You have just given a 'review' of a film!

3 What do you think are the typical contents of a film review? Make a list of *eight* things you would expect a review to include, for example, the names of important actors.

➲ Task

Read this review from the Heart 106.2 website about the film release *Public Enemies*.

Public Enemies

Johnny Depp turns in the performance of his career in this superb gangster drama.

Who's in it? Johnny Depp, Christian Bale, Marion Cotillard

What's it about? The Feds try to take down notorious American gangsters John Dillinger, Baby Face Nelson and Pretty Boy Floyd in the 1930s.

What type of film? Drama

Is it any good? Wow! After watching Johnny Depp camp it up as Willy Wonka and Jack Sparrow I almost forgot what an acting powerhouse he is doing a straight role. Without a doubt this is a career best performance from him and don't be surprised if there are acting nods for him come next February. Marion Cotillard is pitch perfect as his love interest while Christian Bale FINALLY stops doing that Batman Voice for 90 minutes and pulls a stunning performance out of the bag. The supporting cast are also spot on and thanks to the direction of Michael 'Heat' Mann this is as stunning visually as it is emotionally involving … which is, very. The script is not over-egged or too earnest, and all the lines come across as real rather than cliché-riddled monologues which can be the case with gangster movies. Whilst there is a lot of gun action and violent set pieces in this, it's really a piece that is really all about the characters and it is hands down the best gangster movie of the last decade … at least. One of this year's few must see movies.

Marks out of 10? 9

---

1   Which things on your list of typical contents can you find in the review on page 111? How important were any of the aspects you listed, but the website review didn't?

2   If there are any, write down two aspects of the film that the review includes that were not on your list of typical contents. Explain why it might be important to include these aspects in a review.

When you shared your review, you were simply telling your partner about the film, without thinking about how to organise the information. Look again at the *Public Enemies* review. It has six parts: an introduction and five parts, each of which answers a question.

3   Write two further question-style headings. You now have seven headings that you can use to guarantee important aspects of a film are included in a review.

4   Write a plan for a film review of your choice. Use the introduction and question structure to organise your notes. Aim to write about 100 words.

➲ Taking it further

Uncut film review: *Up*

DIRECTED by Pete Docter

STARRING THE VOICES OF Ed Asner, Christopher Plummer, Jordan Nagai, Bob Peterson

Gone are the days when Pixar films could be dismissed as handsome confections for kids. The studio's last film *WALL•E* was a bleak science-fiction vision in the true Kubrick spirit, and the 3D extravaganza *Up* is ... a bittersweet contemplation of ageing and mortality?

You could read it that way – or alternatively see this brisk fantasy as a surreal, sweet-natured comedy about a cranky old man, a flying house and some talking dogs.

Ed Asner provides the voice of elderly balloon seller Carl, who once shared a dream of airborne escape with his late wife. Hitching his balloons to his house, Carl flies off with a bedazzled young Wilderness Explorer (Jordan Nagai) to a lost domain, where they encounter a villainous air ace (Christopher Plummer) and a winningly goofy 13-foot-bird named Kevin.

The humour gets weirder as it goes on and it's among the lightest of Pixar's films, but the first 20 minutes offer the saddest, most poignant sequence seen in an animation film since Bambi's mother died.

JONATHAN ROMNEY

1   Here is an online review of the film *Up* which is just under 200 words. The website host asks its writer, Jonathan Romney, to increase the review to 300 words as there's more space to fill on the web page. What further content could Romney add?

2   Who do you think the target readership for this review is? What evidence is there from how it has been written?

11.2 Writing for an audience

You will consider how reviewers craft what they write to suit their audience, and the publishing context in which their review will appear. You will analyse style choices by focusing on how reviews start.

⟳ For starters

Read this review of *Transformers – Revenge of the Fallen*.

Review A

Transformers – Revenge of the Fallen

1 What's it about? You won't be surprised to learn this is a follow-up to the summer blockbuster *Transformers*. Think huge clunking robots that transform with max noise into all manner of objects and you'll not be far wrong! Sam Witwicky – the 16-year-old from the original – again finds himself involved in huge set piece battles, screen-filling action sequences and ear-piercing sound effects. We're talking serious decibels here! More would be to spoil the plot …

2 Who's in it? Sam is played by Shia LaBeouf, with the lovely Megan Fox playing girlfriend Mikaela. The main characters are the Transformers themselves with Decepticons and Autobots hogging most of the frames. Optimus Prime returns, there's the big baddie, The Fallen, and fans will warm to new 'Formers Mudflap and Skiddy. Heavy metal heaven!

3 What else is it like? Good old mainstream sfx-, cgi-dominated summer-season blockies is what we're talking here. Action. Explosions and fighting. Jaw-dropping speed and frantic camera work. Animation in its screen origins, we're not looking at subtlety of characterisation or brain-busting plotting. This is as in yer face as it gets. Batman crossed with a car-wreck.

4 Why should I bother? Because it is an amazing film that you will want to watch over and over again until your eyes can't take the action any longer. The special effects are breathtaking and the pace is relentless. Wow!!! And Ow!!! At the same time!

5 Why should I stay home and play on my console? Maybe because the cameras are too close to the people, the slow-motion can get repetitive after a while, the plot is a bit pants, the film is overall confusing and when you watch it for the first time at the cinema you will be wondering what's happening because everything is so fast or really slow. But, but … you'll still love it!

6 Cinema or DVD? This is cinema at its loudest, most frantic, most screen-busting. The sound effects, the light and magic, and that slo-mo when it most matters. Huge explosions will be just plain wimpy at home compared to the multiplex megascreen and isn't that why you're there?

Bums on seats score – 7/10.

Who do you think is the most likely audience for the review on page 113? Base your decisions on the way the review is written, *not* on the content of the film itself! For each one, use PEE to explain your thinking.

- **a** males **b** females **c** both
- **a** adults **b** children **c** both
- **a** film experts **b** general readers **c** both
- **a** new viewers **b** Transformers fans **c** both

> **PEE**
>
> make a **P**oint
>
> use **E**vidence
>
> **E**xplain how the evidence supports the point.

⊃ Task

Now look at this extract from another review of *Transformers – Revenge of the Fallen*.

Review B

Transformers – Revenge of the Fallen

Michael Bay, that prince of unsubtlety, rejecter of nuance and repudiator of light-and-shade, has returned with another of his mega-decibel action headbangers. I found it at once loud and boring, like watching paint dry while getting hit over the head with a frying pan. And at two and a half hours, it really is very long. Once again, we are in the world of the Transformers, and again the star is Shia LaBeouf: allegedly a Tom Hanks for the future.

This movie franchise is based on a branded toy manufactured by Hasbro: basically, cars that can transform themselves, with much whirring and clanking, into vast, ungainly and incredibly dull robots. The good ones are the Autobots and they are on our side; the bad ones are the Decepticons, defeated in the first movie, but now intent once more on crushing Earth. For about two-thirds of this mind-frazzlingly dull film, we are led to believe that the 'fallen' of the title refers to this resurgent army. But then we find out it kind of means something else, and the storyline completely transforms itself into something even more boring than it was originally.

Because this film really is quite staggeringly uninteresting, the loud explosions – so densely packed as to resemble a 150-minute drum roll – are the only things keeping you awake. While the Transformers were clanking noisily around, my mind wandered and I found myself thinking about Hazel Blears, swine flu and whether Waitrose was going to take over all the empty Woolworths buildings.

The cherry on this cake of direness is the performance of Megan Fox, playing LaBeouf's sultry girlfriend – a performer so poutingly wooden she makes Jordan look like Liv Ullmann. You'll get better acting and superior entertainment at a monster truck rally.

1 Who do you think is the most likely audience for Review B? Base your decisions on the way the review is written, not on the content of the film itself! For each one, use PEE (see page 114) to explain your thinking.

- **a** males   **b** females   **c** both
- **a** adults   **b** children   **c** both
- **a** film experts   **b** general readers   **c** both
- **a** new viewers   **b** Transformers fans   **c** both

2 Now look closely at the openings of the two *Transformers* reviews. Reread Review A up to the words '… spoil the plot', and Review B up to '… Tom Hanks for the future.' Both are about 80 words. For each question below, answer 'A' or 'B' or 'equally'. Give evidence for each answer.

- Which opening gives readers the most **facts** about the film?
- Which opening gives the most **opinions**?
- Which opening uses the most complicated language?
- Which opening uses the most complicated sentence structures?
- Which opening creates the liveliest **voice**?
- Which opening uses humour the most?
- Which writer comes across as the more reasonable and fair-minded?
- Which writer comes across as the more sneering and dismissive?
- Which writer most engages your interest and attention?

You have analysed these openings closely. You looked at the writers' language choices or **styles**. These choices are influenced by a writer's awareness of their audience and a sense of where their writing will be published. You might not be surprised to learn that Review A is from *Young Voices*, an online arts site for older teenagers, and Review B is from *The Guardian* newspaper.

3 Write a 100–150 word analysis of the opening of either of the reviews, starting in this way: You can tell Review (A or B) is from … and is for … because of …'

⭕ Taking it further

1 Find three reviews from different sources. There are many Internet sites that give film reviews, but remember to look at newspapers and magazines too. Working with a partner, look at the six reviews and choose two that you feel open really well. Prepare a three-minute presentation for the class called 'Grab that Reader – Tips for Review Writers' in which you:

- share the opening 100 words or so from one or two reviews
- explain what impresses you about the opening(s)
- give the class 'six tips for successful openings' based on your analysis of what you have read.

2 Write the opening 100–150 words of a film review. Before you start, think about:

- who you are writing for
- where the review will be published
- the style of writing you will use
- the content of the opening.

> **ⓘ Concept bank**
>
> **Fact:** a statement that, at least in theory, can be checked and confirmed as being true or false.
>
> **Opinion:** one person's thoughts or feelings about something – other people may not agree.
>
> **Voice:** the tone or mood created by a text's writer.
>
> **Style:** the choices about words and sentences that a writer or speaker makes. The choices result from such aspects as word choice, tone, and grammar.

Linking Words and Images

11.3 Writing a review

> You will write a review for a particular audience and context.

⊃ For starters

Look at the table below. One column contains a collection of extracts from reviews of *Harry Potter and the Half-Blood Prince*, while the other column is a list of the sources, but in the wrong order. Match up each review to its source and explain your choices.

Review extracts	Sources
1 **BEST CHARACTER:** Dumbledore is the new Obi-Wan Kenobi – inscrutable. **FAMILY RATING:** One mild swear word, one death, several snogs. **BUM NUMBNESS:** Time flies like an owl. **OVERALL RATING:** Five hats	**A** **Rotten Tomatoes** An Internet forum that organises and collects all of the reviews from a variety of sources (newspapers, online, magazines) and averages them into a single rating.
2 `Dark, thrilling, and occasionally quite funny, Harry Potter and the Half-Blood Prince is also visually stunning and emotionally satisfying.`	**B** *Empire* **magazine** The biggest-selling film magazine in Britain, aimed at movie-goers who are interested in films.
3 It's probably a bit too thin on the action but as a well-crafted film it works well. For the first time a Potter film goes beyond the magic and gives us all something to think about.	**C** *The Times* A daily national broadsheet newspaper published in the United Kingdom since 1785, described as 'UK's leading daily newspaper for business people'.
4 HP7 Part One arrives, ETA November, 2010. We're marking time before the final battle between Good and Evil, with the promised darkness sitting somewhat clumsily with teen romance and humour.	**D** **CBBC** *Newsround* **film reviews website** is based on the BBC children's news programme and was one of the world's first television news magazines aimed specifically at children.
5 But on the evidence of *The Half-Blood Prince* there is a real chance that Potter, like *The Lord of the Rings* before it, will be a fantasy franchise that ends in a bang, not a whimper.	**E** *The Sun* A daily tabloid newspaper published in the United Kingdom with the highest circulation within the UK, standing at an average of 2,986,000 copies a day.

↻ Task

The final step is to examine a review from the website *e-shed*, which features reviews for 'young people who love film'. This suggests that the reviews are written by film fans rather than film experts. Read the review.

1 *Twilight* **Cert:** PG

Run time: 122 min
Cast: Kristen Stewart, Robert Pattinson, Billy Burke, Peter Facinelli
Director: Catherine Hardwicke

2 Based on the first in a series of novels by Stephanie Meyer, Catherine Hardwicke's *Twilight* tells the story of Bella Swan (Kristen Stewart), a broody teen who is forced to swap her life in sunny Phoenix to live with her father (Billy Burke) in dreary Forks, a small town with a mere population of 3120. On Bella's first day of school she meets handsome and mysterious loner, Edward Cullens (Robert Pattinson). The two are instantly attracted to each other but to Bella's dissatisfaction, Edward remains distant. When Edward saves Bella from being flattened by a speeding truck (with his bare hands), Bella makes it her mission to learn more about his mysterious strength. It does not take her long to discover that in fact, Edward is a vampire. On Bella's discovery, Edward explains that he and the rest of the Cullens family are in fact 'vegetarians' (by 'vegetarians', Edward explains, they eat animals, not people), but his desire for her is so strong, that he is not sure if he can stop himself from biting her. Despite obvious dangers (and the disapproval of Edward's vampire family) the couple soon begin a passionate but dangerous romance with real disastrous consequences for all involved.

3 The film as a whole does cause some controversy for me as a viewer – as a thriller/'vampire movie' it does not really work and this is mainly due to the representation of the Twilight vampires and lack of action. Unlike any other vampire movie ever written, these vampires can walk in the sunlight (traditionally, they should combust into flames), and there is not a sharp tooth in sight; eye colour is the only thing that changes when they are about to feed or fight.

4 Of course it is essential to remember that this is a film based on a novel, therefore the characters must be depicted as they are in the series, but hardcore vampire fans and cinema goers who have not read the book (but have seen the rather misleading trailer) will probably feel disappointed.

5 However, not all is lost thanks to Forks local vampire villain, James: what he lacks in vampire props, he makes up for in sadism (as seen in the one and only fight sequence at the end of the film). The main problem is the action that does make it into the film is just not good enough – some dodgy wirework is about all we are offered and you expect more.

6 As a romance, however, the film works well. Edward and Bella's love story is charming and you can't help but be drawn into it. Stewart and Pattinson have an undeniable chemistry and Pattinson in particular does a brilliant job of portraying the broody and angst-ridden Edward. Many of the film's other characters, however, just feel unnecessary and as if they are doing little but getting in the way of the main plot. In particular, Bella's friends are nothing more than irritating (but maybe that is what helps to make Edward so appealing). The Cullens are more enjoyable as the local vampire family, but still there are not really any stand-out performances from any of the supporting cast.

7 Having not read the books, I expected this to be a vampire thriller movie, and that was my problem. As a thriller, it does not deliver, but as a love story, it ticks all the boxes. However, there is nothing really new here – like many films before it and many films to come, it is a story of forbidden love, a story that has been repeatedly retold since Shakespeare's *Romeo and Juliet*. All that said, the two leads do an excellent job of portraying the lust, angst, desire and heartache that would be present in a relationship like this and this is where most of the appeal of the film lies. It does have its exciting moments and will undoubtedly appeal and be worshipped by its target audience of teenage girls. In a nutshell: a pleasant but flawed watch. **6/10**

1 Look at each of the seven sections in turn. Answer these questions in note form:
   - What is the content of this section?
   - What is the purpose of this section?
   - How has the writer used language suited to the website's younger audience?

2 This review uses a paragraph structure with one paragraph following after the other in a series of linked steps. Words such as 'however' are used several times to create these links. Other reviews in this unit have used a question/answer structure. Which way of organising the material do you feel is better? Explain your answer.

3 Imagine you are the *e-shed* website host, and this review is a first draft. List five changes you would make to improve it. You should try to improve:
   - Content – what is in it
   - Structure – how it is organised
   - Style – how it is written.

↻ Taking it further

Write a film review of 500–700 words.

1 Decide who your target readership is. Think about:
   - Age of viewers
   - Gender
   - Specialist or general
   - Sophisticated language user or ordinary
   - Publishing context – which newspaper or magazine? Which website?

2 Decide what structure you will use:
   - Question/answer?
   - Series of linked paragraphs?

3 Decide what 'voice' and style you will use:
   - Reasonable, fair and factual?
   - Whole-heartedly and passionately enthusiastic?
   - Sneering and dismissive?

Themes and Ideas – Family Relationships

Learning aim

In this unit you will look at three poems by William Wordsworth. Each poem shows a different aspect of love within a family. You will analyse the language, structure and form in each one. You will notice similarities and differences, and you will learn about the background to each poem. You will be aware of the key things you need to comment on when analysing a poem.

12.1 'We Are Seven'

You will learn to read and understand a poem which explores a child's view of family relationships. In this section you will need a copy of 'We Are Seven' by Wordsworth.

The Romantic period began towards the end of the 18th century. Romantic literature is characterised by an emphasis on emotion, love and the natural world.

William Wordsworth was born in 1770 and died in 1850. He lived most of his life in the Lake District where he appreciated the outstanding natural beauty of his surroundings. In his poems, he often uses simple, almost childlike, language and regular rhyming patterns. Some of his main themes are love, innocence, beauty and an appreciation of the natural environment. Wordsworth was an important figure in the Romantic movement. The poems you will analyse were published in 1798 in a collection called *Lyrical Ballads*.

⊃ For starters

1 Your first task is to build up a bank of words associated with the theme of family relationships. On your own, spend one minute writing down words (or phrases) that you associate with this theme. Now spend 30 seconds sharing your ideas with a partner.

2 Now spend two minutes sharing your ideas with at least three other people. You should aim for at least 10 different words or phrases.

3 Finally, share and discuss these ideas with the rest of your class, and in doing so, build up a useful bank of words that you will add to during the course of this unit.

4 Look at the pictures on the left. What words or phrases might you use to describe these families? Add these to your word bank.

⟳ Task

1 When you write about poems, there are key words that you will need to use. Match each of these key words with the correct definition and write them down.

Repetition	How the rhymed line endings are arranged
Stanza	The way that lines or stanzas are organised
Simile	A group of lines or unit within a longer poem
Structure	A word or phrase that sparks off the senses, especially visually
Imagery	Key words, phrases, ideas and sentence patterns are repeated to create an effect
Rhyming pattern	A comparison of two things usually using the words 'like' or 'as'

2 Read the poem 'We Are Seven' and underline any words that you are unfamiliar with. In pairs, try to work out the meanings from the rest of the sentence or stanza.

3 Now look closely at the first stanza of the poem on the right.
- What do the underlined words suggest to us about the poem?
- How is the word 'death' emphasised?
- Having read the whole poem, what do you think might be the purpose of this stanza?
- Read stanzas 2 and 3. What kind of image do we have of the little girl? Find and record the words and phrases that help to build up that image. What impression does she make on the narrator of the poem?
- Read stanzas 4–9. What do we learn about the little girl's family?

A <u>simple</u> child
That lightly draws its breath,
And feels its <u>life</u> in every limb,
What should it know of <u>death</u>?

4 Consider each of the words in the box below. Choose the three words that you think best describe the little girl and her attitude to her family.

distant   grieving   united   loving   emotional
loyal   hopeful   innocent   close

5 For each of the three words chosen, find a quotation to back up your point. Then explain your idea more fully using the *point, evidence, explanation* structure. Look at the example below using the word 'close'.

Word	Point	Evidence	Explanation
'close'	The little girl seems *close* to her family. She insists that they are united, even though her brother and sister are dead.	This is shown in the line: 'Seven are we …'	Wordsworth uses simple, child-like language to show the child's simple attitude to the family. He repeats the idea to show how determined the girl is that death has not separated her family.

6 Wordsworth conveys the information about the little girl's family through her conversation with the narrator. How effective is this? What does it allow the writer to show?

7 There are a lot of powerful images in stanzas 10–15. For example:

- the girl sewing and knitting by the graves
- the girl having her supper by the graves in the dusk.

Find at least three more examples of powerful images.

8 Choose one of these images to draw. Underneath your drawing, write the line (or lines) that create this image. With a partner, explain why you have chosen this image and the line (or lines) that support it.

9 Look at the extract on the right of the girl sewing and knitting by the graves. Notice how Wordsworth uses the following ways to create this powerful image:

- Simple words build up a clear image of what the writer is describing.
- Repetition of words, for example, 'my', 'I' and 'there', shows how the experience is personal to the little girl and how important the place is to her.
- There is a clear and simple rhyming pattern.
- Her actions show that she does not really accept that they are dead.

Now look at the final stanza of the poem on the right.

- How does the narrator of the poem behave towards the little girl here?
- How does he feel about her?
- How does Wordsworth show this?
- Compare the structure and rhyming pattern of this stanza with the rest of the poem? How does it differ?
- What effect does Wordsworth achieve by doing this?
- How is the narrator used in the poem to emphasise family love?

10 Look back at your bank of words and your initial thoughts about family relationships. In pairs, discuss whether the ideas shown in this poem fit in with your own ideas.

> My stockings there I often knit,
> My 'kerchief there I hem;
> And there upon the ground I sit,
> And sing a song to them.

> 'But they are dead; those two
> are dead!
> Their spirits are in heaven!'
> 'Twas throwing words away; for
> still
> The little Maid would have her
> will,
> And said, '*Nay, we are seven!*'

⊃ Taking it further

Write two paragraphs to answer the question:

> How does Wordsworth present the relationship between the girl and her brother and sister in 'We Are Seven'?

In the first paragraph, describe the relationship Wordsworth writes about in the poem. In the second, analyse some of the poetic techniques he uses to present that relationship. Remind yourself of the **IF-DISCS** checklist on page 68.

12.2 'The Mad Mother'

You will develop your understanding of the themes of family relationships. You will learn how the writer creates a strong character in this poem. In this section you will need a copy of 'The Mad Mother' by Wordsworth.

In 'We Are Seven', Wordsworth shows family love from the point of view of a child commenting on her brothers and sisters. In 'The Mad Mother', you will see the love of a mother for her child.

⊃ For starters

1 Write two sentences for each picture below describing the relationship between the mother and her children.

2 In pairs, discuss what you think makes a good mother. Write down your ideas.

3 Read the first stanza of 'The Mad Mother' below. Use these words to fill in the blanks but do not write in your book.

> underneath   hair   wild   among   alone   bare   stain

> Her eyes are ......, her head is ......,
> The sun has burnt her coal-black ......,
> Her eye-brows have a rusty ......,
> And she came far from over the main.
> She has a baby on her arm,
> Or else she were ......;
> And ...... the hay-stack warm,
> And on the green-wood stone,
> She talked and sung the woods ......;
> And it was in the English tongue.

What do you notice about the rhyming pattern in this poem? Write down your thoughts.

⊃ Task

1 Below is stanza 2, but every other line has been removed. The missing lines are in the right-hand box. Thinking about what you noticed about the rhyming pattern of stanza 1, slot the missing lines back into stanza 2 in the correct order. It will also help if you look carefully at the punctuation.

```
1  'Sweet babe they say that I am mad,
2  _____
3  And I am happy when I sing
4  _____
5  Then, lovely baby, do not fear!
6  _____
7  But, safe as in a cradle, here
8  _____
9  To thee I know too much I owe;
10 _____
```

> I cannot work thee any woe.'
> But nay, my heart is far too glad;
> I pray thee have no fear of me,
> My lovely baby! thou shalt be,
> Full many a sad and doleful thing:

2 Read the first two stanzas again. What effect does the rhyming pattern create? What impression do we have of the mother? Does the title seem appropriate at this stage?

3 Now read the rest of the poem. Look closely at stanzas 3 and 4 to see how the writer develops the character of the mother and how he shows her state of mind.

4 From the three lines on the right pick out two or three words that best describe her torment. Comment in detail on the effectiveness of each word: for example, 'fire' suggests her torment or even madness because it is something powerful and uncontrollable. Wordsworth perhaps hints at something more sinister because fire is also dangerous and destructive. The word seems to suggest that this is something the mother has struggled with and she tries not to let it overwhelm her.

> A fire was once within my brain;
> And in my head a dull, dull pain;
> And fiendish faces one, two, three,

5 At which point in stanza 3 does her mood change?

6 How might you describe her feelings in stanza 4? Which words or phrases back up your ideas?

7 Now look at stanza 5:

> Oh! love me, love me, little boy!
> Thou art thy mother's only joy;
> And do not dread the waves below,
> When o'er the sea-rock's edge we go;
> The high crag cannot work me harm,
> Nor leaping torrents when they howl;
> The babe I carry on my arm,
> He saves for me my precious soul;
> Then happy lie, for blest am I;
> Without me my sweet babe would die.

In pairs, chose the statement below that you think best describes the mother's feelings. Find a line or phrase to support your choice.

A The baby protects her from harm.

B She feels desperate.

C She feels anxious and afraid.

D She knows that the baby needs her.

E She is brave and defiant.

F She knows no fear when actually she should.

8 In stanza 6, Wordsworth uses two similes to describe the baby. What are they and what effect might these descriptions have on the reader?

9 In the rest of the poem, what animals are mentioned? Why do you think Wordsworth makes so many references to nature in this poem?

10 Read the final stanza again. In pairs, spend two–three minutes discussing these questions:

- Does Wordsworth finish the poem on a positive or negative note?
- What questions do you still want to ask at the end of the poem?

⊃ Taking it further

1 When Wordsworth wrote this poem:

- Women had few rights and were dependent on their husbands.
- Those who were mentally ill would be seen as outcasts and could end up imprisoned.
- Women who had children but were unmarried would also be ostracised from society.
- Divorce was not common and men often sold their wives.
- Women could not own property.

Does this information influence your reading of the poem? What do you think has happened?

2 In the last four stanzas of the poem we find out a few things about the baby's father. Find three different pieces of information about him, then share and discuss these with a partner.

- How do you imagine the father?
- Do we believe what the mother says about him?
- Does he know that the child exists?
- Why has he abandoned her?

3 Decide what the father is like, and show this through either writing a piece of prose (about 150 words) from his point of view, or try to write two or three stanzas, following the same rhyming pattern as Wordsworth uses, giving the father's view of the situation. These phrases might help:

- I begged her to stay but she wanted the baby for herself ...
- She needed peace, she needed calm ...
- Her mind was made up; I was written out of her future and the future of my child ...

↑ *William Wordsworth*

As a class you will probably show the father in many different ways. Read out your work and listen to others to see how different your ideas are.

12.3 'Anecdote for Fathers'

You will explore how the theme of family relationships is presented in this poem and support your ideas with evidence from the text. In this section, you will need a copy of 'Anecdote for Fathers' by Wordsworth.

ⓘ Concept bank

Anecdote: a brief story told to back up or illustrate a point.

⊃ For starters

1 In pairs, discuss how a child's relationship with their father might be different from their relationship with their mother. Write down the main differences (and perhaps the similarities). Be prepared to share your ideas.

2 In pairs, for 2–3 minutes discuss the following statement: Parents can never hope to learn anything from their children.

3 Read the poem '**Anecdote** for Fathers'. What do you think the poem might be about based on the title and your first reading?

4 Look closely at the opening stanza:

> I have a boy of five years old;
> His face is fair and fresh to see;
> His limbs are cast in beauty's
>   mould,
> And dearly he loves me.

- What impression do we have of the boy?
- How does the father feel about his son?
- How does the writer show this?

⊃ Task

1 Read stanzas 3–6.
- How might you describe the father's mood and feelings in this section?
- What image of the father do you have?
- How do the words used to describe nature help you to understand the father's feelings?

2 The poem is based on a question that the father asks the child. Fill in a table like the one below to summarise your reading of the poem. (Use evidence from the poem to support your comments.)

What question does the father ask the child? How does he ask this question?	
What initial answer does the child give?	
How does the father react to this answer? How does the writer show this?	
In stanza 14, the child explains his answer. Why do you think he gives this explanation?	
How does it affect his father? How does the writer show this?	

⊃ Taking it further

1 Now look at the final stanza. How does the father feel? How does Wordsworth show this? Pick out a quotation to support your answer.
2 Thinking about the poem as a whole, discuss these questions:
   - Is the child being good or bad?
   - If you were a father, what might you learn from this incident?
   - Have you ever lied to protect someone's feelings?
3 What do you think Wordsworth is trying to show us in this poem?

> Oh dearest, dearest boy! my heart
> For better lore would seldom yearn,
> Could I but teach the hundredth part
> Of what from thee I learn.

12.4 Review of the three poems

> You will reflect on the importance of the fact that these poems were written at the end of the 18th century. You will consider some of the ways that you can compare these poems.

⊃ For starters

1 At the time that Wordsworth wrote these poems, about 50 per cent of children did not live beyond the age of five – today that figure is nearer 0.7 per cent. Look back at all three poems and for each write one comment that explains how this information affects our reading of these poems.
2 Looking at your initial bank of words about families and family relationships, do these three poems fit in with your ideas? If so, how? If not, how are they different?

⊃ Task

1 Now that you have looked at all three poems on your own, write a list of similarities between them: for example, all three poems focus on relationships within a family; or a more detailed point would be that in 'We Are Seven' and 'Anecdote for Fathers' there is dialogue between an adult and a child but in 'The Mad Mother' it is only the mother's voice that we hear.
2 Are there any important differences between the poems? Add these to your list. Read through your ideas and check that you have included at least one comment on each of these five areas:
   - themes
   - characters
   - relationships
   - language
   - rhyming pattern

⊃ Taking it further

Choose **two** of the three poems you have studied in this section. Write an essay to answer the question on the right.

> How does Wordsworth present family relationships in any two poems?

Presenting People

Learning aim

In this unit you will investigate the techniques that writers use to create character. By analysing description, dialogue and action, you will be able to comment on the presentation of a character and consider what the writer intends the reader to feel in response. This unit will help you prepare for either the Literary Reading Controlled Assessment (English GCSE) or for the Extended Reading Controlled Assessment (English Language GCSE).

ⓘ Concept bank

Description: what the character is like physically.

Dialogue: what the character says.

Action: what the character does; how he or she behaves.

13.1 Creating a first impression

You will look at how a writer uses description, the actions a character performs, and the dialogue given to them to speak to create a character in fiction. You will analyse the character of Curley in *Of Mice and Men*.

⊃ For starters

Look at the painting on the left called 'Snack Bar' by Edward Burra.

1 Discuss with a partner what each of the characters looks like. Agree on five words to describe each.
2 What sort of personality do you think each character might have? Why?
3 Now imagine what might have happened to one of the characters earlier that day. How is he or she feeling? Bored? Miserable? Murderous? Give the character a name and write a paragraph revealing his or her feelings (use third person narrative). Try to use adjectives, verbs and adverbs which help to show your character's mood.

🔗 Grammar link

Adjective – adjectives modify or 'add value' to nouns. They give more information about the noun and can make descriptive writing more interesting.

Verb – the part of the sentence which expresses an action or a state of being.

Adverb – adverbs modify, or 'add value' to verbs. They give more information about the verb and can make descriptive writing more interesting.

Third person narrative – where all the characters in a story are referred to as 'he', 'she' or 'they'.

⊃ Task

Of Mice and Men, written by the American author John Steinbeck in 1937, tells the story of George and his mentally impaired friend, Lennie. George tries to look after Lennie, but Lennie is a liability; he doesn't know his own strength and kills most things he touches.

The story starts as the two men start a new job. But the farm where they have gone to work is a place of high tension. The boss's son, Curley – said to be a good boxer – is agitated because he has just married a 'purty' young wife … whom he does not trust.

The passage below is the first time that the reader meets Curley. George has told Lennie to be quiet and let him do all the talking.

↑ *Curley and his wife. Looking at Curley, how well does he fit the mental image of Curley which Steinbeck's words create in your mind's eye?*

> At that moment a young man came into the **bunk house**; a thin young man with a brown face, with brown eyes and a head of tightly curled hair. He wore a work glove on his left hand, and, like the boss, he wore high-heeled boots …
>
> His eyes passed over the new men and he stopped. He glanced coldly at George and then at Lennie. His arms gradually bent at the elbows and his hands closed into fists. He stiffened and went into a slight crouch. His glance was at once calculating and **pugnacious**. Lennie squirmed under the close look and shifted his feet nervously. Curley stepped **gingerly** close to him.
>
> 'You the new guys the old man was waitin' for?'
>
> 'We just come in,' said George.
>
> 'Let the big guy talk.'
>
> Lennie twisted with embarrassment.
>
> George said, 'S'pose he don't want to talk?'
>
> Curley lashed his body around. 'By Christ, he's gotta talk when he's spoke to.'
>
> **Bunk house:** barn where the farm workers slept.
>
> **Pugnacious:** out for a fight.
>
> **Gingerly:** quickly, sharply.

1 What kind of person does Steinbeck's description make Curley out to be? What five details can you use as evidence?
2 List what Curley *does*. What kind of person does he seem to be?
3 What can we learn about Curley from what he says?
4 If you can, read the story later in the book of Curley's fight with Lennie. What does it add to our opinion of Curley's character?

⊃ Taking it further

Write about how Steinbeck presents Curley at this point in the novel.

Start with a short paragraph summarising what Curley is like. Then write three paragraphs – using evidence and quotations to support your ideas– about Curley's description, his actions and the dialogue.

13.2 Changing perceptions

You will look at how a character develops over the course of a text.
You will look closely at the character of Curley's wife.

⊃ For starters

They say that it takes two minutes to form a first impression about someone, and six months to change it. Share a time when you made a quick judgement of someone you met, but gradually realised that your first impressions were wrong.

⊃ Task

The only female character in *Of Mice and Men* is the unnamed woman who is Curley's wife. At the start of the novel, we see her almost entirely through the eyes of the men on the ranch.

1 Here are some of the words the men use to describe Curley's wife:

> tart   got the eye   tramp   poison   jail-bait

For each, write an explanation of what you think it means.

2 Talk with a partner about *what reasons* the men might have had to speak about Curley's new wife in this negative way. Why was George so keen to persuade Lennie to stay away from her?

3 It is further on in the novel that Steinbeck directly presents Curley's wife to the reader:

> She had full, rouged lips and wide-spaced eyes, heavily made up. Her fingernails were red. Her hair hung in little rolled clusters, like sausages. She wore a cotton dress and red mules, on the insteps of which were little bouquets of red ostrich feathers. 'I'm lookin' for Curley,' she said. Her voice had a nasal, brittle quality …
>
> She put her hands behind her back and leaned against the door frame so that her body was thrown forward.
>
> 'You're the new fellas that just come, ain't ya?'

Analyse how Steinbeck presents Curley's wife in this passage, by looking at his description of her, at what he has her do, and at the dialogue (what he has her say).

4 In what ways does this short extract confirm or modify the impressions you have formed of her so far?

5 Only in the second half of the book does the reader hear about Curley's wife *in her own words*. The first time is when the men – including Curley – have all gone out to a brothel, leaving behind Crooks (a black stable hand), Candy (an old man with one hand), and Lennie. Read the extract on page 130.

↓ *Nancy Allen Lundy plays Curley's wife in an operatic production in 2003. Which illustration better fits the mental image of Curley's wife which Steinbeck's words create in your mind's eye – this portrayal, or the image on page 128?*

'They left all the weak ones here,' she said finally. 'Think I don't know where they all went? Even Curley …'

The girl flared up. 'Sure I gotta husban'. You all seen him. Swell guy, ain't he? Spends all his time sayin' what he's gonna do to guys he don't like, and he don't like nobody. Think I'm gonna stay in that two-by-four house and listen how Curley's gonna lead with his left twice, and then bring in the ol' right cross …

'Whatta ya think I am, a kid? I tell ya I could of went with the shows. Not jus' one, neither. An' a guy tol' me he could put me in pitchers …' She was breathless with indignation. 'Sat'iday night. Ever'body out doin' som'pin'. Ever'body! An' what am I doin'? Standin' here talking to a bunch of **bindle-stiffs** – an' likin' it because they ain't nobody else.'

Bindle-stiffs: poor travelling workers.

Readers often react negatively to Curley's wife. But – if you look carefully at what Steinbeck makes her say in this passage – almost every sentence gives us a new insight into her life, and might make us feel some sympathy for her. Steinbeck uses passages like this to develop his **characterisation** of her.

> ### ⓘ Concept bank
>
> **Characterisation:** the process by which a writer presents and develops a character.

6   Copying the table below, choose four sentences from the passage and explain for each why it makes the reader feel sorry for Curley's wife. To help you, the first one has been done for you.

Quote	Why it makes us feel sympathy for her
1. 'Whatta ya think I am, a kid?'	*The men on the ranch do not treat her as an equal. She has no status; she is undervalued and looked down on.*

7   In Chapter 5, Curly's wife speaks personally to Lennie, and we learn about her background, her dreams and her disappointments. With a partner, skim this part of the chapter to find and list four things we learn here about Curley's wife that might further shape our response to her. How do they strengthen or change our growing perceptions of her? Remember PEE: Point/Evidence/Explanation.

8   After her death, Steinbeck describes Curley's wife (see extract on right). Identify and explain three details here that further shape your perception of Curley's wife. Remember: Point/Evidence/Explanation.

↪ Taking it further

Use the ideas and insights you have gathered in this section to write an essay answering the question on the right.

Create a plan for the essay in four parts:
* first impressions of Curley's wife from other characters
* second thoughts after we first meet her
* further thoughts after her dialogue with Lennie
* conclusions after her death.

And the meanness and the plannings and the discontent and the ache for attention were all gone from her face. She was very pretty and simple, and her face was sweet and young. Now her rouged cheeks and her reddened lips made her seem alive and sleeping very lightly. The curls, tiny little sausages, were spread on the hay behind her head, and her lips were parted.

How does Steinbeck develop the character of Curley's wife in *Of Mice and Men*?

> ### ! Essay tip
>
> Use the 'Good writing techniques' listed on page 48.

13.3 Establishing a character on the stage

You will learn how a playwright uses description, dialogue and actions to create a character for the stage. You will study the character of Mr Birling in J.B. Priestley's *An Inspector Calls*.

⊃ For starters

An Inspector Calls, by J.B. Priestley, is set in 1912. It starts with the wealthy Mr and Mrs Birling and their son Eric, who are celebrating the engagement of their daughter, Sheila, to Gerald, the son of another rich local family.

The family is surprised when Inspector Goole comes to tell them that a poor girl named Eva Smith has killed herself. They claim to know nothing of the girl, but, one by one, Goole shows them how they all helped to cause her suicide – Mr Birling sacked her; Sheila got her sacked from her next job; Gerald had an affair with her then cast her aside; Eric got her pregnant; and Mrs Birling persuaded the local Women's Charity Organisation not to give her any help.

The Inspector's message is the point of the play – that 'we are responsible for each other.' (It is important to realise that the play was written in 1945, at the start of the Welfare State.)

At the end, the traumatised family finds out with much relief that 'Inspector Goole' does not exist; only to be told that a girl has killed herself and the police are on their way …

1 Read the stage directions on the right. Find and explain three words or phrases Priestley uses to describe Arthur Birling which reveal how he wanted him to be presented on the stage.

2 What might we learn about the Birlings from how their house is described?

Stage directions:

The dining-room of a fairly large suburban house, belonging to a prosperous manufacturer … substantial and heavily comfortable, but not cosy and homelike …

The parlourmaid is just clearing the table, which has no cloth, of dessert plates and champagne glasses, etc. …

ARTHUR BIRLING is a heavy-looking, rather portentous man in his middle 50s with fairly easy manners but rather provincial in his speech. His wife is about 50, a rather cold woman and her husband's social superior.

↑ *Inspector Goole*

Presenting People

⊃ Task

1 At the start of the play, Arthur Birling makes these predictions:
   - there would be no more strikes
   - there wouldn't be a war
   - the Titanic was unsinkable
   - by 1940 there would be peace and prosperity everywhere.

   Writing in 1945, Priestley knew that all these claims were nonsense – so why did he have Arthur Birling say them? What impression of Arthur Birling was he trying to create?

2 Working in groups, study (see right):
   - Arthur Birling's speech to Gerald about marrying Sheila
   - his statement to his son Eric about the meaning of life
   - his threat to try to get Inspector Goole to stop his questioning.

   For each speech:
   - Discuss what it tells you about Arthur Birling.
   - Find, and explain the effect of, two significant words.

3 Here are three of the things Arthur Birling does in the play:
   - he boasts to Gerald that he is expecting a knighthood
   - he sacks Eva Smith because she led a strike for higher wages
   - when he finds out that Eric has been stealing money from the firm, his first thought is to cover it up quickly.

   What do these things suggest about Arthur Birling's character?

4 Thinking about what you have learned so far, share ideas about the possible reasons *why* Arthur Birling behaved and talked as he did. Does Arthur Birling's comment to Gerald about marrying into the Birling family (bottom right) give you any ideas?

   Look at the following statements about Arthur Birling at the start of the play:
   - a man of humble origins who has become successful through sheer hard work
   - a capitalist, his sole focus is making profit, whatever the impact on his workers
   - narrow-minded and fails to recognise how business is interconnected to aspects of community
   - impressed by status, power and established wealth, and a social climber.

   With which two do you most agree? Explain your thinking.

⊃ Taking it further

Write a three-paragraph mini-essay answering the question:

> How does Priestley present Arthur Birling in the opening act of the play?

Remember to write about stage directions, dialogue and actions.

Arthur Birling's speech to Gerald about marrying Sheila

'You're just the kind of son-in-law I always wanted. Your father and I have been rivals in business for some time now … and now you've brought us together, and perhaps we may look forward to the time when Crofts and Birlings are no longer competing but are working together – for lower costs and higher prices.'

Arthur Birling's statement to his son Eric about the meaning of life

'A man has to make his own way – has to look after himself … the way some of these cranks talk and write now, you'd think everybody has to look after everybody else … – community and all that nonsense.'

Arthur Birling's threat to try to get Inspector Goole to stop his questioning

'Perhaps I ought to warn you that [the Chief Constable] is an old friend of mine, and I see him fairly frequently. We play golf together sometimes.'

Arthur Birling's comment to Gerald about marrying into the Birling family

'I have an idea that your mother – Lady Croft – while she doesn't object to my girl – feels you might have done better for yourself socially.'

13.4 Developing a character on the stage

You will learn more about how a playwright uses description, dialogue and action to develop a stage character by studying the character of Mrs Birling in J.B. Priestley's *An Inspector Calls*.

⬆ *Mrs Birling*

⊃ For starters

Mr Birling, in *An Inspector Calls*, is a 'do-er' – he is characterised by his words and actions. Mrs Birling, by contrast, is *reactive*; her character is shown in the way she reacts to events and people. The one time she speaks freely is when she is talking to the Inspector – and then she blunders into his trap, ending up asking him to punish the father of Eva Smith's baby (little knowing, of course, that the baby's father was her beloved son Eric).

Mrs Birling *speaks* mainly in short exclamations:

- When Sheila says Eric is 'squiffy' (drunk), Mrs Birling says:
  'What an expression, Sheila! Really the things you girls pick up these days!'
- When Arthur says that Gerald joining the family will be good for business, Mrs Birling says:
  'Now Arthur, I don't think you ought to talk business on an occasion like this.'
- And when the Inspector begins to question her, at first she says:
  'That – I consider – is a trifle impertinent, Inspector.'
- When Sheila suggests that the family had killed Eva Smith, she says:
  (*sharply*) 'Sheila, don't talk nonsense.'
- When Gerald says his relationship with Eva was not disgusting, she says:
  'It's disgusting to me.'

1 Study each of Mrs Birling's five exclamations (left). What do they show about her character?

2 Working with a partner, practise saying each of these statements in the way you think Mrs Birling would have said them. Experiment with different tones and voices, and decide which works best.

⊃ Task

One focus of the play is Mrs Birling's relationship with her son.

Again, this is revealed in what she says:

- When Sheila and Gerald tell her that Eric is often 'squiffy', Mrs Birling says:
  (*bitterly*) 'And this is the time you choose to tell me.'
- When she realises that Eric was the father of Eva Smith's baby:
  (*with a cry*) 'Oh Eric – how could you?'
- And when she finds out that he was stealing money:
  (*shocked*) 'Eric! You stole money?'

1 Study these three lines (left) Priestley gives to Mrs Birling. What do they tell us about her feelings for her son?

2 Mr Birling said that Eric was spoilt; how far do you agree?

And it is Mrs Birling's adoration for her son which leads to the time in the play when she loses her self-control. In the following dialogue, Eric has just found that his mother refused to help Eva.

Inspector	(*with calm authority*) I'll tell you. She went to your mother's committee for help, after she'd done with you. Your mother refused that help.
Eric	(*nearly at breaking point*) Then – you killed her. She came to you to protect me – and you turned her away – yes, and you killed her – and the child she'd have had too – my child – your own grandchild – you killed them both – damn you, damn you—
Mrs B.	(*very distressed now*) No – Eric – please – I didn't know – I didn't understand—

One thing Mrs Birling *did*, of course, was refuse to help Eva Smith:
- Eva had called herself Mrs Birling ('impertinently made use of our name').
- Eva had refused to marry the father ('she was claiming fine feelings and scruples that were simply absurd in a girl in her position').
- Eva had refused money from the father because he was stealing it ('it sounded ridiculous to me').

By the end of the play, Mrs Birling is treating the Inspector's visit as a joke. The last thing she says in the play, when Eric and Sheila refuse to find it funny, is:

'They're over-tired. In the morning they'll be as amused as we are.'

⊃ Taking it further

Playwrights use three devices to establish a character:
- **stage directions** – to create first impressions that shape how the audience might respond to the character.
- **actions** (their actions *and* reactions) – to show their behaviour
- **dialogue** – to present their thoughts, feelings, attitudes and values.

1 List your thoughts about Mrs Birling under these three headings.
2 Use these ideas to answer the question:

How did J.B. Priestley develop the character of Mrs Birling in *An Inspector Calls*?

Remember, for each paragraph to:
- start with a topic sentence stating the point
- provide evidence – in the form of a reference or a quotation – to back up your point
- explain and develop your idea, particularly explaining the effect on you as the audience.

3 Working with two partners, act out the scene between the Inspector, Eric and Mrs Birling. Experiment with different tones, voices and gestures, and decide which works best. How does Priestley use language and rhythmic patterns of speech to suggest something about the characters' emotional state here?

4 From pages 133–134, list all the stage directions given by Priestley about Mrs Birling. What picture of her do they create?

5 What can we learn about Mrs Birling from the fact that she refused to help Eva Smith?

6 Do you think Mrs Birling felt *any* guilt for Eva Smith's death? Did the events change her *at all*?

7 From her speeches on pages 133–134, choose **three** words or phrases Mrs Birling says, and explain how they make you feel about her.

! Essay tip

Write your essay in six paragraphs about:
1 The play's key ideas and themes.
2 What we can tell about Mrs Birling from Priestley's stage directions.
3 What we can tell about her from her actions.
4 What we can tell about her from the play's dialogue.
5 How her character changes as the play goes on.
6 How successful you judge Priestley to be in his presentaion of Mrs Birling.

14 Genres and Form – Openings

Learning aim

In this unit you will look at the opening scenes of *Romeo and Juliet* and *Hamlet*. You will look at the themes and ideas in each opening section; at the characters and how they are presented; and at the language used.

14.1 *Romeo and Juliet* – exploring language and action

> You will analyse what is happening in the opening scene of *Romeo and Juliet,* and examine how Shakespeare creates dramatic interest and impact in it .

⟳ For starters

Has there ever been a time when you have argued or fought with someone?

In pairs, tell each other about a time when you saw a memorable fight or argument on a recent soap or TV programme and explain what happened. Share some of your moments with the rest of the class.

➡ *An image from Baz Luhrmann's film of* **Romeo and Juliet***.*

⟲ Task

Romeo and Juliet opens, as Shakespeare's stage directions tell us, in 'Verona. A public place.' At first the scene is amusing – servants of the two warring families are mixing, boasting and swapping insults. But the atmosphere soon turns violent when Sampson (a Capulet) decides to bite his thumb at the Montagues ('which is a great disgrace to them if they bear it'). In Shakespeare's time, to 'bite your thumb' at someone was a great insult. The situation quickly turns violent …

1   In a group of four, act out or read the scene up until the arrival of Benvolio. Try saying the lines in different ways, so as to achieve different effects, for example:

   • say the words in a very angry and confrontational way, so that the atmosphere is very threatening and violent

   • say the words in a very childish and exaggerated way, so that the affair seems trivial and the effect is to make the men look ridiculous

   • say the words in a very swaggering and cocky way, so that the effect is to make the scene amusing and clever.

   Which interpretation worked best? Explain why.

2   At the start of the scene, Sampson and Gregory both set the aggressive mood for the scene by talking about fighting. Which words can you pick out from the first six lines that can be linked to fighting?

3   Shakespeare often included bawdy language – rude and crude comments – in plays as this would amuse his audience. Find an example or two from this opening scene. Why else does he use it in this scene?

⟲ Taking it further

Based on your study of Act 1, Scene 1, up to Benvolio's arrival, write a mini-essay of about 200–300 words in which you explore how Shakespeare creates mood and dramatic impact at the start of the play. You might include:

• the way the scene gradually builds up

• the way aggressive and crude language is used during the conversation

• how the language gets more aggressive as the scene progresses

• how the scene climaxes with a fight, but not a fight like we might see in the street today – a fight with swords.

🔗 Grammar link

Short sentences – these can make a speaker's words seem to the point, harsh and aggressive, for example:

ABRAHAM   No better.

SAMPSON   Well, sir.

14.2 *Romeo and Juliet* – exploring atmosphere and excitement

You will explore further Shakespeare's use of language and look at what the theatre was like when the play was first staged.

⊃ For starters

As well as including aggressive language and insults, Shakespeare used a number of tricks of the theatrical trade to create a sense of tension and aggression at the start of the play, including:

- short lines
- speed of speech
- the number of people speaking.

Working in a group, for each of the devices above, suggest how it might have helped to create a sense of tension and aggression.

⊃ Task

In lines 60–74, the quarrel that started with Sampson biting his thumb at Abraham continues to escalate until it involves high-ranking Capulets such as Tybalt, mobs of citizens, and eventually the Lords Capulet and Montague themselves.

1 In your group of four, act out or read the section from the entrance of Abraham and Balthasar to the entrance of Benvolio. Really emphasise the key words 'bite my thumb' and 'quarrel' as words of extreme anger, in the way that far more explicit words would be used today. At this time, 'bite my thumb' and 'quarrel' would have been like swear words.

2 Notice how all the characters speak in **prose** until the arrival of Benvolio who speaks in **verse**. Why is this so?

BENVOLIO	I do but keep the peace: put up thy sword,	62
	Or manage it to part these men with me.	
TYBALT	What, drawn, and talk of peace! I hate the word,	
	As I hate hell, all Montagues, and thee.	65

This is verse as both characters speak in an even manner, each line having ten syllables and it reads like a poem does. Note how there is also a rhyme scheme.

> **ⓘ Concept bank**
>
> **Prose:** written as we would normally speak language.
>
> **Verse:** written like poetry. Shakespeare used verse for a lot of his writing – a particular verse style (iambic pentameter) which has ten syllables on each line.

Prose looks like this:

ABRAHAM	Do you bite your thumb at us, sir?	41
SAMPSON	I do bite my thumb, sir.	
ABRAHAM	Do you bite your thumb at us, sir?	
SAMPSON	[Aside to GREGORY] Is the law of our side, if I say ay?	
GREGORY	No.	

Here there is no set rhythm and no evident rhyme scheme. The speech is natural, as would have been spoken at the time. Why do you think Shakespeare uses prose and verse in this way?

3 Reread the whole scene up to the entrance of the Prince (line 74). Find examples of each of the following features. Decide how they create a feeling of tension and aggression in this part of the scene:

- the use of short lines
- powerful/aggressive language
- **speed of speech**
- the number of people speaking.

4 When Tybalt enters (line 59), he sums up the whole aggression of the opening scene. What does he say and how does he say it to really emphasise the aggression? Which words would you emphasise in particular?

5 How would an audience have reacted to the scene then? How would an audience react to it now?

⟳ Taking it further

1 Looking back on this section, write three paragraphs to answer the question:

> How does Shakespeare gain his audience's interest at the start of *Romeo and Juliet*?

- In the first paragraph, write about what happens in the scene.
- In the second paragraph, write about features of language, such as imagery and the use of prose or verse.
- In the third paragraph, explain how he uses other devices (short lines, speed of speech and the number of speakers).

2 Think about what the theatre was like during the time when Shakespeare wrote this play. There was no lighting like we have today; instead there was just natural daylight and maybe the light of candles and torches (from flames). There was little in the way of **set**, with just the items of furniture needed for certain scenes. Sound would have been performed live as there were no facilities to play CDs or mp3s then.

How might dramatic mood and atmosphere have been created in Shakespeare's day, despite the limited scenery, sound effects and lighting available to the company? Have a look at the picture of the Globe Theatre on page 139.

↑ *Tybalt*

ⓘ Concept bank

Speed of speech: how quickly a line in the play is said. The more quickly, the more aggressive a character will come across. Speaking too quickly, however, can't be heard by the audience.

Set: the backdrop, the use of scenery and fixed furniture on stage.

14.3 *Hamlet* – exploring mood and staging

You will work out what is happening and explore how Shakespeare creates **mood and atmosphere** in the very opening scene of *Hamlet*.

ⓘ Concept bank

Mood and atmosphere: the emotional feeling that is created in the scene, such as sad, happy, depressed or tense.

⊃ For starters

↑ *The Globe Theatre where Shakespeare staged some of his plays*

Performances of *Hamlet* in Shakespeare's time might well have been presented in an open-air theatre, in the daytime, with very limited sets and scenery, and with none of the advantages available to present-day directors such as electric lighting and electronic sound effects to enhance mood and atmosphere.

With this in mind, how might a theatre company looking to stage a performance of *Hamlet* in such circumstances get across to the audience the fact that the play opens:

- around midnight
- in a castle
- with guards on duty who are very anxious?

➲ Task

1 The opening scene of *Hamlet* is set on the castle ramparts (the top section where soldiers would have aimed their weapons at invaders) in the dark of night. As you look at the following extract from Act 1, Scene 1 (lines 1–14), think about what the mood and atmosphere of the scene is and how this is put across to the audience:

> **Act 1, Scene 1**
>
> **Elsinore. A platform before the castle**
>
> *FRANCISCO at his post. Enter to him BERNARDO*
>
> | | | |
> |---|---|---|
> | BERNARDO | Who's there? | |
> | FRANCISCO | Nay, answer me: stand, and unfold yourself. | |
> | BERNARDO | Long live the king! | |
> | FRANCISCO | Bernardo? | |
> | BERNARDO | He. | 5 |
> | FRANCISCO | You come most carefully upon your hour. | |
> | BERNARDO | 'Tis now struck twelve; get thee to bed, Francisco. | |
> | FRANCISCO | For this relief much thanks: 'tis bitter cold, | |
> | | And I am sick at heart. | |
> | BERNARDO | Have you had quiet guard? | 10 |
> | FRANCISCO | Not a mouse stirring. | |
> | BERNARDO | Well, good night. | |
> | | If you do meet Horatio and Marcellus, | |
> | | The rivals of my watch, bid them make haste. | 14 |

⟳ Grammar link

Colon – this punctuation mark is often used before a list. In the extract here, what follows the colon is a list of two things – either an instruction:

'Nay, answer me: stand, and unfold yourself.'

or two feelings (the cold and being sick at heart):

'For this relief much thanks: 'tis bitter cold,
And I am sick at heart.'

2 Make some notes on this section. Who are these men? There is clearly something wrong as they are nervous. Shakespeare builds up this nervousness throughout the scene. How?

3 Look again at the opening five lines of the play. How has Shakespeare created tension at the start of the scene?

4 Say these lines in pairs. How is it best to say them? Try them slowly, then try them quickly. Which works best?

5 Lines 6–14 give the audience more information about the time of night. What clues are given as to what time of the day or night it is?

6 What do we learn about the atmosphere from the line 'Not a mouse stirring'?

7 What is the effect of these being short lines?

➲ Taking it further

1 In pairs, act out the opening section up to line 14. Imagine the tension of the moment. Think about the following:

- It's cold – what do you do to show this?
- It's dark so they do not immediately recognise each other – how can you show this?
- It's very quiet – how is this best shown?

2 How did you make your decisions on how to act the scene? Write two paragraphs exploring your decisions:

- What challenges did you face?
- How did you overcome them?

14.4 *Hamlet* – exploring reactions and effects

> You will look at the beliefs and superstitions of those in *Hamlet* and of the audience who watched *Hamlet* when it was first produced.

↑ *David Tennant as Hamlet*

⊃ For starters

1 With a partner discuss whether you believe in ghosts.
2 What problems present themselves to a contemporary theatre company looking to perform a play in which a ghost features to an audience highly sceptical about the existence of such a thing?

⊃ Task

1 Once the atmosphere has been set, we now move on to the first key event in the story. Look at the following lines:

> 'has this thing appear'd again to-night?' *(line 29)*
>
> 'this dreaded sight' *(line 33)*
>
> 'this apparition' *(line 36)*

- What do these lines tell us about what they have seen?
- How is an audience meant to be feeling during this exchange?
- Remember that this would have been performed in daylight, with no special effects, so how is the message that it is night and it is tense conveyed to the audience?
- What does Horatio's line 'Tush, tush, 'twill not appear' tell us about his attitude to it?

Many in the audience would have believed very strongly in ghosts when the play was first performed in about 1601. They were very superstitious and would have taken this very seriously.

2 Read lines 50–63 from the scene.
- What does the ghost look like? Use these lines to help you:

> 'it harrows me with fear and wonder' *(line 54)*
>
> 'fair and warlike form' *(line 58)*
>
> 'majesty of buried Denmark' *(line 59)*
>
> 'like the king that's dead' *(line 51)*

- Pick out a few words and phrases that tell us about its appearance. What does the ghost do? These lines may give you some clues:

  'See, it stalks away!' *(line 62)*

  'Stay! speak, speak! I charge thee, speak!' *(line 63)*

- How do the others react to it? The following line may help you:

  'it harrows me with fear and wonder' *(line 54)*

3 Short sentences are used here to create tension. Identify where **alliteration** is used and say how this adds to the tension of the scene. Note also where there is repetition. What effect does this have?

4 The audience would know what the mood and atmosphere was by how Shakespeare uses language and action and how the actors deliver the lines of the play.

- Act out the whole scene in groups of about four (some of you will have to play more than one part). Remember to think about how Shakespeare creates tension in this scene.

- Once you have acted out the scene and watched some other versions of it, pick out specific words and phrases that show what the mood and atmosphere of the opening scene is.

- A good way to describe the mood of the first scene of *Hamlet* is 'menacing'. Having studied and acted the scene, list all the things which make the scene menacing. Remember to explain each idea, and to support it with a quote from the play.

↻ Taking it further

Write an essay in three sections that compares how the opening scenes of *Romeo and Juliet* and *Hamlet* gain their audiences' interest. What are the main similarities and differences?

- In the first section, compare the scenes of the two plays – writing about such issues as Where? Who? And What?

- In the second section, compare how Shakespeare uses language to create the mood and atmosphere for the play. Remember to support your ideas with quotes from the play, and to explain the effect that his words have on an audience.

- In the third section, write about how Shakespeare uses other devices (such as short lines, speed of speech and the number of people speaking) to make the scene powerful and interesting.

! Essay tip

In a 'compare' essay, you need to split each paragraph into two halves, which are joined by a discourse marker such as 'Similarly …' or 'By contrast …'

For example:

- In *Romeo and Juliet*, Shakespeare …   Similarly, in *Hamlet*, he …

or

- *Romeo and Juliet* is …   By contrast, *Hamlet* is …

ⓘ Concept bank

Alliteration: repeating the first letters of words to create an effect, e.g. 'the seriously sinister snake' – the 's' sound here makes the hissing sound of the snake and emphasises its sinister nature.

⏻ Grammar link

Repetition – used to emphasise a point or an instruction. In the line:

'See, it stalks away!'
'Stay! speak, speak! I charge thee, speak!'

the word 'speak' is repeated three times as Horatio urges the ghost to stay and speak to them.

Attitudes to Spoken Language

Learning aim

In this unit you will consider how we speak. You will learn some of the important terms we use to describe language, and gain the skills you will need for your investigating spoken language Controlled Assessment Task.

↑ *Steven Gerrard has a Scouse accent and Cheryl Cole has a Geordie accent.*

15.1 Introducing accent

> You will investigate the ways in which the pronunciation of words varies between different regions and groupings.

➔ For starters

Some people have an **accent** that depends on the part of the country they were brought up. Do you think you have this kind of regional accent? What makes it different from **Received Pronunciation**?

Everybody has an accent. Our accent depends on a number of things: where we live or were brought up; the way our friends speak; our educational and social surroundings; our sense of self.

➔ Task

Are there people in your class who have a different accent from you? (Don't forget your teacher!) What words do you notice are pronounced differently? Why do you think they have a different accent?

1 Many people are proud of their regional accent because it is part of their identity. Make a list of regional accents that you know (for example: Scouse/Liverpool, Glaswegian/Glasgow, Geordie/Newcastle).

2 For each accent, write down a word or phrase that you would expect to hear from a speaker with this accent. Try to spell the words to represent the accent. Share your answers with a partner.

3 Try this quick quiz. How do you pronounce the following words?

GARAGE	(to rhyme with LARGE or RIDGE?)
GLASS	(with a short A to rhyme with MASS or a long A to rhyme with FARCE?)
ENVELOPE	(with EN or ON at the beginning? Or as EM-VELOPE?)
HOTEL	(with an H at the start or an O? Do you say 'AN OTEL' or 'A HOTEL'?)
SANDWICH	(SAND-WICH, SAN-WICH, or SAM-WICH?)
TUNE	(is it more like TYOON or CHOON?)

> ### (i) Concept bank
>
> **High prestige:** describes an accent or dialect that some people think is spoken by people who have power and status in society.

Compare your findings with your partner. Are they the same or different? Why might this be? Note down your findings.

'Received Pronunciation' is a term used to describe an accent that is often called 'BBC English'. Some people think that people who speak with an RP accent are likely to have more power, have better jobs and be better educated than those who have a regional accent.

4 With your partner, make a list of people you think have power – in your school, in society, in the media. Do they speak with an RP accent, or do they have a regional accent?

5 Discuss this with your partner. Do you think this shows that RP has '**high prestige**'? Do you think it is fair to judge people by how they speak?

⊃ Taking it further

1 Give some older people (perhaps from your parents' and your grandparents' generations) the same quiz as the one at the top of the page. Show them the words written down and listen carefully to the way they pronounce these words. Make notes. Is there a difference between the ways people of your age and people of older generations pronounce these words? Why might this be?

2 Prepare a short presentation on your findings. You will need to:

- introduce the subject by showing the list of words you have used and by talking about how you chose your research subjects – the people you questioned from your generation and older generations

- explain what you found out about the pronunciation of yourself and people of your own age

- compare and contrast what you found out about the pronunciation of people of your own age and those older than you.

- say what you discovered in your research. Did the results surprise you?

15.2 Introducing dialect

> You will explore the difference between accent and **dialect**, and look at the way in which you and other people use dialect words.

⊃ For starters

Speakers from different areas of the country often have words that other areas would find unusual. Here are some examples of **non-standard dialect** words in speech:

A

We was fishing in the rain. If thou seed the line twitch thou'd pull he in.

C

Ah'd say garn yam, but tha'll tek nee notice any road!

D

Mi Mam caught me waggin school and went mental at me.

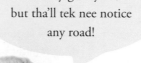

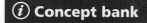

B

Ay up mi duck, ow art?

1 Write down the words that come from non-standard dialects, and note down their meanings (for example, 'yam' in C – in some Cumbrian dialects, 'yam' means 'home').
2 Some dialect forms use non-standard grammar. Can you find any here?
3 Rewrite the four sentences in **Standard English**.
4 Was this tricky to do? Why?
5 How far have you changed the meanings of these sentences as you move from non-Standard to Standard English? Explain why.

Attitudes to Spoken Language

ⓘ Concept bank

Dialect: the choice of words and grammatical construction in speech and writing. Everyone has a dialect. Accent and dialect are very closely linked.

Non-standard dialect: dialect that is different from Standard English.

Standard English: a non-regional English dialect that is often used in formal contexts, such as education and serious media.

⊃ Task

Read the local news article below on dialect. (It is taken from *The Great Harwood Mercury* by Joan White.)

DEAD AS A DODMAN?

Joan White talks about the near extinction of the rural Essex dialect

Ever done a pitch-a-pennie-pie? Seen a dodman? Eaten ingons? You probably have, but if you're a furriner, you won't know it. But when I was young, you only had to walk through any Essex village to hear these words – and many more.

My old Nan were an Essex gal. Although it's many years since she was 'laid by the wall', I still remember the dialect words she used: 'Don't be afeard'; 'Do you need the dunnekin?' (Nan had a ferociously clean outside toilet!); 'Don't goffle your food'.

Accents and dialects remind us that although we are all called 'British', our country is a mixture of different regions and groups, and that's a real strength.

But now regional dialects seem to be dying. It might be because people move around a lot more nowadays. It might be because we have radio and television to let us hear how other people speak. It might be because school teachers insist that children 'Talk properly'. Whatever the reason, I think it's a shame.

So, if you have a grandmother who uses odd words, don't laugh at her. Instead, why not persuade her to keep them alive by recording them? After all, this means that your grandmother – like dialect – will become a national treasure!

1 Write down a list of Essex dialect words from this article. What do you think they mean?
2 Can you find an example of non-standard grammar in the article?
3 Why do you think Joan White calls this article 'Dead as a Dodman?'?
4 Why does Joan White think regional dialects are important?
5 What reasons does Joan White find to explain why regional dialects are 'on the decline'?

⊃ Taking it further

Joan White claims that a lot of dialect terms are dying out. However, a lot of areas still use non-standard forms.

Do you agree that dialects are declining? You might want to consider your own experience of language use, words used by young people as opposed to older people, the influence of modern technology, and so on.

Write a letter to *The Great Harwood Mercury* in which you argue either against or in support of the argument that non-standard dialect words are dying out. You might wish to include paragraphs on:
- words that you and people in your area use that are not Standard English
- words used by young people and not by older people: for example, words used by young people to describe something as good, or words to describe skipping school
- words that have recently entered our language from modern technology.

Lay your letter out as you would for an exam, beginning 'Dear Editor' and finishing 'Yours faithfully'. Remember to use a new paragraph for each new idea or argument.

⊄⊃ Grammar link

The difference between standard and non-standard grammatical forms is often an important difference between formal speech and formal writing, which tend to use standard grammar, and informal speech and informal writing.

15.3 Attitudes to accent in the media

You will investigate the representation of accents in the media.

⟳ For starters

The aural media – in particular radio and television – can be important in establishing our attitudes to accent.

List television programmes which present different accents. You might wish to start with soaps, and then move on to other types of programme, including news and cookery shows. Can you identify the accent being used?

Compare your list with a partner. Discuss whether your lists suggest anything about how the media regards accent.

⟳ Task

The two letters below have been read out on a viewer feedback show on the BBC. The two letters show two different attitudes to non-standard accents. Read the letters, and then answer the questions on page 148.

⬆ The chef Jamie Oliver has an Essex accent

Dear BBC

Well done, BBC! If you intend to 'dumb down' your service until it has lost the little respect it used to have, you've certainly succeeded!

I was shocked when I listened to the *6 o'clock News* last night. The newsreader had such a strong accent that I was totally distracted from what she was saying.

The BBC is supposed to be a quality broadcaster and the *News* your flagship. I'm not saying I couldn't understand the newsreader, but it's a question of standards. The BBC has a duty to preserve correct 'BBC English', and this is especially important for the *News*. Accents are not for serious broadcasting.

Harold Timmins, Potters Bar

Dear BBC

I am amazed and angered that you chose to give airtime last week to the bigoted views of Mr Timmins. What's wrong with having newsreaders talking in their own accents? Mr Timmins understood what was being said, and that's what's important.

Millions of people watch and enjoy soaps like *EastEnders* and *Coronation Street*. Accents here are no problem, so why should it be different for the *News*?

Britain is made up of 60 million people, and most do not have a middle-class Southern 'BBC accent'. Let's show that we value everybody, not just the old fashioned elitists – Mr Timmins and his like. Otherwise, the message you're giving is that people like me who are proud of our accent can't be trusted with serious things like the *News* or current affairs.

Here's for <u>more</u> regional accents on the *News* – then we might really become an equal society!

David Bruce, Aberdeen

1 Write out one sentence from each letter on page 147 that you think shows the attitude of the writer to non-standard accents.

2 Give two words from each letter that show the emotions the writer feels about the subject.

3 Using your own words as far as possible, what is the main argument in Mr Timmins' letter?

4 Using your own words, what is the main argument in Mr Bruce's reply?

5 Write a letter to the BBC explaining your own feelings on this issue. You may choose to argue against or support the views of the writers, or just focus on your own views. You should start your letter with the words 'Dear BBC' and remember to separate your points into paragraphs.

⊃ Taking it further

1 Think about the way accents are used on television. Look at the TV listings for tonight. Make a list of programmes that show strong regional or other non-standard accents. Identify what kind of programmes these are (soap operas, comedy, sports, music ...).

2 Do the same accents appear on the *News* or other current affairs programmes? Try to see part of at least two news programmes to answer this question. It might be interesting to compare different channels.

3 Does your research suggest anything about the attitudes to accent held by the television companies? Write a paragraph that sums up your findings.

Tom Leonard's poem (on the right) is about the way the news is usually read by someone speaking with an RP accent. The poem is ironic – the newsreader makes negative comments about people who speak with a strong accent ... whilst speaking in a strong Scottish accent himself.

4 Which lines show that people tend to look down on people who speak with a strong regional accent?

5 Which lines show how the speaker feels about this? Explain why you chose these lines.

6 Try to read the poem in a strong Scottish accent. Try to read it with an RP accent. Does the use of an accent make the poem more, or less, effective?

7 Write a paragraph summarising what you think Leonard is saying about accent and people's perceptions of it.

'Unrelated Incidents'–No. 3

this is thi
six a clock
news thi
man said n
thi reason
a talk wia
BBC accent
iz coz yi
widny wahnt
mi ti talk
aboot thi
trooth wia
voice lik
wanna yoo
scruff. if
a toktaboot
thi trooth
lik wanna yoo
scruff yi
widny thingk
it wuz troo.
jist wanna yoo
scruff tokn.
thirza right
way ti spell
ana right way
to tok it. this
is me tokn yir
right way a
spellin. this
is ma trooth.
yooz doant no
thi trooth
yirsellz cawz
yi canny talk
right. this is
the six a clock
nyooz. belt up.

15.4 Understanding sociolect

You will investigate how different groups of English speakers use language in different and distinctive ways for varying purposes.

↻ For starters

People who share the same interest, profession, background or belong to the same social group often have their own variety of language. Different groups of people will use specialist terms that other groups will not use: for example, rock-climbers might talk about 'pitons', 'pitches', 'routes' and 'harnesses', as well as terms for different grades of climb such as 'VS' (very severe). This type of shared language is called a **sociolect**.

What special words or phrases might some of the following groups use?

* Football fans
* Teachers
* Drummers (or other musicians)
* Skateboarders
* Doctors

Discuss your ideas with your partner.

> **ⓘ Concept bank**
>
> **Sociolect:** a variety of language used by people with shared interests or belonging to a particular group.

↻ Task

Read the text here and on page 150 written by authors for audiences that share their interests and sociolect.

HOG* HEAVEN!

It don't come better than this: cruisin' down Route 66, helmetless, sunshine highlighting the silver flakes in the Electra Glide's Arctic White glacier-deep paint, accompanied by the iconic throb of the monster Twin Cam powerplant. Forget your Japanese crotch-rockets: Harley, America, the Mother Road – motorbikin' suddenly makes perfect sense again.

(from *HOGBlog*, a Harley-Davidson weblog written by Head Hog)

> ***HOG:** a Harley-Davidson motorcycle or motorcyclist.

DARK IRONIES

Gender, Entertainment (2008)

Post-punk? Goth? Bauhaus? The driving snarebeat and the eerie vocals that open Georgia-based Entertainment's debut album *Gender* blow all categories away. Razorwire ironic lyrics grounded on breakers of sound make this not an experience for the fainthearted. The pulse is visceral and compelling, especially in the aptly named *Confusion of Senses*. Overall, this is entertainment that goes for the jugular. There is no escape. Buy it.

(from *iTunes Reviews*, posted by Livefatsdieyognu)

1 List the specialist terms that the two writers use.

2 List other features that might form part of the writers' sociolect. Give specific examples. You might look at sentence types and non-standard word choices, for example.

3 What is your attitude to the sociolect used by the two writers? Is it positive, negative or neutral? Do you feel included or excluded by the language? Write a paragraph explaining your point of view.

4 You will belong to a number of groups that have their own sociolect. You might think about your sporting interests, hobbies, part-time job or intended career. List three such groups that you belong to.

5 Write a paragraph about one of these. In your paragraph, identify and explain any distinctive language particular to this group. Your audience should be someone who is *not* part of that grouping, so you will need to explain specialist terms that you use.

6 Read your paragraph to the group, and then explain the sociolect features you have included.

⊃ Taking it further

Write your own review or 'blog' entry about the topic you wrote about in task 5. This time your audience will be people who share your interest, so you will not need to explain specialist terms. Remembering the 'Hog Heaven' and 'Dark Ironies' extracts above, try to use as many sociolect features as you can, and highlight them.

Read your writing to at least one other person, and then explain the sociolect features you have included. Ask them for their reactions to the language you used: are they positive, negative or neutral? Do they feel included or excluded?

Grammar link

Look back at the first three sentences of 'Dark Ironies'. Incomplete, or minor, sentences can be an effective way of varying your writing style, and examiners give high marks for variety. Don't overdo it, though – examiners need to see you can use full sentences too!

Speech Types and Genres

Learning aim

In this unit you will gain the skills and knowledge you will need to do an investigation of spoken language for the Spoken Genres Controlled Assessment Task. You will learn about some of the factors which influence spoken language.

16.1 Words in context

You will analyse some of the factors that influence spoken language, including **role**, **context**, purpose and audience.

⊃ For starters

1 Write the words 'Teacher-speak' in the middle of a sheet of paper. Produce a brainstorm of words and phrases that teachers typically use.

2 If you covered up the 'Teacher-speak' title, and showed your brainstorm to someone, how would they guess these were all typical teacher words? What do these words and phrases have in common? Are there any patterns or similarities?

⊃ Task

Scenario: Mike Layton is Head of Year 10. He has just dealt with an incident in the science corridor between two Year 10 boys: Matthew Miles and a classmate. Matthew has been in trouble for fighting before. Mr Layton has spent weeks trying to support him. Minutes later, Mr Layton talks to one of his department colleagues in the staffroom, and then, after break, he phones Matthew's mother.

There are two language contexts:

A In the staffroom with a close department colleague

B On the telephone with Matthew's mother

ⓘ Concept bank

Role: the status, actions and behaviours given to or expected of a person in a particular situation. For example: team captain, brother or teacher. Roles carry expectations of behaviour and of language use.

Context: what the situation is at a particular point in time. For example, talking privately to your teacher is a different context to talking to a group of friends in the canteen.

1 According to the context in which you think these words were used, sort the words and phrases in the box on the right into two groups headed: A – Staffroom colleague; B – Telephone mother.

2 Choose three words or phrases from each group that you are confident you have sorted correctly. Explain why you sorted them as you did. Are there any you struggled to place? Why?

3 In pairs (or as a written script if you are on your own), improvise a 60-second sample of the conversation Mr Layton has in the staffroom with his colleague about the corridor incident. If you have done an improvisation, be ready to perform it, and explain to the class what you were showing about language. How would your audience know from the words you use that this was a teacher talking to a colleague in a staffroom?

Here are four influences on how we use language:

Role – Who?	Context – Where?
How we are required or expected to behave in a situation. For example, Mike as friend, Mr Layton as Head of Year 10, or Mike Layton as husband.	The setting for conversation. For example, in a Maths lesson or at a school disco.
Purpose – Why?	**Audience – To whom?**
The reason for speaking. For example, informing Year 11s about work experience or asking a Year 7 girl how she is.	The person or people to whom the language is directed. For example, to a parent, to a colleague or to the Headteacher.

Analysis of Mike Layton's use of language in your improvisation would discuss how his language was influenced by the fact that:

- he was talking as a colleague (*role*) of another teacher (*audience*)
- he was talking to 'get it off his chest' (*purpose*)
- he was talking in the staffroom; away from students (*context*).

These factors together create the language **register** of Mr Layton's talk.

4 How would the following factors influence Mike Layton's use of language in the staffroom conversation? For each, give a specific example of language use:
- role
- purpose
- audience
- context.

5 Again, either through improvisation or as a script, produce a 60-second sample of the conversation Mr Layton has on the telephone with Matthew Miles' mother. Be ready to perform and explain it to the class if you have done this as drama. What were you showing about the influences on his use of language?

⊃ Taking it further

Write an analysis of the language Mr Layton uses with Matthew's mother. How would the following factors influence Mr Layton's use of language?
- The role Mike Layton was playing.
- The purpose of the conversation.
- The context for the conversation and its audience. (Clue: formality/informality/register.) Give examples of language used.

Confrontation	Apologies for
Contact	Continuing indiscipline
Disciplinary sanction	Endangering
Guess what?	Incident
Lads	Losing patience with
Matthew	Mother
Out of control	Pain in the backside
Students	Put him on report
Required to	Right troublemaker
Scrap	Sick of it
Thug	Typical of him
Bully	Parent
Detention	Regret
Getting stuck in	Ring up
Intimidating	Terrorise
Matt	Yob
Mum	Disappointed

ⓘ Concept bank

Register: the way a text 'speaks to' and addresses its readers or listeners – the text's voice. This could be formal or informal, bossy, amusing, friendly or cold ... or many other registers.

16.2 Voices and choices

> You will learn that speech is influenced by the degree to which it is planned or spontaneous, and by how familiar speakers are with each other.

⊃ For starters

1 Match *three* greetings in the table the with the *three* people who you are *most likely* to greet this way.

Greeting	Person
A 'Hey!'	**1** Headteacher
B 'Hi!'	**2** Form tutor
C 'Right?'	**3** Close school friend
D 'Mornin'!'	**4** Subject teacher
E 'Hello!'	**5** Classmate
F 'Morning, Sir/Miss.'	**6** School bus driver

2 Explain the thinking behind your matches. For example: 'I matched D with 5 because …'

3 What *two* things might this activity have taught us about how we use language?

⊃ Task

Read the following extracts. They are taken from the spoken repertoire of Mrs Marianne Chadwick, Deputy Headteacher and Chemistry teacher at a school in London.

A Hi, Joan. Yeah, sorry … Can I just grab you for a quick minute about Toni Arthur in your form? Won't be a sec … promise … Can I just move your bag?

B Jonty Neville! Don't look away when I'm talking to you. Didn't we have words about this yesterday? Back in line now!

C 8N, quiet, please. Come on … That's it … We, we need just to … to have a look again at yesterday's objectives … that business on atoms and molecules off the whiteboard. Can … Who can remember the difference between a compound and a molecule? Javinder, you?

D Firstly, welcome. It's wonderful that so many of you have turned out to support the school! As you know from newsletters, we've been raising money now for well over 12 months, and it's truly excellent that we're only just a little short of our target.

E I'm expecting nothing but the best behaviour from you all. You are ambassadors for the school, and if there's any nonsense you'll be having a word with me when we get back. Is that clear? I said, is that clear? That's you too, Frances …

F Hello … Mrs Marler? It's Mrs Marianne Chadwick from Midbridge School. Nothing to worry about … Natalie wasn't in registration this morning … I'm phoning to see if there's anything we need to know …

1   Complete a table like the one below to analyse some of the factors that influence Mrs Chadwick's language on page 153.

Extract	Role – In what role is Mrs Chadwick speaking?	Purpose – Why is Mrs Chadwick speaking?	Context – Where is this being said?	Audience – Who is Mrs Chadwick speaking to?
A				
B				
C				

2   Choose *two* of the extracts that show differing language registers (differences in the degree of formality). Describe *how* the language is different in each extract and explain *why*.

Another influence on spoken language is the amount of planning we bring to a speech situation. For example, at one end of the scale is a thoroughly planned speech which is then read out; at the other end of the scale is a casual chat between friends in a spontaneous way.

3   Look at Mrs Chadwick's six extracts. Decide where you would put each one in the Very prepared/Very unprepared spectrum below.

Very prepared and planned				No thought – spontaneous		
1	2	3	4	5	6	7
1	2	3	4	5	6	7
Very familiar				Very unfamiliar		

4   Which *two* of the speech extracts show the most and least planned language? Write about 100 words in which you give reasons for your decisions. For example: 'I can tell this extract is planned from the way she ...'

Another influence on how we speak is how well we know the people we are speaking to: they may be friends we've known for years, or complete strangers we meet at a bus stop!

5   Look again at Mrs Chadwick's six extracts. Where would you place each one in the Very familiar/Very unfamiliar spectrum above?

6   Which *two* of the speech extracts show Mrs Chadwick talking to listeners she was most familiar with and most unfamiliar with? Write about 100 words in which you give reasons for your decisions. Remember to include evidence.

◗ Taking it further

Read the two **transcripts** below that show Miss Powell, a young English teacher, speaking in two different contexts.

Text 1: In class, teaching

People: Miss Powell [P] – teacher, mid 20s; Chelsea [C] – one of the students. The group are about to start writing.

P   Right [.] if you need a pen come and get one from the box on my table [1] gentlemen at the back [2] can I have your attention please [3] [*while the students settle down*] OK right once you have got this written down from the board you can start looking for the quotes [.] Chelsea will you please sit down

C   But Miss [.] you said I could get a pen

P   OK but hurry up [.] I want all this finished by the end of the lesson [3] Rob [.] Shaun [.] is there any danger of you two getting some writing done this side of Christmas [.] you've done nothing but talk since I told you to get writing

Text 2: At a parents evening, talking to the parents of one of her GCSE group

People: Miss Powell [P], Mr Wright [Dad] and Mrs Wright [Mum]

P   Hello [1] you must be Chelsea's mum and dad [*shakes hands*] [2] it's really nice to meet you [2] please sit down [3] Chelsea's doing really well you know [.] especially in her speaking and listening we did an assessment last week and hers was one of the best in the group

DAD   No surprise there [1] she's been good at talking ever since she was a little girl [2] never shuts up

P   And her last piece of writing [1] a description of a place that she knows well was excellent [.] very imaginative and full of excellent descriptive vocabulary [2] at this rate she should at least get a B in her GCSE

MUM   Is there anything we can do at home [.] you know [2] to help her

P   Well if you can just keep encouraging her to read and to get her work done on time cos she has missed a couple of deadlines you know [.] nothing serious but it's not a good habit to get into.

Write an analysis of these transcripts. Write about 250 words altogether in three paragraphs:

- Paragraph 1: what key differences do you notice in the way the teacher talks in each situation? Give some examples.
- Paragraphs 2 and 3: what are the two most important factors (role; context; purpose; audience; planning; familiarity) that cause these differences? How do they influence how Miss Powell speaks? Write an analytical paragraph on each.

Speech Types and Genres

16.3 Represented speech and real speech

You will look at **represented speech** for a TV drama and compare this with a real-life speech situation.

(i) Concept bank

Represented speech: speech written by scriptwriters for TV or film drama. It is not 'real', but might try to sound like it is.

Speech Types and Genres

⟳ For starters

1 With a partner, identify a TV drama programme in which you feel the scriptwriters are successful at making the script sound like real talk. What makes the script sound like real talk?

2 Now identify a TV drama programme where you are far less convinced by the realism of the represented speech. What makes it less successful than the other?

⟳ Task

Here is an extract from *Waterloo Road*, a TV drama set in an English comprehensive school. Andrew Treneman is the class teacher. Russell Millen is a student teacher who makes his first appearance in this episode. An earlier scene reveals that he is an ex-police officer, and that he is very keen to have a go at some real teaching. Mr Treneman has been teaching an English class about nouns.

↑ *Speech in soaps is not representative of real speech*

SCENE 13: ANDREW TRENEMAN'S CLASS, PERIOD ONE, 09:25

Teachers: ANDREW TRENEMAN, RUSSELL MILLEN.
Year 7s: ARON, REST OF CLASS.

Mr Treneman and Mr Millen are walking around the room, checking on the pupils' work. Mr Millen picks up Aron's jotter.

MR MILLEN	'Loyalty – stick.' Stick? How did you come up with that?
	There are a few titters.
ARON (*offended*):	When you're loyal, you stick by somebody, don't you?
	Mr Millen isn't sure how to react but pretends to be on top of things and reads another of Aron's suggestions.
MR MILLEN	'Anger – kettle'.
ARON	You can boil with anger like a kettle. *And now the class is laughing a bit. Aron is mortified.*
MR MILLEN	I don't think Aron's quite got what you were on about, Mr Treneman. *Andrew tries to encourage Russell to help Aron – after all, this is what Russell wanted.*
MR TRENEMAN	Perhaps you could explain, Mr Millen?
MR MILLEN	Yeah, yeah sure ... You see what it is, that you're ... looking for here, Aron, is a word that isn't ... too far away from the words on the board. For example, anger is a word that comes from inside you ... it's a feeling like when your mum doesn't allow you to watch your telly in your bedroom ...

ARON	You mean like 'minging'? *Aron hasn't really understood.*
MR MILLEN	Exactly. Good. *This is not at all good, but Andrew does not want to correct Russell.*
MR TRENEMAN	Although 'anger' is a noun. An abstract noun. *It is obvious Russell's never heard of them.* As Mr Millen says it's about a feeling. Things you can't touch or see or smell or hear. *(To Aron)* Try to think of a word you would substitute for 'anger' in a sentence, Aron. He felt 'anger'. *Aron has a good think.*
ARON	Fury? *Russell gives him a condescending pat on the back.*
MR MILLEN	Give the boy a gold star. *The class laughs perhaps because of Russell's comment. We see a hint of a flicker cross Andrew's face.*

1 In groups of three, read the script several times. The speaking characters are Mr Treneman, Mr Millen and Aron, a Year 7 pupil. As you read, think about how the three actors might perform these lines. The script puts directions in *italics* and gives hints to the actors about their character's thoughts and feelings, and about how lines might therefore be spoken. Be ready to share your read-through with others in the class.

2 Fill in a table like the one below, analysing how the ex-police officer (and now student teacher) Russell Millen is presented in this scene. In the first column, put three words or phrases of your own that describe Mr Millen; in the second, what he says as evidence; and in the third, your explanation (**PEE** – see page 114).

Character words and phrases	Millen's script as evidence	Explanation

3 How realistic do you feel the script is in its presentation of Russell Millen? (Clue: role; context; purpose; audience.) To what degree does he sound real? Write about 100 words, using evidence from the script.

4 Fill in a table like the one below, analysing how the English teacher Andrew Treneman is presented in this scene. In the first column put three words or phrases of your own that describe Mr Treneman; in the second, what he says as evidence; and in the third, your explanation (**PEE**).

Character words and phrases	Treneman's script as evidence	Explanation

5 How realistic do you feel the script is in its presentation of Andrew Treneman? (Clue: role; context; purpose; audience.) To what degree does he sound real? Write about 100 words, using evidence from the script.

⊃ Taking it further

Here is a transcript of a real exchange between a teacher and her Year 7 pupil. (The vertical line shows when the two speakers speak at the same time.)

Text 3: In class, teaching

People: Miss Powell [P] – teacher, mid 20s; Rachel [R] – Year 7 pupil in P's tutor group. These are the only two people in the room.

P   Now then Rachel [.] what was it that you wanted

R   Miss [.] well [.] er Miss [.] it's just that I've got er maths next and I I I'm not sure how to get there

P   What are you like. [.] didn't you get a map on the first day of term [.] and we did a walk round and went to all the rooms didn't we [1] can't you remember where maths is

R   I've left it at home miss [.]| I didn't think

P   isn't there someone else in the form in the same maths group [1] Ellie's your friend isn't she

R   yes [.] but she's gone ahead with the others [.] | and

P   well hurry along after her [.] they're not long gone and you'll soon catch them up

R   Yes miss [1] thanks | miss

P   see you later

R   See you miss

---

1 In what ways is this more obviously a sample of real speech as opposed to the represented speech of the *Waterloo Road* transcript?

2 The represented speech in drama programmes such as *Waterloo Road* is written for our entertainment. Look again at the script extract on pages 156–157. In what ways is the language in the script more entertaining than the real language in the transcript above?

3 Record and transcribe a 60-second sample of represented speech from a TV drama series of your choice. It would be wise to have just two speakers. Look at the three transcripts (Texts 1–3) in this unit to remind yourself of how to set out a transcript. Write a three-paragraph analysis of your transcribed drama extract (about 300 words).

   • Paragraph 1: analyse the language used in terms of who is speaking, why and in what context.

   • Paragraph 2: comment on the degree to which the language used comes across as realistic.

   • Paragraph 3: using your 60-second sample as focus, explore how far it is possible for scripted speech to be realistic as well as entertaining.

Impact of Technology on Language Use

17.1 What is the difference between speech and writing?

> You will learn how technology is affecting the distinction between speech and writing.

➲ For starters

A major factor which is causing language to change is the introduction of new technologies, such as mobile phones and computers.

Look at the list of words below and work out a definition for each one:

*   Internet
*   CD-Rom
*   Wi-fi
*   Modem
*   Fax
*   Byte
*   Blog
*   Facebook.

You could probably identify all of these terms. Were there any you didn't know? Discuss why this might be the case. If you were to look in a dictionary that is over 10 years old, you would probably find very few of the above words. Why do you think this is?

➲ Task

1   You will need to work in groups of three. One of you will observe the other two and make notes on how you perform the task.
    *   Tell your partner the way from your classroom to the canteen.
    *   Write down directions from your classroom to the canteen.

2 What does the last activity reveal about the differences between the spoken and written directions?

3 Complete this table which identifies the features of speech and writing:

Features of spoken language	Features of written language
Conveyed by sounds	
	Planned
	Usually done alone – no interaction
Voice helps show meaning – volume, pace, whispering, etc.	
It is unusual for a person not to be able to speak	
Frequent change of topic	
	The text must be completely clear. The reader can't ask for explanations
Limited range of connectives – most likely to be used is 'and'	
	Usually permanent – can be read again
Facial expressions help convey meaning	
	Well-structured sentences

4 Sometimes it is easy to decide if a text is spoken or written. Looking at the 10 communication forms on the right, it would be easy to place 'a conversation' at one end of the line below, but where would 'a chat-room conversation' go? For each communication form:

• use the continuum to consider how far it is 'speech' or 'writing'
• decide where on the continuum below you would place it.

Speech ⟵――――――――――⟶ Writing

⟲ Taking it further

Find a chat-room conversation. Is it the same as a face-to-face interaction? Answer the following questions and consider the way technology is affecting language.

1 How many topics do people introduce?
2 Do they interrupt each other? How?
3 How do people take turns?
4 Do they produce full sentences?
5 Is the vocabulary formal or colloquial?

Ten communication forms:

1 A conversation
2 A novel
3 A chat-room conversation
4 A written speech
5 A transcript of a telephone conversation
6 An email
7 A message left on an answerphone
8 An audiobook
9 Facebook
10 Subtitles on the TV

⊂⊃ Grammar link

You would want to use formal language when speaking with someone in authority or when you want to create a good impression. You would think carefully about vocabulary and expressions, avoiding slang, for example.

17.2 Texting

> You will explore the features of text language.

⟳ For starters

Make a list of all the text messages you have sent over the last few days. Look at your list with a partner. What do you use texting for? Who do you text? How long are your messages? If your parents completed this activity, how would their findings differ?

⟳ Task

The ways in which we use our mobile phones have changed enormously since their introduction. When mobiles were first used, they were very expensive. Quite often people would use texting to save money. However, a lot of people found it difficult to use and very slow! As a result, people adapted the language they used to speed things up. The introduction of predictive text made sending a message easier although people still use shortcuts.

1   Turn the following messages into texts:

A

> Dear Manjeet,
>
> I will be unable to attend the cinema tomorrow evening. I must remain at home in order to complete my homework.
>
> Yours sincerely,
> Ben

B

> Mum,
>
> Please note I will be late home as I will be spending approximately one hour perusing the merchandise in Primark.
>
> Love,
> Emma

C

> Chris,
>
> Could you please remember to feed the cat?
>
> Dad

What changes did you make? Compare your messages with a partner. You probably began by changing the level of formality and the length. You may also have changed the punctuation and even the spelling.

Impact of Technology on Language Use

2 Text messaging has many special features which are not used in conventional writing. Look at the list. Think of two more examples of each feature.

Initialisms	you put the first letter of each word	brb
Modified acronyms	using letters or numbers in place of words or a phrase	F2F
Emoticons	symbols	☺
Number homophones	using a number as the word it sounds like	8
Letter homophones	using a letter as the word it sounds like	b
Omission of letters	missing out letters	gd
Substitution of letters	using as few letters as possible	wot
Lower case letters	not using many capitals	
No punctuation	not using any full stops or commas	

Concept bank

Acronym: word made up from the initial letters of a phrase.

Homophones: words which are pronounced in the same way but have different meanings.

3 In pairs, write a message using as much text language as possible. Stick it onto a piece of sugar paper. Annotate it to show which features you have used.

4 Where would you place texting on the speech/writing continuum? Explain why.

Speech ◄——————————————► Writing

➲ Taking it further

Write an advice sheet for older people called 'A Guide to Text Messaging'. Think carefully about who you are writing for, what they might know already, and what they need to know.

Structure your advice sheet like this:

- An introductory section that explains what text messaging is and why people might use it.
- Five further paragraphs – select five texting techniques from the table above and write a paragraph on each. In each paragraph:
  - explain what the technique involves
  - give examples to make it clear
  - explain why it is useful, quick and easy.
- A final section that recommends texting as a method of communication, and reassures anxious newcomers.

⬆ *Think carefully about your grandparent and what language they will understand*

! Essay tip

In this advice text, include the writing techniques on page 60, such as:

- appropriate register, including modal verbs ('you should')
- direct address ('you')
- clear explanations, including connectives
- authoritative tone, including facts, examples and specialist words
- enthusiastic adjectives to persuade
- reassurance
- specific suggestions and instructions.

17.3 Attitudes to technology

> You will consider attitudes towards texting and language change.

⊃ For starters

Some people feel that technology is having a negative impact on our language and **grammar**. Read the following two texts and discuss with a friend what you feel about them. Which of the two perspectives is closest to your point of view? Explain why.

> **ⓘ Concept bank**
>
> **Grammar:** the way words are linked together to make a language.

TXTZ RNT GUD 4U – OFFICIAL

Aptly-named Professor Speak, Head of English at Mercia College, believes that texting harms children's writing.

'Text messages teach wrong writing technique,' Professor Speak told *The Advertiser*. 'They omit punctuation. They misspell words. Repetition turns these errors into habits, and suddenly we have undergraduates using text-speak in academic essays … so texting undermines "appropriateness" – the ability to use the right words in the right place.'

'Moreover, young people who use emoticons to identify their feelings, get worse at expressing those feelings in words.'

Professor Speak claims that his research is a wake-up call to educated England. 'We are getting swamped by the language of the street,' he warns. 'We need to act now, before this lazy way of communication takes away altogether our ability to write in proper English.'

Article in a local newspaper

Dear Editor

May I contradict the old-fashioned twaddle that text messages are ruining language skills? In fact, exactly the opposite is the case.

Text messaging helps spelling because abbreviations such as 'txt' and 'wot' force children to think about the structures and sounds of words. And you've *got* to be able to spell accurately to use predictive texting.

At the same time, is not abbreviation a skill we teach pupils to help them make notes; how is it 'wrong' to be able to get down three ideas in 12 letters?

Above all, texting is inspiring youngsters, who previously refused to pick up a pen, to churn out thousands of words of written communication. Texting is teaching us how to write again!

Language changes all the time, n txt MSGs R takN us N2 d fucha.

Yours truly,

Alan Widge

Letter to a magazine for young mothers

⊃ Task

Some people feel that texting is having a bad effect on our language. Others think that texting is really useful and can be very creative.

1 Using the articles on page 163 to help you, work with a partner to think of as many arguments as you can for and against texting. Use a table like this one to organise your ideas:

Texting is the future!	Texting is destroying the language!
Quick and easy, faster than normal writing	Only lazy people use text language

2 How do you feel about texting? Discuss your views with a partner. Can you think of any more ideas to support your views? Using these ideas, write a letter to a newspaper expressing your views on texting. You could research this on the Internet. You'll find lots of articles and websites which express people's views. They often feel strongly about technology and how it is influencing language.

⊃ Taking it further

1 Ask five people how they feel about texting. Try to get a range of ages and gender. Find out if they think texting is a useful shorthand or if they believe it is destroying the language. Use a table for them to complete like the one below, but add three more statements of your own about texting. This will give you eight points of focus.

	Agree strongly	Agree	Disagree	Disagree strongly
Texting is lazy				
Texting leads to poor spelling				
Texting is dynamic (something which changes) and creative (the ability to produce something new and different)				
Texting is quick and convenient				
Texting is destroying English				

2 Write a few sentences on what each person tells you. What conclusions can you draw?

17.4 Email

> You will explore the features of email.

⊃ For starters

We have a wide choice of ways to communicate with other people. You could choose email, a letter, a text or even a phone call. Discuss with a partner which form of communication would be used for each of the following:

- A message from the bank to tell you that you are overdrawn.
- A message to a parent/guardian to let them know you missed the bus.
- A message to invite a number of friends to a party.
- A party invitation to someone you don't know well.
- A message to a wide audience advertising something for sale.
- A message to your boy or girl friend telling them you want to finish the relationship.

What factors influenced which method you chose?

⊃ Task

Do you think there is a language of email? Is there a specific way that emails are written that is different to other ways of writing? There is no doubt that most emails do share some specific features. However, they vary enormously as a result of audience and purpose.

> ### ⓘ Concept bank
>
> **Closing:** the phrase used to close an interaction, e.g. 'Yours sincerely'.

1 Write a short email to your form tutor from your parent/guardian to explain your absence from school.
2 Write a short email from yourself to your friend explaining why you missed school.
3 In pairs, compare the two. Use a chart like the one below, putting a tick in either, both or neither columns where appropriate.

Language use	Email to friend	Email to tutor
Planned?		
Spontaneous?		
Formal language?		
Informal language?		
Salutation ('Dear x ...')		
Closing ('Yours ...')		
Paragraphed?		
Accurately punctuated?		
Accurately spelt?		

4 Investigate the features of email.

Sunday 14th January 2010, 10:42	Inbox	Sent	Junk	Draft

Hi Sam,

Lovely to hear from you! Thanks for emailing me. Can you get there for 6.30 to 7ish? I'll wait for you at the entrance – what film do you want to see? Really looking forward to seeing you and catching up on the goss. Should be kinda fun!

Love, Han xx

- Who is sending it? Who is the audience?
- Is there a **header**? What information is given?
- Is there a **greeting**?
- How formal is the vocabulary?
- Is it in complete sentences?
- Is it in paragraphs?
- How does it close?

5 Where would you place email on the speech/writing continuum? Explain why.

Speech ⟷ Writing

⊃ Taking it further

1 Collect eight emails received by you and your family over the next week. Analyse them using the table on page 165.

2 Present your results in an annotated poster to show the features of emails.

ⓘ Concept bank

Header: information placed at the top of a page, e.g. the date, a reference.

Greeting: the phrase used to open an interaction, e.g. 'Dear Joe'.

ⓓ Grammar link

A complete sentence is a sentence which has a subject, verb and object or adverbial.

Doing Well in the English and English Language Exam

Introduction

This unit will give you information and advice about your English and English Language exam paper. It will help you to answer four questions:

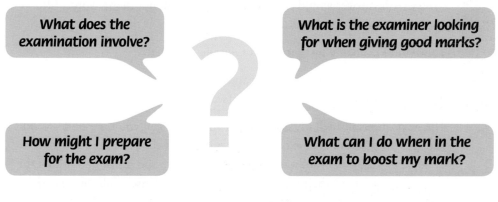

What does the examination involve?

What is the examiner looking for when giving good marks?

How might I prepare for the exam?

What can I do when in the exam to boost my mark?

The English and English Language exam

What does the examination involve?

The exam is called *Unit 1: Understanding and producing non-fiction texts* and is worth 40 per cent of your GCSE. It is a two-hour examination split into two sections. Both sections are worth the same number of marks.

Section A tests how well you can read non-fiction texts. Expect texts such as magazine and newspaper articles, diaries, letters, and autobiographical writing; adverts or parts of leaflets or web material. You will also be given images and other visual items to write about. In this section you will be asked four questions based on three texts.

Section B tests how well you can write. You will be asked to produce two pieces. One will be worth fewer marks than the other. Expect to be asked to write things such as letters, articles, speeches, essays, leaflet material. Basically, anything of a non-fiction kind.

What is the examiner looking for when giving good marks?

Section A – Reading

In Section A the examiner is looking to see how well you can read, absorb and think about the texts you are given.

One question will test whether you can take in the ideas of a whole text and summarise them. So imagine a newspaper article by a writer, Mark Layton, about why dogs should not be kept as pets in a town or city environment. The article, combining facts and opinions, and using language in an argument form, considers why it might not be a good idea to keep dogs in towns or cities. The article is clearly one-sided and shows Layton's firmly presented thoughts and feelings on the subject. A question then might be:

Question

Why is Layton opposed to keeping dogs in a town or city environment?

A very basic answer would simply, and probably in not many words, lift a few reasons straight from the article and not comment on them (see top right).

This would probably just pick up a C-grade type mark.

Students who use their own words and **explain** the reasons are much more likely to pick up A- or A*-type marks (see middle right).

The next questions will dig a bit deeper into how well you have understood and can think about the texts. Imagine another of the texts is a letter to a newspaper. Dean Connolly rather angrily writes to the editor about how the streets and centre of their town are 'no-go areas' because of all the stray dogs:

> ... prowling around in packs! Dogs, dogs, and more dogs! Dogs the size of small horses ... wild dogs, mad dogs. Dogs that look like they'd bite your hand off if you even looked at them. Forget Crufts and friendly Fido. These dogs are more like ones you find in a horror film!

The examiner could ask you:

Question

What are Connolly's thoughts and feelings about stray dogs in his town centre?

The examiner is now asking for more. It's not just enough to know what the text is about. You have to absorb and assimilate the writer's attitudes towards the situation so that you can produce a series of comments about his thoughts and feelings. An answer heading to A or A* might begin as the extract on the bottom right.

This detail and depth of response if sustained across several further comments is likely to earn very high marks.

Layton says it is cruel and not fair on the dogs ... He says that the dogs are left to wander around the streets all day or are left on their own in the house ...

Layton sees the neglect in allowing dogs to roam the streets and regards this as unfair treatment. He disapproves of owners who abandon their dogs in the house all day and shows his disapproval by relating the anecdote about the dog that tore the settee apart. The sarcastic way he likens this to child abuse, by using the phrase 'dog-abuse', shows the depth of his feeling ...

Connolly is clearly angry about the dog situation. His bitter tone, with references to 'packs' clearly suggests the depth of his feeling. This is even clearer when he refers to 'horror films', with all the implications of terror and threat. Later he goes on to argue that more should be done to rid the streets of strays and his depth of feeling is revealed in the sarcasm he uses to attack the 'town council desk jockeys' with a strong sense of disrespect for them.

A further question in this section will ask about the use of pictures or other presentational devices. The examiner must test you on this. So let's imagine the front of a leaflet produced for a charity trying to persuade you to give money to a Rescue Dogs kennel. You can instantly visualise what that leaflet front cover would contain! The droopy-looking dog; big sad eyes; a caption or slogan; possibly a logo for the charity. Got the idea? Here is a possible question:

Top marks will again go to you if you spot several features of the cover, describe them, and explain how they work to make you feel sympathy for that sad-looking, droopy-eyed cutesy little puppy that sits right in the middle of the cover and looks straight into your eyes! Writing then about the logo (probably a doggy-themed shape!) and how it makes the charity seem businesslike and trustworthy, and about how the light-blue lettering creates a sense of calm will earn an A*.

The last question must ask you to compare language use in two of the three texts. Remember all that you have read above, but now simply add words in your answer that link things together because they are similar:

* Similarly …
* Likewise …
* Both texts …
* In comparison …

or words that show how things are different:

* On the other hand …
* In contrast …

If you include in your answer several examples, with some detail, and some compare words, you will pick up good marks. It is worth thinking hard about how and what you might compare – this question is worth the most marks so you will want to do it well. Before you write, put together a planning grid like this:

	Text A	Text B
Purpose		
Audience		
Register		
Style: word choice		
Style: sentencing/syntax		
Structure		
Overall effect		

Writing several sentences on each aspect would give you about a side of A4 in a full answer worth 16 marks, and done in about 18 minutes.

Section B – Writing

Let's think now about Section B. Here it is easier to know what the examiner is looking to give marks for. You will be asked to do two pieces of writing. Both will be some kind of non-fiction. You must do both.

One piece will be worth fewer marks than the other, so the examiner will expect the answer to be shorter. This shorter task is likely to have you informing, explaining or advising. Here is a possible example, keeping to the dog theme:

Question

Write a letter to the manager of a local dog rescue kennel. In the letter, introduce yourself and explain why you want to do your work experience there. (16 marks)

The longer task might be:

Question

Write an article for a school magazine in which you argue that students at the school should get involved in charity work. (24 marks)

In both cases the examiner will want to see certain skills being used well in order to give high marks for the writing:

✔ The writing should be detailed and include a range of ideas, lots of information and a variety of reasons.
✔ It should be obvious that the writing is doing the job asked for. So, it should contain information; it should offer advice; it should give reasons and be persuasive.
✔ The writing should be structured, with some sense of beginning, middle and end. For good marks there will have to be paragraphs or sections.
✔ Interesting words should be used, that show a good vocabulary.
✔ The writing should be in well-punctuated sentences.
✔ Spelling of almost all words should be accurate.

To see how you might do, have a go at either of the example tasks above. Spend no more than about 20 minutes on the shorter one, or about 30 minutes on the longer one. Ask your teacher to mark your work and for some comments that would improve it next time.

How might I prepare for the exam?

Some people say:

> **You can't revise for English!**

> **True, but you can prepare – so no excuses!**

But, there are a number of things you can do in the weeks before you sit the English and English Language exam paper that will make a difference to your confidence on the day. On page 171 there is a bank of suggestions.

Tips for exam success

- Reread this unit to remind yourself about the exam paper, and what the examiner is looking for.

- In sessions of, say, half an hour each, review Units 2, 3, 4 and 5 of this book. If this gets you that all-important A grade, it's worth it. If there is anything you do not remember, or cannot get clear in your head about these units, have a word with your teacher.

- Flick through the Grammar section on page 173–181 – this will help you with any grammar you still do not understand.

- Check out the key concepts in the Concept Bank on page 182–184.

- You will have plenty of notes you made whilst working in class in the past year or so. Remind yourself what is on the exam paper, and have a good look at the relevant notes.

- If you did a mock exam, or any practice questions, and you still have your answers, look again at what you wrote, and any comments your teacher made. Do this to help you spot your strengths and areas for improvement. Then ask for help with what you are most unsure of.

- Have a go at a practice paper or a section or two from one. You would not take your driving test without having some practice drives before, so why do an exam without a trial run? Units 2–7 of this book give you some exam-style questions to work on. Your teacher might have some more, and the AQA website http://www.AQA.org.uk definitely does.

- Share your answers with your teacher. Ask your teacher: 'What can I do that would improve my performance by 3 marks next time?' Listen to what they say!

- Come up with some planning mnemonics – like APPLE. Ask your teacher if they might do this with the whole class to get more ideas.

- Do some honest self-analysis. Ask yourself: 'What do I still find tricky in English?' Here are some prompts. Is it:
  - writing in sentences
  - using punctuation – semicolons impress examiners, but not if you can't use them properly
  - using paragraphs
  - reading stuff quickly
  - explaining how language is used
  - writing about pictures and visual material
  - doing a quick plan before you start writing
  - writing about something in detail?

Find **one** thing that you think you could improve on, and book a five-minute chat with your teacher to talk about it.

So here are 10 positive things you could do before the exam. Suppose you did just six of them. Imagine by doing each one you improved your English skills by just 1 per cent. That would add up to 6 per cent and could easily be the difference between a B and an A.

What can I do when in the exam to boost my mark?

The exam room will feel like a scary place to be: rows of desks; invigilators walking up and down; the demand that you are silent. Not a nice place to spend two hours. But an important two hours, so what can you do in the exam room itself to improve your performance? Read the tips on page 172 now, and again on the night before the exam.

Tips for planning your time

As soon as you open the exam paper write a quick timetable. Remember:

✔ Section A and Section B should each take about 1 hour.

✔ Section A typically has **four** questions, but they will not all be worth the same number of marks. Look at the end of each question and see how many marks it is worth. Then give the right proportion of minutes to marks that the question deserves. So often students spend longer than needed on early questions and rush the bigger one (with more marks!) at the end.

✔ Section B has **two** questions, one worth fewer marks than the other. Aim to spend 25 minutes on one, 30 minutes on the other. More about those missing 5 minutes later.

Tips for Section A

✔ Read the question so that you know what you are looking for.

✔ Then read the passage. But don't just read it! With a pen or highlighter <u>underline</u> or colour over parts of the text where the answers to the question are. Or put 'L' for language next to any bits of language you think you might use when answering about language in the passage.

✔ Quickly read the question again, and then answer it using your annotation to help you. This means the examiner will not be writing 'not relevant' in the margin.

✔ One question will always involve you comparing language. This question will often be worth the most marks in Section A so plan it using the grid suggested on page 169.

Tips for Section B

✔ Section B answers must be planned before you start to write unless you want to risk messing up the structure, running out of ideas, or running out of time. Spend a few minutes before writing each answer scribbling down a few words and ideas. Maybe each one will become the main point of a paragraph.

✔ Examiners often see a strange word like FOREST with a few words next to it in students' exam plans. This is often a mnemonic, a checklist, to remind them, for example, that in a newspaper article that tries to persuade someone about something they should include:

F Facts

O Opinions

R Rhetorical questions

E Emotive language

S Structure

T Triplets

✔ Before the exam, see if you and your class can come up with your own mnemonics. Some plans are lists of words or phrases; sometimes plans can look like brainstorms.

✔ Last but not least, save 5 minutes at the end to check your Section B answers. Read with your pencil hovering over your sentences – this will direct your attention to the page more. Imagine you correct three spelling mistakes. Imagine you catch and sort out three punctuation slip-ups. missing capital letters? No apostrophes or apostrophe's where there shouldn't be? Check those last sentences! That's at least two lost marks saved.

Rereading your answers now might even gain you an extra mark or two if you change a few words for better ones.

> *I am writing this letter angry at the mess our town centre is in …*

could become:

> *I am writing this letter enraged at the shameful state our town centre is in …*

Examiners like self-correcting; it shows them you are thinking about your writing.

Do your best to act on these sets of tips and you should gain at least an A grade. And one last thing – best of luck!

Grammar

The word 'grammar' is used to describe the way in which the words in our language can be combined in order to communicate meaning. Some people describe it as a system of 'rules'.

There are a number of reasons for studying grammar. For example:

- Knowing about grammar will give you more control of your writing, and help you produce and craft it more effectively.
- Knowing about grammar can help you explore how texts work and describe how their messages and effects are created.
- Language is a fascinating subject and understanding more about how it works is very satisfying.

Word classes (parts of speech)

The building blocks of our language

The most basic part of our reading and writing is the **word** – words are the building blocks of our language. If you are to be able to understand and use language in an effective way, you need to be able to recognise the job that each type of word does in the texts that you write and the ones that you read. Ideally, you should be able to recognise what **word class** (or **part of speech**) each individual word in a piece of writing belongs to.

The traditional rhyme on the right gives a brief summary of the main word classes in English.

Every name is called a **NOUN**,
As field and fountain, street and town.

In place of noun the **PRONOUN** stands,
As he and she can clap their hands.

The **ADJECTIVE** describes a thing,
As magic wand and bridal ring.

The **VERB** means action, something done –
To read, to write, to jump, to run.

How things are done, the **ADVERBS** tell,
As quickly, slowly, badly, well.

The **PREPOSITION** shows relation,
As in the street, or at the station.

CONNECTIVES join, in many ways,
Sentences, words, or phrase and phrase.

The **INTERJECTION** cries out, 'Hark!
I need an exclamation mark!'

Find out about nouns

Question	Answer	Examples
What do nouns do?	Nouns identify people, places and things.	*Mr Bean; teacher; London; supermarket*
How do nouns work in sentences?	• Nouns can be preceded by such words as *a, the, some, this, that*, etc. which provide more information about them.	some *money*; a *child*; the *teapot*; this *girl*; that *boy*
	• Nouns can change their form to show how many they are (singular or plural) or to show possession.	*teapots*; the *girl's clothes*; the *children's toys*
What are the different types of nouns?	• **Common nouns** are non-specific people, places and things.	*man; woman; children; town; car; drink*
	• **Proper nouns** are particular people, places and things.	*Cheryl; Kings of Leon; Birmingham; Pepsi*
	• **Concrete nouns** are those people and things that you can physically experience with your senses.	*chair; fish; teacher; train; rain*
	• **Abstract nouns** relate to emotions, qualities and concepts that you can experience mentally or emotionally, rather than physically.	*happiness; fear; speed; trust; love*

How will knowing about nouns help my reading and writing?

Reading: If you are given a passage to read, and you identify a number of **concrete nouns**, you could conclude that the writer is trying to appeal to the reader through the senses (things that readers could see, feel, smell or hear themselves). If, on the other hand, you identify more **abstract nouns**, perhaps the writer is trying to appeal to the readers' emotions.

Writing: If you have a writing task to complete (especially a descriptive piece), you can add variety and interest to it by making sure you use a combination of concrete and abstract nouns. Concrete nouns can make your description detailed and convincing, while abstract nouns can help your readers share your thoughts and feelings about the topic.

Find out about pronouns

Question	Answer	Examples
What do pronouns do?	Pronouns are used to take the place of nouns.	*I*; *you*; *they*; *him*; *herself*; *mine*
How do pronouns work in sentences?	Whenever a noun is used in a sentence, it can be replaced by a pronoun.	*'Maria borrowed Katie's iPod'* could become: *'She* borrowed *her* iPod' or *'Maria borrowed it'*.
What are the different types of pronouns?	There are many types of pronoun in English. The most familiar and probably the most useful type for your reading and writing are the **personal pronouns**.	These are words that can be used in the place of people and things, such as: *I*; *me*; *you*; *he*; *she*; *it*; *we*; *us*; *they*; *them*. If the personal pronouns refer to *I*, *me*, *we* or *us*, they are called *first person pronouns*. If they refer to *you*, they are called *second person pronouns*. If they refer to *he*, *she*, *him*, *her*, *it*, *they* or *them*, they are called *third person pronouns*.

How will knowing about pronouns help my reading and writing?

Reading: If you are given a passage to read which is designed to persuade or to advise, it is often interesting to look at the choice of personal pronoun(s) that the writer has made. For example, in a review of a new film, a reviewer might write:

1 'I thought it was a brilliant, exciting film.'
2 'You really ought to go and see it as soon as you can!'
3 'We all know what to expect from Spielberg, a great film!'
4 'It is a first-class film – the best of its kind for years!'

	Pronoun use	Effect
1	First person (singular)	Clearly identifies the writer's opinion or point of view. It might not be helpful if the readers do not respect the writer's point of view.
2	Second person	Addresses the reader directly. Helps to create a relationship between the writer and reader – almost as though they know each other.
3	First person (plural)	Includes the reader(s) with the writer, and makes them feel as though they are sharing something – creates an even closer relationship.
4	Third person	Makes it look like a statement of fact and so is more likely to convince the reader that it is true rather than an expression of opinion.

Writing: If you are asked to write to persuade or advise, you could keep the above techniques in mind. You could choose to use one of the possible pronoun uses throughout your text, or use a number (or even all) of them at different times.

Find out about adjectives

Question	Answer	Examples
What do adjectives do?	Adjectives are words which give you more information about nouns.	a *good* man; a *fast* car; a *long* life; *beautiful* music; *modern* buildings
How do adjectives work in sentences?	Adjectives can go immediately before the word that they are describing, or following it and a part of the verb 'to be'.	*loud* music *or* The music was both *loud* and *modern*.
What are the different types of adjectives?	There are many different types of adjective in English, for example, adjectives relating to: • age • colour • personality • quality • shape • size.	*old*; *new*; *young* *red*; *white*; *blue*; *pink*; *purple* *angry*; *happy*; *sad*; *calm* *good*; *bad*; *mediocre* *triangular*; *round*; *spherical*; *circular* *big*; *small*; *tall*; *thin*; *thick*

How will knowing about adjectives help my reading and writing?

Reading: Since adjectives are used to give the reader more information about the subject that is being written about, they can also be used to emphasise the opinion of the writer. Some adjectives such as 'beautiful' or 'healthy' carry positive suggestions about whatever it is they are describing, while others, like 'miserable' or 'disgusting', have negative suggestions (or connotations). Understanding this can help you explain how writers use language to be persuasive, or to influence the reader.

Writing: You can enrich and improve your own writing by using adjectives carefully. You can give additional information about people, places and objects, and by selecting adjectives with strong positive or negative suggestions, you can cleverly persuade your readers to agree with your point of view.

Find out about verbs

Question	Answer	Examples
What do verbs do?	Verbs denote an action, a feeling, an occurrence or a state of being.	**Action** – She *danced* all night. **Feeling** – I *wanted* to watch the match. **Occurrence** – It *rained* all week. **State of being** – You *are* my best friend.
How do verbs work in sentences?	Verbs tell you *what* is happening in a sentence, and also *when* it happens, happened, or will happen.	**Present** – He *is watching* the game. **Past** – He *watched* the game. **Future** – He *will watch* the game.
What are the different forms of verbs?	Verbs sometimes have a different form depending on who is performing the action in the sentence.	I *go* to town on Saturdays. She *goes* to town on Saturdays. He *likes* football, but you *like* rugby.

How will knowing about verbs help my reading and writing?

Reading: A verb is a very important word class as no sentence is complete without a verb. The most important aspect of verbs is the type of verb that writers use. Have they selected verbs because they have particular strength or express a particular feeling? For example, think about the difference between the verbs *like*, *love* and *adore*. They all have the same basic meaning, but some are stronger than others. The same is true of *dislike*, *hate* and *despise*. These stronger, more powerful words are known as **emotive vocabulary** because people use them to show more emotion about the subject they are writing about.

Writing: In your own writing, if you want to show how strongly you feel, or if you want your readers to share these feelings, you could use emotive verbs; you could choose stronger alternatives to commonly used verbs such as *say*, *go* and *get*. For example, 'The teacher *said*, "Stop talking now"' is much less powerful than 'The teacher *bellowed*, "Stop talking now."'

Find out about adverbs

Question	Answer	Examples
What do adverbs do?	Adverbs give more information about (or modify) verbs, adjectives or other adverbs.	I *completely* agree; a *totally* awesome experience; *quite* loudly
How do adverbs work in sentences?	Adverbs normally go next to the word that they give more information about. In most cases this is before the word – but occasionally afterwards for special emphasis.	I *distinctly* heard you speak. That is *completely* unacceptable. I will support you *totally*, whatever happens.
What are the different types of adverb?	The most widely used types of adverb are adverbs of: • **Manner** which answer the question *how*? • **Place** which answer the question *where*? • **Time** which answer the question *when*? • **Frequency** which answer the question *how often*? • **Degree** which answer the question *how far*?	She sings *beautifully*. I always drive *carefully*. We saw you *there*. I can't find them *anywhere*. I've been there *before*. He is *still* at school. We are going for a pizza *afterwards*. I *often* miss the bus. You *always* give me a hard time. She *sometimes* forgets her homework. We *almost* won the lottery. The weather was *quite* good. There was *hardly* any snow last winter.

How will knowing about adverbs help my reading and writing?

Reading: Since adverbs are used to give the reader more information about the subject that is being written about, they can also be used to suggest the opinion of the writer and to influence the reader. Using adverbs such as *obviously* or *clearly* suggests that the writer is sure that what they are saying is true, while the use of adverbs such as *perhaps* or *possibly* casts doubt upon it.

Writing: You can enrich and improve your own writing by using adverbs carefully. You can suggest additional information about people, places and actions by selecting suitable adverbs. As with adjectives, you can influence your readers without being too obvious about it.

Grammar

Find out about prepositions

Question	Answer
What do prepositions do?	Prepositions are words that express a relationship between nouns or pronouns and other words in a sentence.
How do prepositions work in sentences?	The most common prepositions are small words related to: • **Direction** – They are going *to* the match. • **Location** – He hid *under* the bed. • **Time** – She left for work *after* her breakfast. • **Possession** – The Queen *of* England.
What are the different prepositions? (a detailed but not complete list)	**Simple prepositions:** *above; after; at; before; below; by; for; from; in; near; on; over; round; since; till; to; under; until; with* **Prepositional phrases:** *according to; ahead of; apart from; as well as; because of; except for; in addition to; in favour of; in spite of; near to; on behalf of*

Find out about connectives

(For an explanation of terms marked with an asterisk, see the Phrases, clauses and sentences section on pages 178–179.)

Question	Answer
What do connectives do?	Connectives are words that join two or more words, phrases* or clauses*.
What are the different types of connectives?	**Coordinating connectives** The most common of these are *and*, *but* and *or*. They join words, phrases or clauses when all of the parts being joined together are equally important. For example: The Long *and* the Short *and* the Tall. (single words) Football shorts *or* a pair of swimming trunks are necessary. (phrase) She locked the door *but* left the window open. (clause) **Subordinating connectives** These help to show connections in meaning between main clauses* and dependent (or subordinate) clauses*. • **Simple subordinating connectives** include such words as: *although; as; because; before; if; since; though; unless; until; when; whenever; while.* • **Complex subordinating connectives** are made up of more than one word and include: *assuming that; in case; in order that; insofar as.*

How will knowing about connectives improve my writing?

As connectives are the main way in which words, phrases, clauses and sentences can be joined, knowing about them allows you to choose the length and complexity of your sentences. This allows you to vary the effects that your writing can have on your readers. For example, a series of long and complex sentences can make your writing seem sophisticated. A short, simple sentence following a number of longer and more complex sentences can have a considerable impact. A variety of sentence lengths and types can also add variety and interest to your writing.

Find out about interjections (exclamatories)

Question	Answer
What do interjections do?	Interjections (or exclamatories) are words or phrases that are put into written text to express strong feelings or emotions. Writers often include them at the start of a sentence to denote feelings such as joy, disgust and excitement. They also use them as links or fillers in speech.
How do interjections work in sentences?	<ul><li>Exclamations such as: *Fantastic!*; *Cheers!*; *Hurrah!* (notice that writers often make use of exclamation marks to demonstrate the force of the emotion they are expressing).</li><li>Formulaic expressions in speech such as: *Hello*; *See you*; *Goodbye*.</li><li>*Well* can also be used as an interjection when it is put at the beginning of a sentence or utterance.</li><li>Many taboo (or expletive) phrases are interjections.</li><li>Polite words and phrases such as: *Excuse me!*; *Sorry!*</li><li>Expressions that are not strictly 'words' such as: *Oh!*; *Wow!*</li><li>Some experts consider such words as: *yes*; *no*; *amen*; okay to be interjections, as they have no direct grammatical connection with other words in the sentence.</li></ul>

Advice on using interjections in your writing: Don't overdo it! You could use them when you are writing dialogue (speech) to make it sound realistic. You could use the occasional interjection to demonstrate that you have strong feelings on the topic about which you are writing. However, if you use too many examples they will lose their strength, and your writing will not be convincing.

Phrases, clauses and sentences

This section looks at how you can put words together to get your meaning across to your readers or listeners. You make sentences, which are built up from words, phrases and clauses. The table explains the process:

You can combine		
words	**phrases**	**clauses**
word: the representation of a sound in writing which communicates a meaning	phrase: a group of words which belong together but do not contain a verb	clause: a group of words which go together and contain a verb
to make sentences.		

What is a sentence?

A **sentence** is a piece of language which generally starts with a capital letter and finishes with a full stop, an exclamation mark or a question mark, and which makes sense. In order to make sense, it has to follow the accepted rules of grammar.

What are the different types of sentence?

There are two ways of looking at types of sentence.

1   Consider the *sort of meaning* a sentence puts across:

Statement (also known as **declarative**) This type of sentence gives information.	This is a statement.
Is this a question?	**Question** (also known as **interrogative**) This type of sentence asks for information.
Command (also known as **imperative**) This type of sentence gives instructions.	Look at this sentence.
What a great sentence!	**Exclamation** (also known as **exclamative**) This type of sentence expresses strong feelings.

2   Consider *how complicated* the sentence is:

Simple This type of sentence is made up of a single part (usually called a **main clause**).	This is a simple sentence.
This is a compound sentence but it is not very long.	**Compound** This type of sentence is made up of two or more main clauses, joined together with *and*, *but* or *or*.
Complex This type of sentence is made up of at least one main clause and at least one other clause starting with such words as: *if*; *when*; *where*; *because*; *that*; *unless*; *as*; *while*, etc. These are called **subordinate** or **dependent clauses**.	This is a complex sentence, because I have added this extra clause to it.

How will knowing about sentences help my reading and writing?

Reading: Writers use different types of sentences depending on the purpose of their writing. They will use *statements* when they are writing to *inform*; *questions* when they are trying to *involve* the reader (and perhaps to *persuade* them); *commands* when they are providing *instructions*; and *exclamations* when they *feel strongly* about the subject (and perhaps as part of a description in a piece of writing to *entertain*).

A writer may choose to use a mixture of simple, compound or complex sentences for a number of reasons. A writer might choose to use mostly simple or compound sentences to make sure important points are very clear to the reader. If a writer wants to appear well educated and well informed, they might choose to use a series of complex sentences, in order to sound like an expert! If a writer wants to emphasise a point, they might write a series of long and complex sentences and then finish with a short, simple one. The contrast will draw attention to the final, short, sentence.

Writing: You can use any of the techniques (or all of them) in your own writing. Variety is a good way of keeping your readers' attention.

Punctuation

Another important weapon in the writer's armoury is **punctuation**. Punctuation can be defined as 'the use of marks and signs in writing to divide words into sentences, clauses and phrases in order to make their meaning clear to the reader'.

Punctuation mark		Function	Examples
.	**Full stop**	• A full stop indicates the end of a sentence. • A full stop is sometimes used to show that a word or phrase has been abbreviated.	*We arrived in New York in the afternoon.* *Dr. Lewis O.B.E.; Mrs. Doyle*
?	**Question mark**	• A question mark is used to show that a sentence is a question. • Sometimes the sentence might look like a statement, but the question mark shows that it is meant to sound or act like a question. • If the sentence needs an answer, then it also needs a question mark.	*'Will that be everything, madam?'* *'So that is the best you can do?'*
!	**Exclamation mark**	• An exclamation mark shows that a sentence is carrying some form of strong feeling.	**Anger** – *'Get out of my sight!'* **Forcefulness** – *'Never again!'* **Surprise** – *'I don't believe it!'* **Strong dislike** – *'That's gross!'* **Commands** – *'Do it now!'* **Joy** – *'That's fantastic!'*
,	**Comma**	• A comma is used to separate words, clauses or phrases in a sentence. These could be parts of a list. • Commas are used when there is extra material in a sentence which is not part of the main clause. • If a sentence includes some information before the main clause, there is normally a comma after that information. • In written speech, commas usually separate the words that are spoken from the person who is speaking them. • A comma is used if you start a sentence with the name of the person or people you are talking to.	*He asked for bacon, egg, sausage, hash brown, mushrooms and baked beans.* *It was, without doubt, the best day of her life.* *Even though he hated maths, Mike passed his GCSE.* *'That will be £17.99,' said the shop assistant, 'Would you like a bag?'* *'Lucy, have you handed in your homework?'* *'Year 11, please lead out first.'*

,	Apostrophe	The apostrophe has two main uses: • To show that something belongs to something else (possession).	To show that something belongs to a noun that is singular, put the apostrophe *before* the *s*: *Peter's dog; the teacher's pen* To show that something belongs to a noun that is plural, put the apostrophe *after* the *s*: *Footballers' Wives; the passengers' luggage* **EXCEPTION:** if a plural word does *not* end in an *s*, you must treat it like a singular noun and put the apostrophe *before* the *s*: *a children's story; men's clothing* **Note:** the words that mean 'belonging to her, us, you and them' (possessive pronouns) do *not* have apostrophes. They are written as: *hers; ours; its; yours; theirs* *The monster raised its ugly head.*
		• To show that a letter or a group of letters have been missed out (omission).	This usually occurs when you are writing speech, or writing in an informal way, trying to make your writing sound like the actual words that people say. The apostrophe goes in the place where a letter or group of letters have been left out: *I am* becomes *I'm* *She will* becomes *She'll* *You could have* becomes *You could've* *It is* becomes *It's:* *It's Friday at last!*
" " • • •	**Speech marks**	If you use speech (the exact words that people say) in your writing, it is important that you use speech punctuation accurately: • The speaker's exact words are placed inside speech marks (they are also known as *quotation marks*, *quotes* or *inverted commas*). • When the speaker changes, start a new paragraph. • There should always be a punctuation mark at the end of a piece of speech. • Each new piece of speech should start with a capital letter. • If a phrase such as 'asked Jane' or 'she asked' appears in the middle of a piece of speech, the 'a' of 'asked' or 's' of 'she' is not a capital letter, even if the piece of speech before ended with a question mark or exclamation mark.	*"Where are you going?" she asked.* *He replied, "I'm going to the paper shop, if that's OK with you."* *"Fine," she said, "Pick me up a pint of milk while you're there, please."* *"Is that the one with the green top?" she asked, "Because that's what I usually have."*

How will knowing about punctuation help my reading and writing skills?

Punctuation is a system which is understood, accepted and used by almost everyone involved in reading and writing. This means that if you follow the system in your writing, other people will know exactly what you mean. In the same way, you know what writers mean when you are reading, because they are following the system!

Concept Bank (Glossary)

Accent: the way in which words are pronounced.

Acronym: word made up from the initial letters of a phrase.

Adjective: a word which describes a noun (a thing, object or person).

Alliteration: repeating the first letter of a word to create an effect.

Analysis: In English, analysis is the careful investigation of language to see how it works.

Anecdote: a brief story told to back up or illustrate a point.

Argument: the presentation of all sides to a debate, with relevant facts and figures.

Audience: the intended readership of a particular piece of writing.

Characterisation: the process by which a writer presents and develops a character.

Cliché: a tired or worn-out phrase or saying. They are not original and should be avoided.

Closing: the phrase used to close an interaction, e.g. Yours sincerely.

Code: all texts (written, spoken, visual, non-visual) use codes to communicate meaning. To analyse a text we can break it down into the codes it uses to communicate.

Cohesion: the means by which we make links within and through a text, such as through connectives.

Colloquialism: informal words or phrases, including slang.

Connotation: the idea or meaning suggested by a word or image.

Context: what the situation is at a particular point in time.

Contrasting pair: where two ideas opposite in meaning are held next to each other.

Couplet: a pair of lines which belong together in some way, often rhyming.

Dialect: the choice of words and grammatical construction in speech and writing. Everyone has a dialect. Accent and dialect are very closely linked.

Dialogue: what the character says, and how he or she interacts with other characters.

Editing: changing a photo to increase the emotional impact of a picture.

Ellipsis: dots showing where words have been omitted.

Emotive language: words or phrases which describe the writer's emotions and/or make the reader feel a certain way.

Enjambement: the carry-over of a phrase or sentence into the next line or stanza.

Explanation texts: often contain facts and figures like information texts, but they can also be subjective and biased.

Fact: a statement that can, at least in theory, be checked and confirmed as being true or false.

Figurative language: descriptions in which one thing is compared with another to create interesting or powerful images. Examples include similes, metaphors and personification.

Form: the way in which subject matter is presented, or its conventions and rules.

Formal/informal: we can consider the degree to which a text comes across as somewhat distanced from and 'above' its audience, or as 'close to' and involved with its audience.

Genre: comes from French and means style or type.

Grammar: the way words are linkd together to make a language.

Greeting: the phrase used to open an interaction, e.g. Dear Joe.

Half rhyme: rhymes in which the last consonant(s) are the only things that rhyme, the vowels do not, e.g. little/scuttle.

Header: information placed at the top of a page, e.g. the date, a reference.

High prestige: describes an accent or dialect that some people think is spoken by people who have power and status in society.

Homophones: words which are pronounced in the same way but have different meanings.

Hyperbole: where an idea is exaggerated.

Imperative: a sentence which commands the reader to do something.

Impersonal/personal: we can consider the degree to which a text comes across as detached and impersonal, or as more emotionally involved and personal.

Lexical: refers to the words of language that help shape texts and construct meaning.

Lists of three: where a speaker repeats something three times to emphasise the point being made.

Metaphor: much more direct comparison between two things.

Mood and atmosphere: the emotional feeling that is created in the scene, such as sad, happy, depressed or tense.

Non-standard dialect: dialect that is different from Standard English.

Onomatopoeia: where words sound like what they are describing, such as 'squelch' or 'boom'.

Opinion: one person's thoughts or feelings about something – other people may not agree.

Oxymoron: combining contradictory terms to create an expressive or amusing phrase such as 'same difference' or 'extremely average'.

Pathetic fallacy: where the weather or surrounding landscape reflects the mood of the scene.

Persona: where poets write as if they are characters, not themselves. We should be careful of always thinking that the 'I' in a poem is the poet.

Personal address: where a listener or reader is directly addressed as 'you'.

Pitch: a short speech where you attempt to persuade someone to buy a product. Often given to a group of people from businesses.

Presentational devices: features of presentational design and organisation that help a text communicate its information, ideas and feelings.

Prose: written as we would normally speak language.

Received Pronunciation (RP): a non regional English accent that is often used for serious television and radio programmes and in formal contexts. Since it is used for 'serious' matters in the media, some people regard it as having 'high prestige'.

Register: the way a text speaks to and addresses its readers or listeners – the text's voice. This could be formal or informal, bossy, amusing, friendly or cold … or many other registers.

Represented speech: speech written by scriptwriters for TV or film drama. It is not 'real' but it might try to sound like it is.

Review: a critical report and evaluation of a film, book, play, performance or concert. Often found in newspapers, in magazines or on the Internet.

Rhetorical language: language used in a crafted way to achieve an impact.

Rhetorical questions: are asked for dramatic effect and/or to make an audience think. They do not require an answer.

Rhyme scheme: a regular pattern for end rhymes which can be represented by letters, each standing for one rhyme position, e.g. ABAB, where first line rhymes with third and second with fourth.

Role: the status, actions and behaviours given to or expected of a person in a particular situation.

Set: the backdrop, the use of scenery and fixed furniture on stage.

Shot: the way in which a photographer chooses to show the subject in a photo.

Similes: compare one thing with another using 'as' or 'like'.

Sociolect: a variety of language used by people with shared interests or belonging to a particular group.

Speed of speech: how quickly a line in the play is said. The more quickly, the more aggressive a character will come across. Speaking too quickly, however, can't be heard by the audience.

Standard English: a non-regional English dialect that is often used in formal contexts, such as education and serious media.

Style: the choices about words and sentences that a writer or speaker makes.

Syntax: the structure or 'shape' of a sentence.

Text: How we define a text is changing. Once, the word 'text' meant simply longer writing such as novels, but now texts include images and film as well as written and spoken texts.

Transcript: the text that is made when a speech is recorded and written out.

Verse: written like poetry.

Visual aid: an object, poster image, film clip or prop that will help you to present information in a visual way so that other can **see** what you are talking about.

Voice: the tone or mood created by a text's writer.